SHORT ESSAYS

ON FINDING HOPE
IN OUR FRAGILE WORLD

40 Days Of Exploration

Graham Albert Logan

MMed Sc, BScHons, Dip Th, Dip Pastoral

To all those with smashed hopes.
To all those who have lost hope.
To all those who earnestly seek hope.
To all those who lead us to hope.
To all those who inspire us to hope.
To all those who find the true source of hope.

CONTENTS

ACKNOWLEDGEMENTS

My sincere thanks to the publishing team for all their help and support.

My thanks to my faithful companion, Barney, the wonderful harrier hound who is by my side most of the time and disciplines me to walk every day, a welcome break from the pen and the keyboard.

FOREWORD

A Fragile World

The front cover sets the scene. Our world in the shape of an egg and it's cracked. Whether we view it globally, internationally, nationally, locally, or personally, we do live in a fragile world. Whichever which way we look, we live in uncertain times and our world could be shattered in an instant. The cracked egg is a powerful visual representation of such fragility. Plutarch wrote: *'The future bears down upon each one of us with all the hazards of the unknown. The only way out is through.''*

When we hear the nursery rhyme 'Humpty Dumpty,' we probably visualise an egg. Whether we think of him as an intact egg on the wall or a smashed one at the bottom of it, this may reveal something about ourselves. Our hopes can be dashed. Here are the lyrics:

Humpty Dumpty sat on a wall.
Humpty Dumpty had a great fall.
All the king's horses and all the king's men,
Couldn't put Humpty together again.
The oldest known lyrics (1797)

Humpty Dumpty sat on a wall,
Humpty Dumpty had a great fall.
Four-score Men and Four-score more,
Could not make Humpty Dumpty where he was before.

Humpty has been depicted as an egg for a hundred and fifty years, but how did he end up as an egg? Apparently, we have Lewis Carol to thank because in 1872 he published a novel entitled *'Through the Looking Glass.'* And so, today, when children recite the rhyme, the image of Humpty as an egg is etched on the mind for another generation.

We do know, however, that the original Humpty Dumpty was not an egg. In fact, there are at least four theories that have done the rounds. The rhyme has been said to be a riddle about breaking things. Another suggests it's an allusion to King Richard III, whose brutal 26-month reign ended with his death in the Battle of Bosworth in 1485. King Richard III's horse was supposedly called "Wall," off which he fell during battle. He was bludgeoned so severely his men could not save him; becoming the last king to die in battle. Another story is that Humpty was a siege engine around the year 1643.

According to historians, Humpty Dumpty was in actual fact a cannon used in the English civil war (1642–1649). In the year 1648, at the siege of Colchester, one of the cannonballs fired by the enemy managed to destroy a wall Humpty was positioned on. The cannon came tumbling down, and due to its massive size, all the king's horses and all the king's men couldn't put Humpty together again. So, there you have it, and yet we will probably continue in the vein of Lewis Carol and think of Humpty Dumpty as an egg.

So, what has all this to do with hope? The author suggests that if we are to find hope in a fragile world, then it would need to be a real, true, and lasting hope; not a Humpty Dumpty hope that is easily smashed to pieces. It would need to be able to withstand the march of time and the metaphorical cannonballs of the sceptics, as well as the onslaught of adversities and opposition.

Herein is the challenge to the reader. You now have 40 short essays on hope and 40 days and more to explore these. The questions posed to you by the author are these: *'Is it a real hope? It is a true hope? Is it a realistic hope? Is it a sure-fire hope? Is it a lasting hope? Is it a reasonable hope? Is it a rational hope? Has the author done it justice? Or not? Or is it another Humpty Dumpty hope? The essays have been written and it's now over to you to take up the challenge and decide for yourself. Bon voyage!*

PREFACE

RAISON D'ÊTRE

A hope beyond Shakespeare's anthesis of hope

Sir Walter Scott and the mystery of mysteries

Today, perhaps more than ever before, our world cries out for hope. In the midst of wars, catastrophes, and global pandemics, the positive thinkers shout *'Keep hope alive.'* We might retort, *'Where there's life there's hope.'* The gloom merchants respond, *'You have two hopes, Bob Hope and no hope.'* Sadly, for many, hope has either died or is on a life-support system. The reality is we all need hope to survive; to make life worth living. To lose hope and to feel we have lost it can lead us into the dark caverns of hopelessness, bleakness, and a meaningless, languishing existence. *What's the point?* is the cry of the soul that bleeds for hope. That's where billions find themselves today, living in a state of restless despair and dis-ease engulfed by a sense of chronic despondency and desperately needing to find hope.

Anyone who genuinely seeks to offer hope to the hopeless truly deserves our admiration. Whether it be food for the hungry, a place for the homeless, housing refugees from war-torn lands, support for those facing a health crisis, rescuing those who have been trafficked, and bringing freedom to those who have been abused; to offer even a glimmer of hope is surely worth it all. How we need people who offer hope and can light the candle of hope in the dark tunnel of despair. People

1

who can throw the lifeline of hope to those who are drowning in their plight, even if it's just helping to give that precious life the will to stay afloat and eventually start for the shore of hope again. We all need hope in our everyday lives and in our own personal and unique set of circumstances.

It may be viewed as tantamount to blue-sky thinking, but in our short essays we are exploring a hope that claims to endure and triumph in all seasons and circumstances. What if we could lay hold of a hope that is lifeproof, shockproof, crushproof, stormproof, timeproof, waterproof, bombproof, and even deathproof? A tall order and impossible you might say. It's almost audacious, even outrageous, to even contemplate such a hope. The concept of hope by its very nature usually means it's certainly not a certainty, rather we live in hope.

Furthermore, is anyone actually offering this kind of hope today? And if so, we would want to know their credentials. There are more than enough quacks and scammers around with pop-up hope stalls and fake-it-till-you-make-it books and programmes. And what of the great fields of education, science, philosophy, medicine, psychology, or any other 'ology'. Is there anyone in any of these fields living today to whom we can turn and find such hope? Is there anybody out there? Or has anyone ever lived and offered such hope? Has any book ever been written that not only claims such hope exists but claims to offer it and we can actually obtain it in the here and now? A certain hope.

And yet, if the truth be known, and it seems it is not commonly known, it's not far from any of us, no matter who we are, what we are, where we are, or what we have done or left undone. Wishful thinking indeed. It needs extensive exploration. Our purpose in these short essays is really fivefold, namely, does such a hope actually exist? If so, what is it? Who claims to offer it? And how on earth can it be on offer given our human condition and the uncertainties of this life? And for the sake of argument, let's say we are able to get our hands on it, what substantial difference would such a sure and steadfast hope make to us living our everyday lives here on earth? We are going to meet a number of people along the way who may be able to aid us in our explorations. There are names instantly recognisable, others less so. These include Marilyn Adamson, Emma Bevan, Ruby Wax, William Shakespeare, Sir Walter Scott, Friedrich Nietzsche, Voltaire, Sir Isaac Newton, Napoleon Bonaparte, Jean Paul Sartre, and many others. Quite a variety of people who were passionate in their views and belief systems. We come across such viewpoints as atheism, deism, theism, existentialism, and humanism to name but a few. Most people may not be aware of the philosophical movement called deconstructionism which questions assumptions about certainty, identity, and truth, but we do, however, live in a world where a form of deconstructionism takes place and people question everything. The author sees this as positive rather than negative. Perhaps a better word for us is re-examination. If we are going to believe in something with a passion then it is worth deconstructing or re-examining it extensively to ensure it's not a Humpty Dumpty belief system in terms of its certainty, its identity, and its truth.

A well-known Australian apologist and presenter said in one of his podcasts that he is often asked the question, *'What are you reading at the moment?'* To which he would reply, *"Have you got a pen? Take this down, I'm reading Genesis and Exodus and Leviticus and Numbers and Deutornony and so on … I'm reading the Bible."*

For many of us that's the cue to shut up shop, close our ears,

3

and stop reading too. But as we shall see, some of the greatest minds have been interested in and seriously considered the Bible; sceptics, atheists, and believers alike. Any serious exploration of our subject will need to include the Bible and that is our intention here; to employ it in our quest.

However, the forty short essay reflections are not just some blessed thoughts that one had at the bus stop on the way to Hopeful City, no! This is a genuine attempt to see in the dark and look for the light. We look into the blackness of the sky at night – nothing. It's all black on black, but then there is a twinkle and there's another one and then there's another and another and we can see and there are treasures of darkness. So, keep reading as you have nothing to lose and everything to gain. You can judge for yourself if it's valid and plausible and not some kind of Humpty Dumpty hope that will fall to pieces at the first challenge from the honest sceptic.

You can be sure that no matter what book you name in the world, you will not get a more shocked, startled, and negative reaction from many people if you were to say, *'I'm reading the Bible'*. It's as if it's a no-go area, it's so outdated and what relevance does it have in our postmodern technological age, God-is-dead world? I don't need to reiterate all the usual suspects in the arguments against it. Well, it's the last place on earth many would look at or even consider, and yet it's a collection of books that claims to offer humanity true hope. It declares hope, it defines hope, it describes hope, and it displays hope. It claims to bring us to the true source of a hope which is described as both sure and steadfast.

Therefore, it is not beyond reason why anyone who is on a genuine quest for hope – and, let's face it, who isn't? – would avoid a book that claims to offer a fool-proof hope. Given its claims, surely it's worth consideration despite what the critics say. And perhaps there are some big surprises awaiting us in our considerations.

The author has just been offered access to over forty books on self-improvement each month, giving access to loads of material. Very attractive indeed. I fell for it of course. The vast majority of them are about finding happiness and virtually nothing about finding hope; although the theme throughout is finding happiness within yourself, and one could then deduce that one finds hope in oneself. By creating your own sense of happiness, you create your own sense of hope in self-expression and self-fulfilment in the context of our existential existence. Happiness is based in the self; therefore, hope is based in oneself.

The thing that strikes me is the number of genuine people seeking to make some sense of it all and offer their take on self-help, people of all persuasions from all walks of life with different outlooks, different experiences, and different belief systems. It is so commendable and encouraging to one who seeks to write. When you pick up a book it's like a prism, you come to it with your own thoughts and knowledge and the book can open up new ideas and new things, just like a prism diffuses light.

Having spent over twenty years working in mental health psychiatric hospitals, one learns how important even a little hope is to the person who is reaching up to touch the bottom of their world which has fallen apart. All of us look for even a chink of light and we will leave no stone unturned in our quests. Yet when the Bible is mentioned, this can be a major obstacle. If that is you, perhaps it's time to get over those impediments and give it a go. This is your golden opportunity.

The pandemic of Covid-19 and the war in Ukraine has made many people think again. Life is so uncertain and unpredictable.

Is there a hope we can cling to? The YouVersion Bible App celebrated 500,000,000 – that's 500 million – installs in November 2021. Quite an achievement. Millions use it every day. Why not download it and you can follow what the author has called 'the prism of the word' each day and get over the obstacles, whatever they are and whatever their source, to at least have a look. If it's hope we are after, true hope, then the Bible has to be at least considered in that quest. We are going to find a counterintuitive argument to the self-actualization found in self-help literature; rather than hope being *based* in us, hope is *placed* in us. It's a gift that is given to us. This will become clearer as we go on in our journey.

We all need hope in the great everyday of life. These are mortal hopes; mortals need hope. These are at best temporal hopes. A higher hope demands more. Immortal hopes. Immortals hope. Yes, eternal hope. Is that possible? Is that available? Can a mortal who needs temporal hopes be immortal with an eternal hope? Mortal hope and eternal hope! And so, our exploration begins.

William Shakespeare (1564-1616) so eloquently describes the very antithesis of hope in Hamlet's "To be or not to be" soliloquy.

Whether 'tis nobler in the mind to suffer
The slings and arrows of outrageous fortune,
Or to take arms against a sea of troubles
And by opposing end them. To die – to sleep,
No more; and by a sleep to say we end
The heart-ache and the thousand natural shocks
That flesh is heir to: 'tis a consummation
Devoutly to be wish'd. To die, to sleep;

6

To sleep, perchance to dream – ay, there's the rub:
For in that sleep of death what dreams may come,
When we have shuffled off this mortal coil,
Must give us pause – there's the respect
That makes calamity of so long life ...

The soliloquy has several themes including doubt, uncertainty, life, and death. In essence it's about life and death: 'To be or not to be' means 'To live or not to live' or 'To live or to die'. Hamlet considers the misery and pain of human existence and how death would be preferable, were it not for the fearful uncertainty of what comes after death. The words, 'ay, there's the rub' may come from bowling, where *rub* refers to an unevenness in the ground that impedes the ball, an obstacle.

The phrase refers to an obstacle or difficulty, in Hamlet's case referring to death. Hamlet contemplates death by suicide but there was no hope for him in life or in death, not even the remote chance of sleeping and dreaming. And yet there is a book that is so daring and audacious as to outrageously offer a hope and challenges the notion of 'the calamity of so long life' before 'we have shuffled off this mortal coil.' A hope that is placed upon us in the here and now, yet transcends time and is ultimately timeless.

You will find the prism of the word at the beginning of each short essay for additional reading. Wherever 'prisms' are brought to bear upon your mind in the course of your day and influence your thinking, here is 'the prism of the Word' i.e., the Bible; it may be familiar to you, or utterly foreign to you. But it's given for you to begin to think about hope, perhaps in a way you have never done so before. If real hope is worth having, this is worth considering as you consider the challenge – is it real or is it a Humpty Dumpty one?

The Apostle Peter, as a leader, was a dealer in hope. Any dealer in hope needs to be able to name the hope they have and its source. Peter was no different; against a tidal wave of suffering, which his readers were experiencing, and which Peter acknowledges throughout his first letter, he nevertheless boldly waved the flag of hope. *Vexillum logia.*

The first usage of the word 'vexillology' was in 1959, referring to the study of flags. It was the Persians who used cloth banners to symbolise their armies. It would seem, however, that it was the Romans who first made widespread use of these symbols to represent their armies. These banners, known as a Vexillum, were used to represent each army unit as far back as 100 BC. Peter had one flag in mind – the flag of hope. He raised the standard of hope in the battle for the soul. He names this hope, and he also names its source.

Our priority is to explore this hope. Does it have any validity? And as to its relevance after 2000 years from the quill of a former unlearned and unschooled fisherman, who at one point waved the white flag of surrender and denied he knew Jesus of Nazareth at all; why would we even take it under our notice? He denied Jesus with swearing and cursing, so why would we believe him? Is he reliable? That's asking a lot. Is this genuine or fake? Is it real or fantasy? Or was Peter eating too many magic mushrooms, as one modern 'scholar' suggested? A famous old Ulster Preacher, having studied this hope for years, said; "I'm afraid it wasn't Peter who was on the mushrooms. That scholar must have had a quare feed of them" ('quare' is an Irish word with a wide range of meanings, in this instant meaning a lot). In considering this hope we will be checking in with Peter from time to time to consider the basis of his claims as a dealer in hope.

Sir Walter Scott (1771–1832) is known worldwide as an historian, biographer, novelist, and poet. He is considered to be the inventor and the greatest practitioner of the historical novel. He made his name and won enduring fame by writing fiction. His most popular work was *Ivanhoe*, published in 1819. From his earliest days he was a voracious reader and his love for reading took him into all kinds of literature including poetry, romance, drama and Scottish ballads. He was also a devout reader of the Bible. He spent his last days on earth in Abbotsford. As his illness worsened and he was on his deathbed, he said to his son-in-law, "Mister Lockhart, bring me that book."

"What book?" Mr. Lockhard asked.

"There is but one Book," replied the famous author. "Read to me out of the Bible." Sir Walter wrote in the flyleaf of his own personal Bible:

Within this awful volume lies the mystery of mysteries.

Happiest they of human race to whom their God has given grace

To read, to fear, to hope, to pray; to lift the latch and find the way.

And better they had ne'er been born, that read to doubt, or read to scorn.

Students of English literature have noted that Sir Walter certainly did 'lift the latch' for numerous plots and subplots, and characters in his novels are drawn directly from the Bible. For example, Abraham and Sarah are readily identified in his novel *Kenilworth* published in 1821. Perhaps we should take a 'leaf' out of the life of Sir Walter's book in this respect; that we too become avid readers of the Bible for ourselves. At least give it a go as it declares a unique and unparalleled kind of hope. It claims to offer us true hope.

We are on a journey of exploration into this hope and given the assertion of the Bible to be a Book of Hope and its message of hope, it does need to be seriously considered. Again, we hear voices raised in earnest, but is there any validity to its claims? We shall certainly seek to answer this question, and in addition give consideration to any other obstacles and indeed any malevolent sources behind such obstacles and difficulties. Is there something more sinister that lies beneath the opposition of turning to an ancient book of literature and wisdom that offers hope?

And what of other writers in the ancient world? What we find is that ancient authors tended to regard hope as a dangerous thing, the reason being it could set us up for practical or moral failure. In addition, since they saw hope as an emotion or an attitude, hope could be good or bad.

It was, however, the New Testament writers who declared hope as being an unqualified good and dwelling in a specific object of desire, eternal life in Christ. This good hope included an eschatological dimension. For Rome, hope was seen in terms of empire and the future ruler. The philosophical schools of antiquity developed the case against personal hope, unlike the teaching of Jesus and the apostles where hope is not only a collegiate one found in the Kingdom of God, but also a personal one, gifted to the followers of Jesus who are invited into the kingdom, the Kingdom of hope.

All need to be examined as to their truth and their validity. Let's get it all out on the table. Let's at least look into that which is being offered by way of Peter's prism (day one), then the decision will be ours as to what to do with it. Rather, what will we do with Him, who claims to be the custodian of True Hope. The desire of the author is to signpost the reader to the book of hope that claims to be the Inspired Word of God. It makes astounding claims about hope and its antithesis, hopelessness. Any quest for hope and the discovery of true hope for us as individuals, and indeed for the human race, must take into account what the Bible says. Then we can choose what to do with it.

DAY ONE

A PRISM OF HOPE

The prism of the Word: 1 Peter 1.1-25

Sir Isaac Newton and the study of light

In 1665 a young student studying science at Cambridge University in England became very interested in light and colours. As he sat in his room, he decided to close the window shutters and, in the darkness, he made a small hole that allowed a beam of light to shine through. Then he placed a prism in the path of the beam of light and to his amazement the result was a spectacular multicoloured band of colours like that of a rainbow. His name was Sir Isaac Newton (1643–1727), and he was the first to prove that white light is made up of all the colours we can see.

The rainbow that we see in the sky happens as a result of sunlight being scattered by water droplets. The process is known as refraction, and this describes how the sunlight changes direction, spreads out, and is reflected back to us, thus we observe the marvellous beauty of the multicoloured rainbow; red and orange and yellow and green and blue and indigo and violet. As children we had the hope of finding that elusive pot of gold at the end of the rainbow. Perhaps the notion of that pot of gold still lingers every time a rainbow appears.

Newton is world famous not only for his discoveries and theories in relation to optics and the composition of white light;

his work still forms the basis for current scientific thought on light, colour, and optics. But it is his work on mathematics and the formulation of the three laws of motion which form the basic principles of modern physics for which he is most famous. We all know how the story goes of Isaac as a young man sitting under an apple tree when he was struck on the head by a falling apple. This is said to have inspired that 'eureka moment' and prompted him to suddenly come up with his law of gravity. We don't really know if this story is true or not.

What we do know to be true about the life story of Newton is the significance of the Bible in his daily routine. Newton had many versions of the Bible, and we know he studied them meticulously. Throughout his busy and productive life, he had a passionate desire to know the God of the Bible. This was a major driver in his quest for understanding, if not more than physics, the natural world, and mathematics combined. The following quotes give us something of insight into the mind and the thinking of the inquisitive genius.

"If there exists a God, He has to be extremely powerful, absolutely present, and unique."

"The more I study science, the more I believe in God."

"This most beautiful system of the sun, planets, and comets could only proceed from the counsel and dominion of an intelligent and powerful Being."

"Gravity explains the motions of the planets, but it cannot explain who sets the planets in motion."

"Atheism is so senseless. When I look at the solar system, I see the earth at the right distance from the sun to receive the proper amounts of heat and light. This did not happen by chance."

13

"I can calculate the motion of heavenly bodies but not the madness of people."

"What we know is a drop, what we don't know is an ocean."

"Tact is the knack of making a point without making an enemy."

What on earth has all this to do with finding true hope? Well, for many in the world today, finding true hope seems as elusive as that pot of gold at the end of the rainbow. No matter how much we search for it we can't find the hope that gives us real certainty and total assurance. Perhaps we are a bit like Sir Isaac Newton when he pulled the shutters, and we are in the darkness. Perhaps we have almost given up on finding true hope. But bear in mind that hope may well be within our grasp as we have embarked on our journey of discovery. The reason we began with Newton's discovery was more than just an intentional 'grab your attention' introduction on day one of our travels.

There is something very profound here and it involves the imagery of the prism. A prism is a transparent object, often a polyhedron, made of glass and, as we have noted, it can refract light into a rainbow of colours. If we take that analogy of the prism and apply it to, say, opening a book, we come to it with our own preconceptions, knowledge, and experiences. We may come with the scars of dashed hopes and disappointments. We come with our restricted, individualistic, and perhaps negative view of the world. We come with our preconceived notions and prejudices. We all do this if we are honest. We come with all the influences of all the other prisms we have ever gazed into, and these have shaped our thinking and our outlook, and even our belief systems.

This book, like any other book, also has the potential to act like a prism and, just like the rainbow of light refracted through the prism, so there is the possibility of enlightened prismatic moments as we seek to expand our understanding and knowledge together in the quest for finding a sure and steadfast hope. That's a tall order, but that is the 'hope' of the author for the reader. The author would be the first to admit that this is indeed a flawed and imperfect prism, and yet an honest attempt to share hope.

The good news is that its purpose is to point us to the greatest prism in all of literature, the most perfect prism ever written, which, if we allow ourselves to look into, we shall be confronted with the greatest hope on earth. It claims an eternal dimension that will not fade or gather rust. It is so robust and assured that it need not be discarded for the next fad that comes our way. That prism is the Bible of Sir Isaac Newton and Sir Walter Scott. We are also going to meet others on the journey who investigated the prism of the Word of God and they too found therein a hope beyond their wildest dreams.

Anyway, in our quest for hope, we do well to ask whose peddling it? And if they are, what is the basis for such claims? What is the bedrock on which it's based? Or does it need blind faith to 'hope' for the best? Enough said, all the reader is asked to do now is to continue on and not disembark because here is something that has the potential to turn your night into day, your darkness into light. You might be the owner of a new coat, the hope coat of many colours that can endure any storm as well as the transient nature of life on earth for the transcendent and eternal nature of God. An awesome prism awaits us and the possibility of profound prismatic moments if we take the time to look and listen.

Look and Learn was a British weekly publication that ran

from 1962–1982. It was educational and informative, covering a wide range of topics from volcanoes to the Loch Ness Monster. It also had a science-fiction comic strip called the *Trigan Empire*. Some rare copies can now fetch hundreds of pounds. Let us be willing to look and learn. What is truth and what is fiction? And let us listen too for the voice of hope.

There is the sense in which the whole world acts like a prism; the things we watch and the stuff we read; everything is reflected and is absorbed either consciously or unconsciously into our minds. The problem is that unfortunately these may not be the bright hopeful colours we seek but the dark ones, making our darkness greater rather than diminishing it, exacerbating our hopelessness rather than giving us real hope. Marcus Aurelius is quoted as saying: *"The soul becomes dyed by the colour of its thoughts."*

He elaborates further on this in his meditations by saying: *"Your mind will take the shape of what you frequently hold in thought for the human spirit is coloured by such impressions."*

The deepest desire of the author is that this book acts as a prism to enable the reader to not only explore and expand their knowledge of true hope but to find it and get into the awesome prism of the Word of God and discover what we thought to be beyond our reach. Too good to be true? Don't let the scepticism of the age and the voices that demand you *'don't give any credence to this nonsense'* influence you. It's our time to explore. This could be our time to find true hope. And we can decide if it's a Humpty Dumpty phenomenon or if it's actually in the clear light of day, phenomenally true! The real deal!

DAY TWO

IS HOPE THE MOST EVIL OF ALL EVILS?

The prism of the Word: Psalm 130 and Peter 1.3-5.

Nietzsche, Voltaire, Spurgeon,
and an antiquarian curiosity seeker

Nietzsche was born on 15th October 1844 in a Lutheran manse in a village near Leipzig. His parents decided to name him after King Friedrich Wilhelm IV of Prussia, who celebrated his birthday on the same day. It was the King who had been responsible for the appointment of Nietzsche's father as the local minister.

Sadly for Nietzsche, his father died when he was only four years of age and within six months, his two-year-old brother, Joseph, also died. These events had a profound impact on Nietzsche. Being exposed to the suddenness and finality of death left him with a deep sense of uncertainty about life and the seeming injustice of it all. He would, in later years, refer frequently in his publications to the utter despair of our existential existence and the finality and calamity of death. The following is an example of the pathos and hopelessness of his outlook on life: *"Let us beware of saying that death is opposed to life. The living is merely a type of what is dead; and a very rare type."*

At the age 19, Nietzsche attended the University of Bonn. He was intending to study theology and classical philology (the study of language from ancient written texts). However, after only one semester he abandoned theology and lost whatever faith he had. The following quotation gives an insight into his thinking and his replacement of God, and aligning himself with philosophers such as Schopenhauer, who was regarded as the 'philosopher of pessimism.' He had an ardent follower in Nietzche.

> ... [I]n the place of an all-powerful, all-knowing, and all-good God at the ruling centre of the universe, Schopenhauer substituted a blind, aimless, and fundamentally senseless energetic urge that he could describe as nothing more than the blind force of sheer will.

Nietzsche had exchanged the Christian view of God with that of the superman. Nietzsche's superman represents the highest principle of the development of humanity and the affirmation of man's full potentialities. One can see why the Nazis made selective use of Nietzsche's philosophy. Indeed, Hitler needed a philosopher, like all dictators, and he chose Nietzsche's work which he used as a blank cheque for his megalomaniac empire building; enter the superman of Nazism. It is believed that Nietzsche's sister, Elisabeth Förster-Nietzsche, who joined the Nazi party, and who published her late brother's work, did him no favours. There are doubts over her work on 'The will to power' and that she forged it to blacken her brother. Elizabeth is one of the most despised women in all of German history.

Yet what is fascinating about Nietzsche's 'superman' is its profound religious implications. Despite Nietzsche's rejection of the Christian faith and his attack on God and religious moral ideals, his concept of the superman fails in stripping humanity/man of his religious and spiritual nature. He replaced the God of Hope for another God, the god of self – man is god, man is superman. Mankind needs a superman. He rejected the God Man. Hope, for Nietzsche, is now based firmly in man, not placed in man from an outside source, i.e., God. Nietzsche declared God to be dead, and identified himself with Dionysus, the Greek god of wine and excess. In denying God, he argued, we are then in a position to deny any accountability. To trace the life of this genius madman is to observe the sad and inevitable descent into hopelessness and despair.

The experience of being human and living in a world of which hope can be hard to find led this great German philosopher to state his opinion on the subject: *'Hope is the most evil of all evils because it prolongs man's torment.'*

Thus, Nietzsche fell into a nihilism and despair. For him there was little chance of his 'reality' of despair changing and his final descent into madness vividly demonstrates his incorrigible condition. Yet while calling hope an evil he also pleaded longingly for its rehabilitation. The reality is we all need hope to enable us to survive. One writer on the subject of Nietzsche's failure to kill God said:

Did no one explain to the young Nietzsche that this world is not the way God originally created it, that sin entered and caused a cursed world – that God the Judge, whom Nietzsche hated so much because he was accountable to Him, was also the loving God who sent His own Son, the Lord Jesus Christ, to die on the cross and rise again, so that He could justly forgive us for our sins?

19

In his book *The Anti-Christ*, as well as in many other books, Nietzsche shows he was quite familiar with these concepts but vehemently rejected them. Many have rejected the concept of future judgement by claiming that there are no absolutes of right and wrong. Nietzsche, however, had a more fundamental approach: he announced the death of the Judge! In denying God we can thus deny any accountability whatsoever.

The Bible, the ultimate book of Hope, not only declares God to be the righteous Judge, but also the God of Hope. It defines hope, it describes hope, and it declares here is where hope is to be found. Millions have discovered this hope. And yet while many long for hope and seek it under every 'nook and cranny,' biblical hope is rejected in the quagmire of a world without God. The Bible is either rejected outright or is decidedly off limits for a sceptical and secular world that refuses this prism which claims to diffuse light for darkened minds.

Sadly, Nietzsche suffered psychiatric illness, coupled with depression and a progressive cognitive decline into chronic dementia, exacerbated with strokes. He died of pneumonia in 1900.

Over a century before, Voltaire (pseudonym, François-Marie Arouet, (1694-1778) made his prediction about the Bible. In 1776 the French sceptic said: *"One hundred years from my day, there will not be a Bible on earth except one that is looked upon by an antiquarian curiosity-seeker."*

Many make the assumption that Voltaire was an atheist, but this was not the case. One of Voltaire's favourite sayings was: *"If God did not exist, it would be necessary to invent Him."*

Unlike Nietzsche, Voltaire believed in God but did not believe in a God personally involved in people's lives. He did not accept the concept of personal God of Hope. The following is a fascinating quote from his quill.

> *The astronomer who watches the motions of stars, established according to the laws of the most profound mathematics, must adore the Eternal Geometer. The physicist who investigates a grain of wheat or an animal body must recognize the Eternal Craftsman. The moral man who seeks a support point in virtue must admit the existence of a Being as fair as He is supreme. So, God is necessary to the world in every way, and we can say, together with the author of the Epistle to the scribbler of a vulgar book on the Three Impostors, 'If God did not exist, it would be necessary to invent Him'.*

As a Deist, the philosophical system in which Voltaire operated allowed both he and other intellectuals of the time to reconcile a belief in some form of God which incorporated their overwhelming passion for reason. In addition, Deists believe that the God who created the universe does not interfere with any natural processes on Earth. This ideology reconciles a belief in a Supreme Being with belief in scientific reasoning. As such, Deism generally rejects the concept of miracles along with any other supernatural occurrences, such as the divinity and resurrection of Jesus. Thus, we can see that people like Voltaire and Nietzsche came up with their own views, one with no God, and one with an absent God, with neither having hope in the God of hope.

After his death, the presses that were used to print Voltaire's books printed Bibles and Voltaire's house was used by the Geneva Bible Society to distribute Bibles. One hundred years from the time of Voltaire's prediction, the first edition of his work sold for .11¢ in Paris, but the British government paid the Czar of Russia half a million dollars for an ancient Bible manuscript.

Research on Voltaire's vast array of writings reveal a comprehensive knowledge of Scripture, and biblical quotations permeate his works, including those which have no apparent connection to Christianity. He is seen to respond positively to the Bible, almost despite himself, and shows insights beyond the perceived wisdom of the day in terms of its composition. It's a book that must not be ignored.

One hundred years after Voltaire, a contemporary of Nietzsche, a man called Charles Haddon Spurgeon, was preaching in London. One of his famous quotes about the Bible was: *'Scripture is like a lion. Who ever heard of defending a lion? Just turn it loose; it will defend itself.'*

Charles Spurgeon (1834–1892) is still referred to today as 'The Prince of Preachers.' A Wikipedia search will reveal that he preached thousands of sermons, wrote many commentaries and books, including devotionals, as well as publishing magazines, poetry, and hymns. He pastored the Metropolitan Tabernacle in London for almost 40 years. It was the mega-church of its day with a seating capacity of 5,000 and standing room for an additional 1,000 attendees. The place was packed to hear him preach. Spurgeon understood the full range of human emotions and often preached on them. He suffered from depression throughout his life but his preaching always returned to what the Bible had to say about us and about God. Here's one of the things Spurgeon had to say about the subject of hope:

My hope lives, not because I am not a sinner, but because I am a sinner for whom Christ died. My trust is not that I am holy, but that being unholy, Christ is my righteousness. My

*faith rests not upon what I am or shall be or feel or know –
but in who Christ is, in what He has done, and in what He is
now doing for me. Hallelujah ...*

Here is an example from one of his sermons: 'Patience,
Comfort, and Hope from the Scriptures', Charles Haddon
Spurgeon July 20, 1879, Scripture: Romans 15:4, From:
Metropolitan Tabernacle Pulpit Volume 47.

THE HOPE OF THE SCRIPTURES:
*"That we through the patience and the comfort of the
Scriptures might have the hope." You have noticed, I daresay,
that the matters which concern our salvation are always
spoken of as the objects of faith. A man does not obtain the
pardon of his sins by hoping for it; he is not regenerated
because he hopes to be born again; justification is not given
to him because he hopes for it; all these things are matters of
faith, not of hope. We are justified by faith; it is by faith that
we receive the forgiveness of our sins. Faith has to do with
the past – with what Christ has accomplished; but hope looks
forward to the future. Hope is for those who are saved, and
hope comes to us, and is strengthened in us, by the patience
and the comfort of the Scriptures.*

Without a personal God, the God of hope, Nietzsche offers
us the 'super human' – superman. Voltaire offers us an absent
God who does not get personally involved with humans.
Spurgeon offers the God of the Bible who is a personal God
offering us salvation hope. The argument from Scripture is that
hope is not based in us by atheism or by deism, but theism
offers us a hope that is placed in us by Almighty God, it's only
source.

Is *'Hope is the most evil of all evils because it prolongs man's torment'*? It all comes down to what we believe and what we embrace and espouse. To be given hope by the God of the Bible is to obtain a hope of which Isaiah refers to: *'But those who hope in the LORD will renew their strength. They will soar on wings like eagles; they will run and not grow weary, they will walk and not be faint'* (Isaiah 40.31).

The Psalmist David had his own personal struggles in life and its vicissitudes. At a time of depression and being downcast we find him saying: *'Why, my soul, are you downcast? Why so disturbed within me? Put your hope in God, for I will yet praise him, my Saviour and my God'* (Psalm 43.5).

DAY THREE

OUR VOYAGE OF EXPLORATION

The prism of the Word: Psalm 62 and Romans 15.4.

Social psychology, hopeless optimism, and Coran Deo

Hope is pictured as an anchor in Hebrews 6.19 and is described as both sure and steadfast. But what is hope? We would do well at this juncture to define what hope actually is, so we know exactly what it is we are looking for.

Hope has been associated with and indeed is often synonymous with optimism. Any comparison of the various dictionary references will suggest quite an overlap in terms of the meaning. Hope can be seen as being optimistic about our situation, our relationships, our circumstances, and our future. Or sometimes in the face of trouble and uncertainty we hear ourselves saying, *'Well, all we can do is to hope for the best.'*

We all know the well-worn phrase, *'Hope for the best, prepare for the worst.'*

The reality is that no matter how hopeful and optimistic we are we can have our hopes dashed. We get up each morning with a hopeful attitude, optimistic about a certain outcome, and we may be devastated when it doesn't materialise or work out as we had planned. We know from experience that nothing is totally certain in this life.

Sitting in my upper room, musing on and grappling with the meaning of the great and sometimes elusive concept of hope, the thought came to me: *'In two days' time the world will be recognizing the importance of good mental health and celebrate world mental health day.'*

Having worked in the field of mental health for almost a quarter of a century and walked the corridors of psychiatric inpatient hospitals, speaking with patients in acute and intensive care wards, one knows how important hope is in the recovery journey. Whether it be recovery from mental illness or recovery within the illness to a better quality of life. Whilst living with mental illness, whether it be a single episode or a long-term condition, hope is central to the wellbeing of the individual.

One of the pillars of the recovery ethos in the mental health arena is hope. There is the need to cultivate and establish hope. Hope is seen as the growing ground for recovery. The 'healer' needs to be a dealer in hope, and more often than not is a wounded healer. Social psychologists grapple with and seek to research the concept of hope. Given that none of us are getting out of here alive, one of the ideas they have come up with is *'hopeless optimism'*. As mere mortals we need to cultivate a sense of optimism about our existence whilst on earth. Sir Winston Churchill would have agreed with this viewpoint. He is quoted as saying: *'I am an optimist; it does not seem to be too much use being anything else.'*

One knows from experience the importance of hope and optimism in the life of a person who has lost hope in themselves, hope in the system, and in everyone around them. One has discovered the vital importance of learning to adopt an empathetic and attentive listening approach, valuing the person and really tuning in to the cries of helplessness and hopelessness from the bleeding soul. It is in these moments of authentic connection that hope can germinate and eventually flourish. We are talking here in the natural realm of humanity and human experience. And for all of us on the journey of life we need hope in everyday life to be able to function and cope so we are able to manage our struggles and difficulties. The emphasis is more so on hope, however, than on optimism, or even hopeless optimism.

The relationship between hope and optimism has been well considered by Arthur Brooks, who writes a weekly column on 'how to build a better life.' He seeks to tackle questions on the meaning of happiness. In one of his articles, he sheds tremendous light on the important distinction between hope and optimism. He gives the example of U.S Navy vice admiral, James Stockdale, who was imprisoned for over seven years during the Vietnam war. The vice admiral carefully observed his fellow inmates and noticed a surprising trend: some prisoners survived appalling conditions, whereas others did not. Those who didn't tended to be in the most optimistic group. These were the prisoners who, with hopeless optimism, stated that they were definitely getting out by Christmas. But Christmas would come and go, then another and then another. Stockdale then saw them die in prison of a broken heart. Brooks himself observed that those who have struggled the most during the Covid-19 pandemic were the optimists who were always predicting a speedy return to normality, only to be disappointed as the pandemic dragged on. Brooks states:

> There's a word for believing you can make things better without distorting reality: not optimism, but hope. Just as Stockdale found – and I've found in a less dramatic way during the pandemic – optimism often isn't the best way to improve your well-being. The research shows that hope is a far more potent force. We can all get better at it as we work

toward recovering from the pandemic, and benefit from our
improved skill for the rest of our lives.

Brooks notes that most philosophical and religious traditions regard hope as an active choice, and even a commandment. He is of the view that it is a theological virtue in Christianity as it implies voluntary action, not just happy prediction.

Teresa of Avila, writing in the 16th century, put it this way:

Hope, O my soul, hope. You know neither the day nor the
hour. Watch carefully, for everything passes quickly, even
though your impatience makes doubtful what is certain, and
turns a very short time into a long one. Dream that the more
you struggle the more you prove the love that you bear your
God, and the more you will rejoice one day with your
Beloved, in a happiness and rapture that can never end.

Whether you are a hopeless optimist or a hopeful pessimist, the Bible emphatically declares a hope that is beyond the limitations of earth and the human condition and is supernatural in nature. It claims that it originates in the author of truth Himself, God. Trust in God is what makes the great paradigm shift from chronic despair to confident hope in the eternal, not just in the ephemeral. Paul encourages the followers of Jesus: *'I pray that God, the source of hope, will fill you completely with joy and peace because you trust in Him. Then you will overflow with confident hope through the power of the Holy spirit'* (Roman 15.13).

Notice the words carefully, God, source, hope, joy, peace, trust, confidence, power. And that's what the Bible claims. That's what God, as revealed in the Bible, declares. God is identified as the giver of a sure and steadfast confident Hope.

We shall find out that is exactly what the Apostle of Hope, Peter, tells us in his opening remarks in 1. Peter 1.3, our prism of the Word meditation for today.

Just to be clear, and to reiterate the differentiation in the usages of the word 'hope'. We typically use the word 'hope' in our everyday vocabulary to refer to hope in times of uncertainty. The team that has just appointed their new manager hopes that success will now be their destiny. It's a hope, but it is not certain. When the Apostles speak of hope they are declaring a sure and certain hope.

The Apostle Paul refers to this sure and certain hope in relation to resurrection. This hope is about a confidence that is based upon the Word of God and the fulfilment of its promises. Biblical hope is about certainty; the hope of salvation as it is referred to in his first letter to the church at Thessalonica, an ancient city of Macedonia in northern Greece which today is the city of Thessaloniki.

'But since we belong to the day, let us be clear-headed, putting on faith and love as a breastplate, and the hope of salvation as a helmet' (1 Thessalonians 5.8).

The Believer can be confident, living in the triad of faith, hope, and love. Paul contrasts the unbelief of the world with the believer's faith in God and love for others. In addition to demonstrating faith and love, those who believe are to adopt the hope of salvation and live in the light of the return of Jesus Christ. Living authentically in the present with an eye on the future.

We will find that the hope Peter refers to in his opening chapter of his first letter is also described as a salvation hope and this is interwoven into the five chapters. The dominant theme is a salvation hope in the opening chapter; it's a living hope. The essence of this living hope is summed up in the Latin words 'Coram Deo'. Biblical hope is manifested in the reality of Coram Deo, literally, 'in the presence of God.'

This is the big idea in Christianity and captures the essence of the hope and optimism that is declared throughout the canon of Scripture. This is a hope that is about our eternal welfare and our eternal wellbeing. This hope is a treasure to have and to hold and to experience it in life as flourishing in the light.

'We now have this light shining in our hearts, but we ourselves are like fragile clay jars containing this great treasure. This makes it clear that our great power is from God, not from ourselves' (2 Corinthians 4.7).

The source of our hope is key. A sinner who knows he or she is beloved of God and made the benefactor of Christ's sacrifice on the cross is a person of hope. Hope indwells this person because the perfect sacrifice for all avails for him or her and they are clothed in His righteousness. True hope isn't based on our feelings. Instead, it's based on, as Spurgeon put it, *'... who Christ is, in what He has done, and in what He is now doing for me.'*

DAY FOUR

THE LEADER IS A DEALER IN HOPE

The prism of the Word: 1 Peter 1.1-3.

Napoleon Bonaparte and the book that surpasses all others

Emperor Napoleon Bonaparte (1769–1821) was born into a relatively modest family on the provincial island of Corsica, far from the centres of power. From humble beginnings he became one of the greatest military and political leaders of all time. The leadership philosophy that enabled him to achieve this was very simple. He said: *'A leader is a dealer in hope.'*

In battle, Napoleon carried himself with an aura of victory, even in the worst situations. He exuded confidence to his troops, inspiring them and assuring them that victory was certain. Another of his famous quotes is: *'Moral force rather than numbers, decides victory.'*

His fighting men believed in him, and he was immensely popular for this was a man who had turned their country into a world power. They were led by one of the greatest generals in world history and he inspired hope and optimism in everyone. He believed passionately in the power of hope.

In our chaotic world as we fight the enemies of pandemics and fear, we need people who will inspire hope and tell us that there is hope. There are more than enough merchants of doom and gloom. And as for dealers who say they deal in hope we need to be careful because not all dealers have a good reputation, nor are they offering that which is good, even if it seems good. Is it the genuine article? The Apostle Peter has been described as a dealer in hope, who, in the face of adversity and even death by execution, espoused a lifeproof, deathproof hope.

Peter as a dealer in 'sure-fire' hope does so by giving his readers something to believe in, and he establishes the foundation for such. In fact, it is more than that, he gives his hearers, and us his readers, someone to believe in. Peter draws our attention to a person, and he is saying categorically that hope is found in a person. That person is God. As a dealer in hope here are ten things that Peter talks about which can undergird and inspire our hope today.

A secularist will, on the other hand, take each of these and apply them in a way that takes the humanistic approach. As one who has worked for over twenty-two years in the secular world in the mental health field, one is not at liberty to proselytise and one can see the benefits of seeking to aid and support one of the most vulnerable groups in society in these terms in that way and in that context.

When we delve further, however, into this true hope, we will find that this lasting hope of which Peter and his fellow writers speak is only possible if we have the right foundation. Peter points to Jesus Christ.

1. Connexity

The secret to finding true hope is connexity – we need connection with others. Social isolation is not conducive to good mental health. Peter emphasises this in the context of fellowship. The first of the five-a-day for mental health/good wellbeing is about connection. You may have come across the five-a-day; they are:

1. *Connect with other people. Good relationships are important for your mental wellbeing.*
2. *Be physically active. Being active is not only great for your physical health and fitness.*
3. *Learn new skills.*
4. *Give to others.*
5. *Pay attention to the present moment.*

Our relationships with other people are fundamental to our sense of wellbeing and happiness. Close relationships with family and friends can yield love, support, and a sense of meaning in our lives.

Peter and the Bible writers go further and emphasise that the key to lasting hope is connection with God. We will find that Peter tells us that we connect with God through His Word, the Bible. Here, it is claimed, are the very words of God to our generation and every generation. If you have been led to believe that this book is outdated and irrelevant, watch this space. This book tells us how connection is possible, given that the relationship has broken down. It presents to us the person of Jesus Christ in the incarnation 'Emmanuel, God with us'. More on that later in our short essays. The Apostle John, as an eyewitness, said, *'We proclaim to you what we ourselves have actually seen and heard so that you may have fellowship with us. And our fellowship is with the Father and with his Son, Jesus Christ'* (1 John 1.3).

2. Challenges

The secret to finding true hope is acknowledging the challenges of life. We need to begin with an honest analysis of who we really are and what we really are. The big challenging questions are really, who am I? Where did I come from? And where am I going? The launch of NASA's $10 billion James Webb Space Telescope on 25th December 2021 from French Guiana has caused great excitement because it is believed it could mark a triumph in a journey that thousands of astronomers have been following for a generation. The basic reason for its launch is to answer the question, where did we come from? The Bible analysis of humanity answers this question and many more and shows our need for God as the source of all hope through the Saviour of the world, Jesus Christ. Peter is going to tell us about this too in his letter of hope. Paul reminds his readers of their past life before they found true hope, where they are now, and where they are going.

In those days you were living apart from Christ. You were excluded from citizenship among the people of Israel, and you did not know the covenant promises God had made to them. You lived in this world without God and without hope. But now you have been united with Christ Jesus. Once you were far away from God, but now you have been brought near to him through the blood of Christ (Ephesians 2:12-13).

Earlier he refers to the eternal dimension of this unique hope in these terms:

… But God is so rich in mercy, and he loved us so much that even though we were dead because of our sins, he gave us life when he raised Christ from the dead. (It is only by God's grace that you have been saved!) For he raised us from the dead along with Christ and seated us with him in the heavenly realms because we are united with Christ Jesus. So

God can point to us in all future ages as examples of the incredible wealth of his grace and kindness toward us, as shown in all he has done for us who are united with Christ Jesus. God saved you by his grace when you believed. And you can't take credit for this; it is a gift from God. Salvation is not a reward for the good things we have done, so none of us can boast about it. For we are God's masterpiece. He has created us anew in Christ Jesus, so we can do the good things he planned for us long ago (Ephesians 2.4-10).

3. Compassion

The secret to finding true hope is to find out about compassion. Many feel utterly lost today in the darkness of the present world. Lost, needing direction from one who has compassion for us. I remember a lorry driver telling me of driving in a certain country and getting lost. He asked someone and they gave him very clear directions. He followed them closely, but he ended up on a narrow road that became a dirt track and after some miles he had to go back. He had to reverse that articulated truck back to where he had started. He has been deliberately given the wrong directions. The deceiver had a great laugh but for John, the driver, it could have led to fatal consequences.

Then a compassionate and genuine individual offered to travel with him to get him on the right road to reach his destination. We may have taken the wrong road and we may have done so because we were given the wrong directions. No doubt our arch enemy had a hand in it. Do we have an arch enemy? We will be checking this out too in our explorations.

Peter tells us there is one who is so compassionate and wants to get us on the right road and travel with us and give us the hope of fulfilling our destinies and eventually reach our destination. *'The LORD is gracious and merciful, slow to anger and abounding in steadfast love'* (Psalm 145.8).

4. Contribution

One of the five-a-day for good mental health and wellbeing is to give. Doing good is good for us. Helping others makes us feel needed and valued. This can reinforce social connectedness and give us a sense of purpose. One of the elements that promote hope is to know that our lives have purpose and meaning, and our contributions are of immense value. Each of us can make a difference for good. The biblical perspective emphasises this and we are required not only to do good and but to take this further. The prophet Micah gives us a divine mandate for living; one that gives a balanced answer to today's spiritual and political questions. *'What does the Lord require of you? To act justly, and to love mercy and to walk humbly with your God'* (Micah 6.8).

The amplified Bible makes this mandate even clearer.

He has told you, O man, what is good; And what does the LORD require of you except to be just, and to love [and to diligently practice] kindness (compassion), *and to walk humbly with your God [setting aside any overblown sense of importance or self-righteousness]?*

This relationship with God was broken but it can be restored and within this there is a divine plan. A plan for mankind, but also Scripture reveals to us there is a master plan for each of us and we all have our part to play in it. Peter is going to outline this masterplan so be prepared for something astounding and matchless in comparison to anything you have ever dreamed or imagined. Prismatic moments to come! In the meantime, here is a great word of encouragement for you today. *'"For I know the plans I have for you," declares the Lord, "plans to prosper you and not to harm you, plans to give you hope and a future'* (Jeremiah 29.11).

The interpretation and primary application of this statement applied to Jews living in exile in Babylon and whom Nebuchadnezzar had taken captive. This message came to encourage them. However, given the theme of Divine plans in Scripture, we can readily apply this to our lives in our submission to the King, to whom we bow the knee. He has a plan for us, and that plan includes the practice of justice, love, kindness, and compassion, as we walk humbly with God.

5. Consecration

The secret to finding true hope is to focus on what is real and genuine and authentic. We need to get real and not live in cloud-cuckoo-land. We have had enough of the counterfeit. There is an arch enemy that Peter tells us about that seeks to rob us of real hope and to confuse as he desires for us to set our hopes on that which is only transitory. In a world of hopeless desperation, we need to seriously consider what Peter has to say. Don't let the enemy pull your strings any longer. The words of the Lord of Hope come to mind: *'The thief comes only in order to steal and kill and destroy. I came that they may have life, and have it in abundance – to the full, till it overflows'* (John 10.10).

6. Capacity

The secret of finding true hope is to know that you have the capacity to reach for that higher hope, to find true hope, to actually have an assured and certain hope and to fulfil the purpose for which we were put on this earth to do. You have the capacity to be who you really are and to become what you long to be. Whatever your mess is and no matter how you have messed up, you have the potential to become a masterpiece. It's worth using the quote from Paul's pen again. *'For we are God's masterpiece. He has created us anew in Christ Jesus, so we can do the good things he planned for us long ago'* (Ephesians 2.10).

The amplified Bible puts it this way:

For we are His workmanship [His own master work, a work of art], created in Christ Jesus [reborn from above – spiritually transformed, renewed, ready to be used] for good works, which God prepared [for us] beforehand [taking paths which He set], so that we would walk in them [living the good life which He prearranged and made ready for us] (Ephesians 2.10).

7.   Communion

The secret of finding true hope is to be in communion with God. It is not the case that God is nowhere but rather God is now here. And He wants us to know Him. That's the invitation of the Bible. This is the claim of the Bible; we can know God and have a personal relationship with our Creator.

We will get into the origins of it all and the various views that tell us we don't need the notion of a Creator, never mind one who would need to be infinite to create the universe, and even if He did, how on earth would He or could He have a relationship with you and me? It's all too big and He would be too big for it to be otherwise.

We are encouraged by many to commune with the infinite universe and with nature, but to suggest that we commune with the eternal Being who made it all is regarded as an impossibility, and it's just about the brain's need for certainty. We will look into this. One thing is certain: we long for love and intimacy and communion. *'Our souls are restless until they find their rest in you'*, wrote Augustine. The Psalmist wrote: *'O God, you are my God, earnestly I seek you; my soul thirsts for you, my body longs for you, in a dry and weary land where there is no water. I have seen you in the sanctuary and beheld your power and your glory'* (Psalm 63.1).

8. Celebration

The secret of finding true sure-fire hope is to celebrate its reality, joy in its source, worship God in its possession and to live daily in its truth and so fulfil its potential and possibilities and the plan we were born for. Even in a world that is foreign to sure-fire hope and where adversity and opposition to such a seemingly ludicrous belief system is commonplace, we can, according to the Bible, know this true hope. *Why am I discouraged? Why is my heart so sad? I will put my hope in God! I will praise him again – my Saviour and my God'* (Psalm 42.5).

9. Conflict

The secret to finding true hope is to realise who the enemy of hope really is, and who is still plying his evil trade and is still in the obscene business of seeking to stifle our grand desires and will stop at nothing to thwart our discovery and possession of true authentic hope. But there is a hope that is triumphant and available through Jesus Christ. *'Now thanks be to God who always leads us in triumph in Christ, and through us diffuses the fragrance of His knowledge in every place'* (2 Corinthians 2.14).

10. Clarity

The secret of finding sure-fire hope is to conclude that the message of the Bible is true and true hope is found in God alone. *'Simon Peter answered him, "Lord, to whom shall we go? You have the words of eternal life"'* (John 6.68).

So are you up for the challenge then? We are not hiding behind pious platitudes or blind belief. Then you can decide for yourself if sure-fire hope is a runner for you and where you will place your hope and your faith. Most of us will want more than hopeless optimism. But it has to be credible. And there are times in life when the credible is also incredible. The Merriam-Webster dictionary asks the question, does incredible mean not credible? And here is the answer: *The in-prefix in incredible did initially imply "not," as the original definition of incredible was "too extraordinary to be believed," thus "not credible." However, over time the meaning of incredible weakened and is now taken to mean "amazing." This is similar to the weakening of the word 'unbelievable'.*

Let's see what Peter the dealer in hope is offering along with his fellow writers. Credible and incredible? Authentic and amazing? Or implausible and untenable? Flummoxing and baffling? The Humpty Dumpty variety or the genuine article?

Napoleon was a voracious reader with an insatiable desire to learn. Even as a child he gravitated towards books about leaders and how they dealt with the world. He wanted to understand leadership in action and how they strategized.

On the Bible Napoleon said: *'The Bible contains a complete series of acts and of historical men to explain time and eternity, such as no other religion has to offer.'*

'The Bible is no mere book, but a Living Creature, with a power that conquers all that oppose it.'

'The Gospel is not a book; it is a living being, with an action, a

power, which invades everything that opposes its extension, behold! It is upon this table: This book, surpassing all others. I never omit to read it, and every day with some pleasure.'

'The more I consider the Gospel, the more I am assured that there is nothing there which is not beyond the march of events and above the human mind. Even the impious themselves have never dared to deny the sublimity of the Gospel, which inspires them with a sort of compulsory veneration.'

What Napoleon said about Jesus:

'From the first day to the last He is the same; majestic and simple; infinitely firm and infinitely gentle. He proposes to our faith a series of mysteries and commands with authority that we should believe them, giving no other reason than those tremendous words, "I am God."'

'Superficial minds see a resemblance between Christ and the founders of empires and the gods of other religions. That resemblance does not exist.'

DAY FIVE

HOPE FOR A HOPELESS CASE

The prism of the word: 1 Peter 1 and 1 Timothy 1.12-17.

A hopeless case who, with hope restored, turned the world upside down

Peter describes himself as *'an Apostle, on assignment by Jesus, the Messiah...'* (1 Peter 1.1a). I got to thinking about the word 'assignment' that Eugene Petterson uses in his wonderful paraphrase, the Message Bible. As an Apostle, Peter was very much on assignment as God had a specific task for him to complete; but it had been all up in the air years before. Dreams were shattered and all his hopes evaporated that cold dark night as he warmed his hands at the world's fire, in the courtyard outside the place of trial, and denied he had anything to do with Jesus Christ, and did so with oaths and curses. You can read the account of Peter's denials in Luke chapter 26.69-75. We are told by physician Luke in his account of the events leading up to the crucifixion: *'The Lord turned and looked straight at Peter. Then Peter remembered the word the Lord had spoken to him: "Before the rooster crows today, you will disown me three times. And he went outside and wept bitterly.'* (Luke 22.61)

An immense cloud of hopelessness hung over his life. Any consideration of the life of Peter will encounter what was tantamount to gross failure. It is more commonly known as 'Peter's denial;' his total denial of Jesus Christ. Peter must have seen himself as one big failure. In fact, as we visualise that gloomy betrayal night, so vividly portrayed by Luke, we cannot help but feel empathy for Peter as we see him going out and weeping bitterly. Such was his chagrin that having been such an ardent follower of Jesus, and a member of the inner circle and spokesman for the twelve, he totally blew it. He had given up his fishing business, his livelihood, and followed Jesus for over three years. He had literally given up everything. Now it was all over as far as he was concerned.

He then made up his mind about his future and decided to go back to his old job, fishing. Time to escape to the sea again and to fade into the background and hopefully not have to face the public again.

Oh, the shame of it all. Oh, the hopelessness of it all. It was cold comfort for Peter, but he was not alone in his failures. The other boys – the other disciples – had experienced the same gross failure on the night of betrayal and had run away; all of them. When Peter announced his intentions on returning to his old occupation, the others said, 'We will go with you.'

And this is the Apostle of hope? Yes, but here is the very point we need to make; the hopeless can find hope, and Peter is a prime example of it. So much so that he is writing over thirty years later to encourage others, who for different reasons find themselves in the pit of hopeless despair. You can read all about it in our 'prism of the Word' readings for today. Hope lost can be hope restored.

Peter's humility is displayed in the writing of Mark's Gospel. We have good scholarly reasons to believe Peter was the source behind it. Mark 14.66-72 records the actual betrayal and we get this interesting touch when Mark records Peter's thoughts on the night. 'And when he thought about it, he wept.' We can be sure it was recorded so that those of us who have failed, or lost our way and have lost hope, can be assured that all is not lost. We may think it's lost but hope can be found again; or rather, hope can find us.

The story of Peter's recovery shows hope found him after a fruitless night at sea when he had caught nothing. Jesus stood on the shore and beckoned to him, and at a warm fire when breakfast had been prepared by Jesus Himself, Peter was restored and so was hope.

Having his hope restored, Peter was a changed man. He stands out in the testimony of Scripture, teaching us that even hopeless cases can find hope. Peter had to return to the Source of Hope – the very one he betrayed. To find true hope we have to go back to the true source of hope. If our hopelessness has arisen because of our own failures, we have taken the wrong road; Peter stands out as a shining example that failure is not final. The God of hope and restoration and recommissioning can fill us with all hope and joy and peace in believing. You can be assured that God is not finished with you yet.

The first ten chapters of the book of Acts are replete with this rejuvenated, powerful man emboldened by the Spirit of God. Peter now lived fully and effectively in the spiritual world – he knew that his fight involved spiritual warfare. In fact, he had been told that his arch enemy, and ours, had wanted to sift him as wheat and suck every ounce of hope out of his life and soul. To the world at large he was a big former fisherman, now a passionate street preacher and many would not have given him a second thought; but he was on an assignment from God to spread the Gospel of Hope. And boy did he do so! Peter, who almost went under, became an agent of hope on assignment for Jesus the Messiah ... to proclaim a living hope.

As this undercover agent, so to speak, engaged in undertaking an undercover assignment, he was engaged in a warfare that the watching world knew nothing about. He refers to this spiritual battle we are engaged in by telling his readers in his letter of hope to prepare our minds for action and exercise self-control. He then tells us to put all our hope in the gracious salvation that will come to us when Jesus Christ is revealed to the world (1.13), when every wrong will be put right for ever.

The battle for the mind is raging today and never more so with the ascendency of social media and the constant bombardment from enemy forces to sift us like wheat and keep us from finding the source of true hope. The enemy seeks to keep us from the book of Hope, the Hope Manual, the Bible. Peter, who had been through the mill and experienced it first hand, tells us that the arch enemy is on the move. We need to stay alert! We need to watch for our great enemy the Devil *'who prowls around like a roaring lion, looking for someone to devour'.* (1 Pet 5.8)

The awesome letter of hope written by the big fisherman from Galilee, the humble and devoted Servant of Jesus Christ, has been preserved for us to read. This is the same Peter who Dr Luke records (Acts 4.1f) was arrested along with John after the healing of a poor penniless man. We can listen to Peter's dynamic message of hope and the need for us all to turn in repentance to the source of hope, God.

The religious leaders of the day were very disturbed by what they heard and how Peter preached the resurrection of Jesus from the dead. After an overnight stay in prison, they brought Peter and John before the Jewish Council to be cross examined and to explain by what power, or in whose name, they had worked such a miracle. As we say in our part of the world, *'they knew righty'* by what Name; they were the ones who had Jesus condemned to death several weeks earlier. They just wanted the opportunity to tell Peter and John in front of everyone to never ever speak or teach in the Name of Jesus ever again; it was to shut them up. No chance! These are among the men and women who Dr Luke records *'turned the world upside down.'* (Acts 17.6)

Luke records that the members of the council were amazed at the boldness of Peter and John. In fact, they could not understand that these men had no special rabbinical training – they were seen as unlearned and ignorant men, in their view. They marvelled and they recognized them as men who had been with Jesus (Acts 4.13). Another translation in up-to-date language says Peter was regarded as an unlearned, ignorant, ordinary, uneducated, unschooled, untrained man. How wrong they were; Peter had sat at the feet of the Greatest Teacher to ever grace the broad acres of earth. His accusers recognised, however, that he had been in the school of Christ. Bible versions give various renderings of the inspired text such is the richness of the original language; but almost every translation you can turn to uses the same wording – *'They had been with Jesus.'* For three and a half years they had heard every word that Jesus had spoken. He taught them and they were well taught. Peter had been to school, and he had graduated in a masters so to speak because he had set at the feet of the Master. They had been with Jesus.

That is the secret for us who read the letter of hope. We need to spend time with Jesus. He is the great Teacher. *'Behold, God is exalted in his power; who is a teacher like him?'* (Job 36.22) I am not decrying education; we need education but the person with education and without hope in Christ is an educated fool. Here is hope for dopes and the intelligent too, even for those who regard themselves as intelligent and are high on the dope of delusion as to mankind's mastery and godlike status; the Nietzschean 'superman' mentality.

'The fool has said in his heart there is no God. They are corrupt.' (Psalm 14.1)

The word 'fool' does not mean mental inability but rather moral and spiritual insensitivity. The phrase *'no God'* suggests a practical atheism and living as if God is irrelevant and as if He does not exist. The next phrase says of such individuals *'they are corrupt'*. The idea here is one of soured milk. Those who reject God, the source of Hope, will sour and their degeneration will not be recovered without Him. They are fools because they have turned away from a personal relationship with the Lord of Glory, the Source of True Hope, and the Author of Eternal Life.

There are things only He can teach us in the secret place, a knowledge that only He can impart that cannot be found in all the great halls of academia put together. If you feel like a hopeless case, you have come to the right place. Jesus specialises in rescuing hopeless cases. Look at Peter. No matter how far you have fallen or failed or lost faith, or never had any faith whatsoever in the first place, Jesus stands alive and well to give you salvation hope. There's much more to take in as we proceed on our journey of finding hope in a fragile world.

DAY SIX

HOPE IN A HOPELESS PLACE

The prism of the Word: Luke 22.31-34, 54-62,   and John 21.1-19

Seamus Heaney, 'Hope and history rhyme', and the Divine

Peter, this man on a mission to spread the message of hope, addresses those whom he describes as exiles who have been scattered to the four winds. He actually calls them 'elect' exiles of the Dispersion in Pontus, Galatia, Cappadocia, Asia, and Bithynia (1 Peter 1.1b).

The location is now known as Northern Turkey. Check out how Peter introduces his letter of hope against the backdrop of suffering and adversity. It's one thing to have hope and live with great optimism and expectations when we are feeling good and all is going well. We are in good form, and it all seems so right, and our dreams and aspirations are still intact. We are hopeful. We are positive and we are on the crest of the wave. The Hope Express is on track so to speak. It's a different matter when we are facing a potential or a sudden derailment.

A young woman came to live in my part of the world. She came from a different country to find a better life. In fact, according to the media, she lives some nine miles from the town where I reside. Her dreams have been shattered and her hopes have been derailed because of hate crime and constant attacks on her home; windows smashed, doors kicked in, and the house plastered with all kinds of obscene graffiti. It is totally appalling, and words of unequivocal condemnation rightly come from all quarters, but if they are not followed up by positive and meaningful action, they are somewhat empty and worthless. Words are fruitless and futile if not accompanied by positive actions.

But why did it happen? Xenophobia? This dear young woman and her children have been targeted because they are seen as foreigners, from an ethnic minority. They are hated by horrible individuals because they are not from here and are not welcome here by the Neanderthals and have been told to get out and go home to where they came from. Her plight, in a sense, albeit for different reasons, is not dissimilar to the dilemma the recipients of Peter's letter found themselves in.

They are 'foreigners'; exiles from what he calls the dispersion. On reading through the letter, we find that these 'exiles' had been uprooted from their homes and scattered across the world. They had lost everything and now they were foreigners with an uncertain future. They were at risk from all kinds of attacks. But why? They did not fit in, they were different, and they had some 'weird' views and practises too, allegedly. History records, as does the history of the Troubles in my own country, Northern Ireland, that if you depersonalise and dehumanise a person or a group it gives the ruthless and the violent the permission to do anything to them.

Once, these exiles had been accepted in their communities and were very much a part of the social fabric and cultural scene. Now they were rejected and marginalised and abused. They were very dangerous. In my part of the world Van Morrison, the world-famous Ulster musical artist, is being sued by a Northern Ireland Government Minister because he said at a public event that our health minister, Robin Swan, *'is very dangerous.'* Now the health minister is suing him and saying *'Van the Man is very dangerous'*. You could not make this stuff up. This was in the context of governmental restrictions due to the Covid pandemic. One of Van's songs ironically is called *The Healing Game*. Some healing needed there then. He sang this song on a compilation album called *Across the Bridge of Hope* which was created and recorded in support of victims of the Omagh bombings. A dear friend of mine was seriously injured in that explosion, just standing a few feet away from the car bomb, and miraculously survived. His young shop assistant, however, standing beside him, was blown to pieces. Another Ulster man, Liam Neeson, took part in the album and recorded a recitation of a poem by the Irish poet and playwright, Seamus Heaney, entitled *Doubletake* from his volume *A Cure at Troy*. Here are the lyrics.

Human beings suffer,
they torture one another,
they get hurt and get hard.
No poem or play or song
can fully right a wrong
inflicted and endured.

The innocent in gaols
beat on their bars together.
A hunger-striker's father
stands in the graveyard dumb.
The police widow in veils
faints at the funeral home

History says, Don't hope
on this side of the grave.
But then, once in a lifetime
the longed-for tidal wave
of justice can rise up,
and hope and history rhyme.

So hope for a great sea-change
on the far side of revenge.
Believe that a further shore
is reachable from here.
Believe in miracles
and cures and healing wells.

Call the miracle self-healing:
The utter self-revealing
double-take of feeling.
If there's fire on the mountain
or lightning and storm
and a god speaks from the sky.

That means someone is hearing
the outcry and the birth-cry
of new life at its term.

Seamus Heaney (1939–2013)

To understand the poem, we need to have some cognizance of the background to it. Heaney had adapted Sophocles' play, *Philoctetes*, written in the fifth century. Philoctetes was a mythical Greek archer and hero, who had been banished to a remote island because of a festering foot wound.

His bow was believed to be an instrument of immense power and symbolic of heroism and victory. This highly prized bow was much sought after and was needed to secure victory in the Trojan war. Men were sent to get the bow, but eventually Heracles came down from Olympus and persuaded Philoctetes to fight, and in return his foot would be healed. The hero fought with his magical bow, which never missed a target, and the victory was won. This is the backdrop to the poem. All seemed hopeless but with the hero in the frame, bow in hand, hope and history rhymed.

This is powerfully expressed in Heaney's *Doubletake*. The first stanzas begin with human suffering of the kind inflicted by humans on each other. The miseries of war and suffering are to the fore and the hurt and hopelessness of humanity caught up in such conflict is palpable. But then the poem turns, hence the title. In essence, the poem can be taken to mean that history can be full of misery and dashed hopes. History is personified and seems to say, 'there is no hope.'

As we read the 39 lines, we find that Heaney does not remain submerged in despondency and despair for long. The melancholic downtroddeness gives way to a sea change on 'the far side of revenge.' There is reason to hope, and change can take place even once in a lifetime. Heaney said he had Nelson Mandela's twenty-seven-year imprisonment in mind with this poem. One can also see a fleeting reference to the conflict in my own country that dragged on for thirty years, referred to as The Northern Ireland Troubles, where more than 3,500 people were killed.

Hope for Heaney is underscored by endurance and grace. Justice can prevail and when we do the right at all costs, hope can prevail. In spite of the human condition, things can change and we can 'make hope and history rhyme.' This has become one of the most quoted lines of Irish poetry this century.

How does this fit with our quest for hope in our short essays, you may ask? And how does it fit with the Divine? We need to move beyond the mythical and the magical, and even beyond human frailty. For the Apostle Peter and his fellow writers, 'Hope and History rhyme', but not in a mythical Greek figure. It is in Jesus Christ that hope and history rhyme, for He is the Lord of Hope and the God of history.

C S Lewis says that: *"The Son of God became the Son of Man that the sons (and daughters) of men might become the sons (and daughters) of God."*

God entered the world in human form and in the incarnation, the perfect life, the sacrificial death by crucifixion, in the resurrection, and in the final consummation of all things God will make hope and history rhyme, in the Kingdom of God, the kingdom of righteousness and justice, the Kingdom of the Prince of Peace, Emmanuel, God with us.

The emblem of hope for Peter is the cross. A crucified Saviour, in his death brings redemption and salvation and, in His resurrection, brings a lasting hope. Here we find hope for a fragile world. *'Yet, He was despised and rejected by men, a man of sorrows and acquainted with grief. And we hid, as it were, our faces from Him; He was despised, and we did not esteem Him'* (Isaiah 53). He was viewed as a dangerous outlaw by the chief priests, the scribes, and Pharisees of His day. The religious leaders were the instigators of His murder on the cross. And yet in the foreordained plan of God, He fulfilled what was written of Him; the Hope of the Nations and each individual who places their trust in Him. The original readers to whom Peter was writing did so, and they also experienced the same rejection.

The society to which the original readers found themselves made them unwelcome and viewed them as very dangerous people to be avoided. There was no justice here. They were viewed as a sect, a dangerous sectarian movement. They were in fact Christians who believed that God had not only spoken but came into the world and lived on earth. His name was Jesus Christ, and Peter knew Him oh so well. The word 'Christian' is only found three times in the New Testament; in 1 Peter 4.16, Acts 11.26 and Acts 26.28. It was to this group of people that Peter writes about hope.

How could Peter possibly write to people who had lost everything and who faced a bleak and uncertain future and speak of hope? Peter writes to encourage them in such a hopeless place. The truth is that these people, in spite of all they had lost and all they were facing, were exhorted to rest in a sure-fire hope. Even though they were caught up in a tsunami of hate and persecution. It is in such circumstances that true hope can truly be found.

You know where *you* have been and all that you have suffered. All of us have experienced the dark clouds of dread overhead; fear and despair become our constant companions. Yet in the darkness, Peter's prism comes to shine the light of true hope. The actual word 'hope' is mentioned four times in Peter's first letter. We will look at these in due course.

Have your hopes died? Has your 'Hope Express' been derailed and you live in a state of constant catastrophization? Our hopes can imperceptibly evaporate in the daily grind or quickly implode in the face of crisis. The hope that Peter proclaims is described as a living hope (1.3). Then he reminds his first audience, the exiles, that they have placed their faith and hope in God. Well, surely that must have posed a problem for at least some of them, you might say. A hope in God? And look at all the trouble they were in. However, at this juncture let's seek to complete the following statement.

I put my hope in …

The reality is we are all looking for some kind of hope to get us through the journey called life. We long for certainty in uncertainty. We look for hope in a hopeless place. So where is our hope? Or do we have no hope? Is it no wonder that hope is either in the ED or ICU when we are constantly served up large helpings of the godless goulash of guesses and guesstimates from the so-called 'experts' in every field; no wonder we are drowning in the word-soup of sceptics and God-deniers. We are expected to swallow grand hypotheses and bow before their grandiose architectural edifices to the gods of self and human wisdom, all washed down into our very souls with a poisonous sorbet of hopelessness, the very antithesis of edification and real hope. The best on offer in the secular world is hopeless optimism. We are left empty and indoctrinated to the extent that even to contemplate a higher hope, a sure-fire hope, never mind seeking it, is viewed as preposterous and even madness by the most fervent in the so-called Voltairean, *'God is dead'* camp.

I came across an advert recently and it was an advert for hope. It was called 'Hope Express' and the subtext was *Thriving in a complex world*. That's it! That's exactly what Peter is telling us in his first letter. If you want to know how to thrive in this sick world, then let us stick with our journey of exploration of hope as set out in Scripture. We have nothing to lose and everything to gain. For Peter, hope and history does rhyme as the God of Hope is the God of history and His master plan of salvation cannot be thwarted.

The references to Hope in 1 Peter are:

1.3. A living hope – real and relevant

1.13. A confident hope – confidence and clarity

1.21. A sure hope – sure-fire and steadfast

3.15. A rational hope – reasonable and reasoned

DAY SEVEN

BRIGHT HOPE FOR DARK DAYS

The prism of the Word: Philippians 2.1-11 and 1 Peter 1.3

Existentialism's spirit of hopelessness and the challenge of true hope

To the watching world they were a bunch of Jesus followers who were forced to flee because of persecution and the threat of death. In fact, the reason for their predicament was their allegiance to Jesus Christ as Lord (1 Peter 3.15). They were 'the dispersion' to the world at large, but in reality, they were much more than that. Chance and random does not come into it, according to Peter (1.2msg).

> *Not one is missing, not one forgotten. God the Father has His eye on each of you and has determined by the work of the Spirit to keep you obedient through the sacrifice of Jesus. May everything good from God be yours.*

At this juncture it is important to point out that when we say, 'according to Peter', we mean more than the fact that he was the author. This was not some strange letter cobbled together by an eccentric obscurantist in an obscure hideaway in Rome. The letter forms part of what is called the *'Canon of Scripture,'* which is made up of 66 books that form the Bible. Suffice to say at this point that this book claims to be the Living

Word of the Living God, God's hope manual for humanity. We will say more in other essays. It boldly claims to be God's revelation to us.

In his second letter Peter tells us that his letter and all the other books are not *'cunningly devised fables',* and that they are not of some private interpretation, meaning of private origin. Rather, Scripture's origin is from God Himself. Peter and the other writers and prophets did not give their own private solutions or interpretations as to the mysteries of life; rather God spoke through them, and He alone is responsible for what is written in Scripture. No mere mortal could write this. God chose men to write down His thoughts given to them by God the Holy Spirit. This is what Peter means when he says: *'Holy men of God spoke as they were moved by the Holy Spirit'* (2 Peter 1.16-2.3).

It is this marvellous prism of God's Word that gives us the brightest of hope against the backdrop of life's adversities. There are powerful and prismatic moments of wonderment to be experienced in the reading and study of The Divine Hope Manual. In his opening words of greeting, Peter presents several great teachings of the Christian Faith. In succinct fashion and with a few strokes of his inspired quill, Peter gives us the embodiment of faith and hope in rich doctrinal truths that will take our breath away. The great doctrines of the faith are unveiled like an exquisite masterpiece of grace in vivid and vibrant colours. There are prismatic moments for those who will take the time not only to read but also to listen.

We have noted already that Peter refers to this band of Jesus followers as 'elect exiles'. But they are in fact designated as God's chosen people. Peter notes that they have a particular and unique identity; they are God's people and God has chosen them.

And if that is not enough to get our heads round, they are further described as having been chosen a long time ago according to the foreknowledge of God, in eternity. Now that is staggering by any stretch of the imagination. This is in a similar vein to the words of Peter's fellow Apostle when he wrote to the Ephesian church and told them that even before God made the world, He loved us and chose us in Christ (Ephesians 1.4). Just to be absolutely clear about what Peter is saying, here are the words of Peter as rendered in the NLT: *God the Father knew you and chose you long ago, and His Spirit has made you holy. As a result, you have obeyed Him and have been cleansed by the blood of Jesus Christ. May God give you more grace and peace.* (1 Pet 1.2)

This is a lot to take in, but the essential thing is the Scriptural 'given' that God is up close and personal and has chosen a people for Himself. By His Spirit He makes His people holy. He expects obedience and He cleanses His people from their sins through the sacrifice of His Son Jesus Christ by His blood. He gives His grace and His peace to His people. He is the bestower of true Hope. He is not a remote and impersonal God but a God at hand.

Having trained in the field of psychotherapy and witnessed the importance of what is referred to as the *'talking therapies'*, of which there are many varieties, instilling a sense of hope is an important part of therapy. This enables people to develop not only optimism but also a sense of agency in their lives. Agency is one of the buzzwords for taking personal responsibility and really means taking control over actions and their consequences. Talking about hope in the context of the therapeutic environment is important in searching for and identifying hope. Not all therapies take this approach. For Freud, the best he could hope for in relation to his clients was to turn *'neurotic misery into general unhappiness'*.

One particular talking therapy is 'existential psychotherapy,' which is based on four 'givens'. These are death, meaning, isolation, and freedom. If we take, for example, isolation, this is the 'given' which says if we are to live authentically then we need to accept the fact that we are born alone, live alone, and we die alone. The individual must wrestle with the dilemma of trying to reconcile the internal sense of aloneness with the need for others. It was Orson Wells who said: *'We're born alone, we live alone, we die alone. Only through our love and friendship can we create the illusion for the moment that we're not alone.'*

Surely any insightful person will be thinking that there must be more to life than the creation of an illusion to cope with reality as expressed in existentialism. The stark contrast between the Scriptural 'given' and existentialism could not be more striking. The word 'given' means to accept that something is true and not expect it to change. Peter informs his readers, 'you are not alone'. In our reaching out for a higher hope, the God of Hope has reached down to us, and He has done so in the person of His Son, Jesus Christ, in the incarnation. God has come to earth and taken on human form in an actual body (John 1.14). God is the God of Hope, and He offers us hope through the incarnation. We are not alone in our struggles and adversity because God is with us in it all, so we need to put our hope in Him. Peter's compatriot, Paul, said, *'May the God of Hope fill you with all joy and peace as you trust in Him, so that you may overflow with Hope by the Power of the Holy Spirit'* (Romans 15.13).

We need to put our trust in Him. Given that we have briefly considered two 'givens', which 'given' do we plum for? God or man? Christianity challenges existentialism's spirit of hopelessness, affirms that all that is broken and disordered will finally be put right; evil will be vanquished from the cosmos and Christ will return and rule over all. Christianity affirms a hopeful and future reality of resurrection and everlasting life and complete sanctification. All are freely given by the grace of God and sure-fire hope can reside in our hearts and souls today (Romans 6.23).

The Father elects, The Spirit sanctifies, and the Son redeems. The interpersonal nature of the Godhead is focused on a bunch of elect exiles whom no one would have given a second thought to. Yet they are the subject and the centre of the intense love and interest of the Triune God. They are not immune from trials and tribulations, but God is with them, as He is with us, and He will never abandon us. He is building His Church and the gates of hell will not prevail against it. The world is in turmoil and mankind's desire to rule and govern the world has failed miserably. The responsibility that we took on in our federal head, Adam, for governance and justice and good and fairness and equality has also failed. Just look at man's inhumanity to man and many of us are bystanders who do nothing. A world of disorder and chaos groans for redemption. But God's work goes on, quietly and imperceptibly in a world of madness and mayhem. And Jesus the Lord of all will return and make it right, and every person who has ever lived will give an account to God. He alone offers us true hope today.

Do you not know that the Triune God has your interests and every part and every facet of your being – body, soul, and spirit – in His heart? Your past, your present, and your future matter to Him. You matter to God. And you did so even before you were born. You mattered to Him before the foundation of the world. You mattered to Him in the eternity past. Before there was even a universe you were on His mind. And that's just the first two verses written by a big unschooled fisherman from Galilee whom Jesus called and equipped and used to change the world. And he has a plan for you too and what do you need to do? Just do what He says – *'follow me!'*

DAY EIGHT

A NEW START IN LIFE OR A NEW LIFE TO START WITH

The prism of the Word: 1 Peter 1.1-3 and Romans 8.18-25.

De-baptism and the increasing abandonment of the church

The rise of atheism in Italy has led to an increasing number of people deciding to officially de-baptise (*sbattezzo* in Italian) from the church. The process is relatively simple. Mattia, a young 25-year-old man from the northern city of Bologna, is a typical example. He grew up with the teachings and sacraments of the church in parochial school. Now in adulthood he decided the time had come to leave the church behind. He filled out a form that he had found online, and accompanying it with an explanation of his reasons, sent it off to the parish in his hometown. Two weeks later, a note was put next to his name in the parish baptism register, formalising his abandonment of the Catholic Church. Mattia became one of an increasing, though hard to quantify, number of Italians who have been officially 'de-baptized'.

One writer has estimated that 100,000 people have gone for de-baptism from the church and the numbers are growing year on year. The church does have a problem with this, however, since it is not possible to erase a baptism because it's a fact that historically happened and was therefore registered at the time. What the procedure does, however, is formalise the person's abandonment of the church.

According to canon law there are severe consequences for de-baptism because it is deemed to be committing the crime of apostasy. The apostate faces immediate excommunication from the church without need of a trial, is excluded from the sacraments, and may not become a godparent and will be deprived of a Catholic funeral. The church sees a substantial difference between the sin of apostasy and the crime of apostasy.

An atheist commits the sin because it's an internal decision, and they can be forgiven if they repent. An apostate, instead, manifests their will to formally abandon the church externally, so they face the severe legal consequences for their decision. People give many different reasons for de-baptising. One young man said he made the decision because he asked himself, 'do I believe, or do I not believe?' and the answer led to his de-baptism.

There is compelling evidence that if all the people who don't truly identify as Catholics were to be de-baptized, the official percentages of Italian Catholics would be significantly lower. The latest data seems to back this up. In 2020 the Italian Catholic Bishops Conference financed a large sociological study which concluded that 30% of the Italian population is atheist; that's around 18 million people.

One wonders what the Apostle of Hope, Peter, would think. I honestly don't think he would lose any sleep over the baptism or de-baptism issue, and I don't say that lightly. You see, Peter's position is radically different from both sides of the argument, to be baptised or to be de-baptised?

The answer is given to us in the third verse in chapter one of his first letter. In fact, it has nothing whatsoever to do with being baptised into a church. It's got nothing to do with religion and religiosity with all the pomp and splendour and outward show that goes with much of it. Let's hear exactly what he has to say to his readers desperately looking for hope.

Blessed [gratefully praised and adored] be the God and Father of our Lord Jesus Christ, who according to His abundant and boundless mercy has caused us to be born again [that is, to be reborn from above – spiritually transformed, renewed, and set apart for His purpose] to an ever-living hope and confident assurance through the resurrection of Jesus Christ from the dead, [born anew] into an inheritance which is imperishable [beyond the reach of change] and undefiled and unfading, reserved in heaven for you, who are being protected and shielded by the power of God through your faith for salvation that is ready to be revealed [for you] in the last time. In this you rejoice greatly, even though now for a little while, if necessary, you have been distressed by various trials, so that the genuineness of your faith, which is much more precious than gold which is perishable, even though tested and purified by fire, may be found to result in [your] praise and glory and honour at the revelation of Jesus Christ. Though you have not seen Him, you love Him; and though you do not even see Him now, you believe and trust in Him and you greatly rejoice and delight with inexpressible and glorious joy, receiving as the result [the outcome, the consummation] of your faith, the salvation of your souls. (1 Peter 1.3-9)

It is not only important that we understand what Peter is saying, but also imperative. To grasp the concept of biblical hope, and more importantly to obtain it, we need to understand with the utmost clarity what the Bible is saying to every generation. A first reading makes it clear that it has nothing to do with baptism and the church. I remember being teased at school because I was not baptised as an infant. 'You don't even have a name', they said, 'because you weren't baptised'. My parents didn't believe in infant baptism. One can smile now but it was painful at the time to be called 'No name'. Here comes 'No name.'

Notice the words that Peter is using. He tells us that this hope, which he describes as an ever-living hope – a hope that can never die or fade away, is actually brought about by being 'born again' because of the abundant and boundless mercy of God the Father. In fact, the word he uses is 'caused' by God the Father. When the priest goes to the record in Italy, he sees the registry and the name of the person and the date they were born. Every Church and authority and Government keeps records.

'No name' actually has a birth certificate. I can prove when I was born. I have a birthday in December. We record birthdays and we celebrate them. Peter is saying we need a second birthday because we need to be born again to have this living hope. Does God have a register of those who have been born from above?

John writes in the book of Revelation: *'Yet you have a few people in Sardis who have not soiled their clothes. They will walk with me, dressed in white, for they are worthy. He who overcomes will, like them, be dressed in white. I will never blot out his name from the book of life but will acknowledge his name before my Father and his angels'* (Rev. 3:4-5).

We each have a physical birth; Peter says we need a spiritual birth. For some this does not make sense. We can't make ourselves to be born again. Of course, we cannot do this any more than we can make ourselves be born physically. So, what does it all mean? That's a lot to take on board in one day, but we are now beginning to get into the depth and reality of what is written by the Apostle of Hope. We will need to explore further and find out more from those who use the same language. Have a think about this question. Can I have two birthdays, a physical one and a spiritual one? The Bible says yes! The world says 'Oh no you can't', the Bible says, 'Oh yes you can.'

DAY NINE

BORN AGAIN INTO A LIVING HOPE

The prism of the Word: John chapter 1.1-18 and John
chapter 3.1-21

A top religious leader seeks the truth and finds hope

Arguably the street preacher's favourite text is *'You must be born again.'* It's a strange statement for many. On the streets of the land where I live it is a regular sight and a familiar cry, *'You must be born again.'* As people go about their business some nod in agreement, others find it an annoyance that should be banned, and others are somewhat bemused. What on earth does it mean anyhow? How can you be born again? It does not make sense, or does it?

The best commentary on the Bible is the Bible itself and the only way we can understand it is to allow the complementarity of Scripture to explain itself. The words from the quill of Peter and John, and the written account of the conversation between Jesus and Nichodemus, a top religious leader and a member of the Jewish Supreme Council, tells us a lot about being 'born again'. Nichodemus too would have concurred with the people in the street. How can a person be born when they are old, can they enter a second time into their mother's womb and be born? And anyone who has problems with the street preacher does well to note that Jesus' answer to Nocedemus was: *'Do not marvel that I say unto you, you must be born again.'* To grasp its meaning, we need to look at the context. We notice from the words of Jesus Himself that being born again is a Divine work.

Being born again happens by the work of the Spirit of God

Jesus said, *'The wind blows where it wishes, and you hear its sound, but you do not know where it comes from or where it goes, so it is with everyone that is born of the Spirit'* (John 3.8).

Being born again has to do with spiritual birth, not physical birth. Previously Jesus said, *'That which is born of the flesh is flesh, and that which is born of the Spirit is Spirit'* (John 3.6).

Thus, we now know that being born again is a spiritual birth and it takes the movement of God the Holy Spirit for this new birth to happen.

Being born again is by means of the Word of God

This is what Peter tells us in 1 Peter 1.23. Peter tells his first readers, *'Since you have been born again, not of perishable seed but of imperishable, through the living and abiding Word of God.'*

So the means God uses to bring about the new birth is the Word of God, the Bible. Faith comes by the Word of God.

Being born again is by the Mercy of God

'Blessed be the God and Father of our Lord Jesus Christ! According to His great mercy, He has caused us to be born again to a living hope through the resurrection of Jesus Christ from the dead ...' (1 Peter 1.3)

It's all to do with God's mercy which flows from His infinite love. It is as a result of mercy signifying God's attitude towards us and also our unworthiness and undeserving nature and our need of spiritual new birth. We are all in need of divine mercy.

We all need a new birth, a spiritual one.

Being born again is by the Mystery of the Grace of God
John shines more light on this subject by telling us, *'But to all who did receive Him, who believed in His Name, He gave the right to become children of God, who were born, not of blood, nor the will of the flesh nor of the will of man, but of God* (John 1.11,12).

Eugene Peeterson, in the Message Bible, paraphrases the text in this way:

> *The Life-Light was the real thing:*
> *Every person entering Life*
> *He brings into Light.*
> *He was in the world,*
> *the world was there through him,*
> *and yet the world didn't even notice.*
> *He came to his own people,*
> *but they didn't want Him.*
> *But whoever did want Him,*
> *who believed He was who he claimed*
> *and would do what he said,*
> *He made to be their true selves,*
> *their child-of-God selves.*
> *These are the God-begotten,*
> *not blood-begotten,*
> *not flesh-begotten,*
> *not sex-begotten.* (John 1.9-13)

When you put all this together, it's all of God and yet this is where the mystery is seen in the hope of salvation. It's what one writer, Sidlow Baxter, referred to as *'His Part and ours'*. It is the work of God from start to finish, but human responsibility on our part involves believing in Him. This involves what we could call 'appropriation' and means:

We must respond to the Spirit of God.

We must respond to the Word of God.

We must respond to the Mercy of God.

We must respond to the Grace of God.

We must respond to the Mystery God.

When the Spirit of God moves, we will know it. And His word comes alive and His boundless mercy reaches down to us and His matchless, all-sufficient grace comes to lift us out of our hopeless condition and we must bow the knee and repent of our sins and embrace Jesus Christ as our very own personal Saviour and Lord of our lives. In the mystery of God and His sovereignty and human responsibility, we are born again into this living hope. We obtain this hope by virtue of the new birth. And we worship Christ as Lord of our lives (1 Peter 3.15). It is indeed not only a new start in life, it is much more than that, it's a new life to start with. It's a spiritual life. It's new birth, it's being born again.

Human responsibility means the 'appropriation' by faith of the sure and steadfast hope God has for us in the Son of God, Jesus Christ our Saviour. It's about obedience to Jesus Christ. This is emphasised in Peter's First Letter of Hope. In the first chapter note the following references:

(1.1) *You believe in Him …*

(1.8) *… obtaining the outcome of your faith, the salvation of your souls …*

(1.9) *Now because we have a living hope we can set our hope on the grace that will be brought to us at the revelation of*

Jesus Christ …

(1.13) … and we act as the obedient children of God …

(1.14) … because we have been born into God's family. We can call God our Father …

(1.17) … having been ransomed from futile ways …

(1.18) … by the precious blood of Christ …

(1.19) We through Him are believers in God who raised Him from the dead and gave Him glory, so that your faith and hope are in God …

(1.21) … and this involves the purifying of the soul by our obedience to the truth.

What an awesome teacher Peter was and the Word lives today because it is the inspired Word of the Living God; God's word to us today in the here and now. Towards the end of the first chapter of the letter we read these words: *For you have been born again, but not to a life that will quickly end. Your new life will last forever because it comes from the eternal, living Word of God. As the Scriptures say, "People are like grass; their beauty is like a flower in the field. The grass withers and the flower fades." But the word of the Lord remains forever* (1 Peter 1.23-25).

We must be born again and that's what the Giver of Hope, Jesus Christ, said as did His dealers in Hope, Peter and John and all the other Bible writers.

'You must be born again.'

The writings are more than writings, they are inspired writings. In fact, they claim to be the very Word of God. How do we know this? Well, Peter the Dealer in Hope tells us this in no uncertain terms. Let's listen in to his words carefully again, this time in the AMP…

For you have been born again [that is, reborn from above – spiritually transformed, renewed, and set apart for His purpose] not of seed which is perishable but [from that which is] imperishable and immortal, that is, through the living and everlasting word of God (1 Peter 1.23).

Today we have sought to explore the miracle of being 'born again' into a sure and steadfast hope. And we have noted the declarations of Scripture. We have noted that we are told at the very beginning of Peter's first letter that this living hope is found in being born again. This happens through the seed of the living and everlasting Word of God and the first chapter ends with the words *'And this is the word of [the good news of salvation] that was preached to you'* (1.25).

So, it's not just the word of Peter that we are reading, it claims to be the Word of God. Being born again into this living hope comes with a certain assurance. Peter is dead and gone. Well, that's not true, his body is in the grave, but he lives on in eternity. This letter and this book lives on, the book they tried to burn and ban and belittle and banish, and still do so. But it's still here. Do yourself no harm – it's all here! And it speaks into a hopeless world and troubled hearts and all the hopeless places declaring here is a sure and steadfast hope. If you have not done so already, it's time to appropriate by faith the salvation that God has for you. As to being born again, that's His work, your responsibility is to believe as the Spirit of God strives with you. But remember, His Spirit will not always strive ...

Blessed be the God and Father of our Lord Jesus Christ! According to his great mercy, he has caused us to be born again to a living hope through the resurrection of Jesus Christ from the dead, to an inheritance that is imperishable, undefiled, and unfading, kept in heaven for you, who by God's power are being guarded through faith for a salvation ready to be revealed in the last time (1 Peter 1.3-5).

Jesus went back to heaven to prepare a place for us. A prepared place for prepared people. And Peter gives us a glimpse of what awaits those who believe. We have an eternal inheritance, and it is a God-given inheritance. There will be no fighting over wills in heaven because our Testator lives, and He gives to us an inheritance that is described as *unspoilable, undefiled, unfading, untouchable.*

Reserved – kept in heaven for you. It can't be spoiled or defiled or fade or touched – it's reserved, and it's got your name on it. And who has reserved it for you? God has – that's how much He thinks of you. And the day is coming when you will have it all. In fact, we have it all now in Christ our Hope.

We began today with the street preacher. The Bible records the preaching of Peter in Acts 1. Peter preaches and he quotes from the Old Testament: *'And in the last days it shall be, God declares, that I will pour out my Spirit on all fresh ... and it shall come to pass that everyone who calls on the Name of the Lord shall be saved'* (Joel 2.28-32).

Have you called yet? Now is the day. If you have already, then rejoice in the hope you have in Jesus.

DAY TEN

THE GREATEST CONSPIRACY IN HISTORY

The prism of the Word: 1 Peter 11.21-25, John 1.10-13, John 3.8.

L N Goenka: Aristotle and 'Does the atom have a designer'?

The world is full of conspiracy theories, and many are avid followers of the latest fads. It's a good question, but what is the greatest conspiracy ever concocted? There are many to choose from, and these could include flat earth, the 'fictitious' moon landings, the lizidardisation of certain members of the establishment, or even as I write, the conspiracies abounding in relation to the Covid pandemic, chip technology, vaccinations affecting our DNA, the mind control of whole populations and the entire world, even eradication of huge swathes of populations. There are indeed a lot to choose from. Given what we are considering in our reflections about the hope that is declared in Scripture, my conjecture here, and I believe it is more than a conjecture, is that the greatest conspiracy in world history is that the Bible is a book of lies, the Book of Hope is a book for dopes, and any idea of a personal God on a divine throne is really a make-believe fantasy.

Here's the gist of it, if being born again into a living eternal hope is really true, and let's say there is an arch enemy who does not want anyone to obtain salvation and the hope that goes with it, and if that enemy is so hellbent on keeping the absolute truth from the masses, then there will invariably be an all-out vociferous, vicious, vitriolic, and protracted attack. We would then expect this to be intensified throughout history and even more so as time begins to run out for our ageing planet and our disintegrating universe, and our ever increasingly troubled war-torn world.

The enemy will even make himself invisible and non-existent in plain sight in the desire to strengthen the conspiracy for people to think they are really clever and that they are the masters of their own destiny; that belief is God is a nonsense, never mind this strange born-again thing. The indoctrination by the enemy has convinced many that if God ever existed, He has left the stage, and given that we live in a suffering world which is in such a hopeless mess, He could not have existed in the first place. Yet, all the while it's the enemy who has caused the mess and mankind is guilty of the culpable homicide of hope by buying the lie that the Word of God is a lie. Such is the sinful nature of fallen mankind that we not only buy the poison, we consume it, and pass it on and sell it in all manner of ways. It's an international global industry of God defiance and denial and Thanatos. Men and women love darkness rather than light.

This undermining of the means of hope, i.e., the Word of God, has led to all kinds of beliefs and belief systems. We are all here by chance. We are just the result of random interacting forces and here we are in a world that is just a chance phenomenon in the universe, and now there is the postulation of a multiverse and it's all random. And yet if we start to unpack all this chance theory in our exploration, we need to take a serious look at the Atomic System. This is the fundamental building block of the universe whose structures and interactions produce multiple levels of functionality that enable the functioning of the universe and everything in it. Let's drill down into this a bit further.

Dr Lakhi N. Goenka, a secular researcher and expert, in his brilliant book *Does the Atom have a Designer?* explores the atom in depth. Having done this, he applies the 'why' questions related to the atom and its causality. Having set out the complexities of the atom, along with its functionality and purpose, he then applies Aristotle's theory of causality. He notes that in Aristotle's metaphysics and physics, the theory of causality was developed to show there are four related causes or explanations needed to explain change in the world. The search for causes is really a search for answers and any complete explanation of any material change will use all four causes. The explanatory conditions to answer the why question about an object, in our case, the atom, are set out by Goenka as follows:

1. Material cause – Energy, with its ability to behave in different ways both as a wave and a particle.
2. Formal cause – the quantization of Energy into subatomic particles consisting of matter with multiple and complex functionality including interactions and purposeful quantum behaviours with stability and reversibility features.
3. Efficient cause – an underlying intelligence that produces and directs multiple independent causes (material and formal) to create the atom with its complex structures and interactions.
4. Final cause – The structural electromagnetic, chemical, nuclear, and biological functionalities of the atom to realise the workings of the universe. The atom makes the universe function.

Dr Goenka comments on this:

Aristotle's four causes together point to an underlying intelligence as the only plausible explanation for the causality of the Atom (note also that the Atom is Irreducibly Complex). The Atom makes the Universe function. The Atom realises the structural, electromagnetic, chemical, nuclear, and biological functionalities necessary for the workings of the Universe. Almost every aspect of the Atomic Structure and its quantized interactions is necessary to realise one of the many functions of the Atom. The Atom is the product of an underlying intelligence that produces and directs multiple independent causes to enable its proton-neutron-electron structure with its quantum interactions to realise the workings of the Universe. The Atom must have a Designer (God).

Since God is revealed in the Bible as transcendent and thus fundamentally different from the created order, the Designer did not need a Designer for He, the Transcendent and Almighty God, created the Universe and everything in it. Dr Goenka goes on to say: '*Every worldview must believe in a cause that itself is uncaused, and people understand this uncaused cause to be the Creator God.*'

God and God alone, who is not only the explanation for the beginning of everything but for the existence of all past, present, and future, He is the One who is Source of sure and steadfast hope. Again, the anti-God brigade in the belligerence and denial of the reality of God posits the multiverse idea with an infinite number of universes, why has such a hypothesis been proposed? It is used mainly as an argument against design and well, we just happened, and it so happens that we have what is needed to support life. Talk about blind faith and obscurantism.

And yet when we think about it, even the whole concept of being able to think should really make us think and if we do still believe the chance idea, then we will believe anything. Let me use a simple illustration. My daughter and I went into a charity shop one Saturday morning. I spied a small writing desk and loved it. My daughter insisted on buying it for me for Christmas. The choice was between a night away for a break in a hotel with my beloved harrier hound, Barney. Barney and I are more than happy in our little study; he's on his couch and I'm at my desk. As long as there is good coffee and dog biscuits on the go, we are more than happy. No contest then, the desk would fit perfectly into my little upper room study and it's my favourite place in the entire world. And you've guessed it, upon my desk is the Book of books in different versions along with my little Chromebook. What I am about to say is very simple and you probably know what's coming. Well here goes. Mum is asleep when I arrive home with my newfound joy in the boot of my car.

I can't wait to get it in the house, give it a clean and some polish and get it up the stairs, which I just about manage on my own. There it is, installed and in pride of place and I try it out and set my stuff on it. It's well made and it's sturdy and perfectly proportioned for height. Well, it's fantastic and it will serve me well for my purposes for as long as I am able to use it. Eventually my mum pops her head round the door, as she does, to give me the latest weather report. She sees the desk and the conversation goes something like this:

'What's that in your study?'

'It's a time machine, Mum!'

'Cheeky monkey,' Mum responds.

'It's a desk, Mum, I think I will call it Desk.'

'Well I can see that, how did it get here?'

'Well Mum, it got here by chance.'

'Likely story, how did you get it up the stairs? And what do you need it for anyway? You don't need it.'

'I need it to write books on it, Mum.'

'You're just a pen pusher, and that dripping tap needs to be fixed. Time machine indeed. Cheeky monkey.'

You can see the point. But what if I were to go further and tell my mum not only do I not know how it got here and that it appeared here and came about by chance, but no one made it. That's right, no one designed it, no one planned it, it's the result of a big bang explosion in a furniture factory in Belfast. Never mind the big bang, we had enough big bangs in Belfast during the Troubles with bombs going off almost daily at times. Here is the outcome – a perfectly made, perfectly proportioned functional desk. It has a purpose and in fact it meets all my requirements for many years of 'desktop' study. 'You're mad', would be Mum's reply and that would be yours too. You would be absolutely right.

When you strip away all the sophistication and so-called intelligent arguments you arrive at the same conclusion. How on earth can we believe that there is no God? How can we not accept the reasonableness of the belief that God is the Creator and the universe is His design? And how can we say that the Bible is not the Word of God but a book of lies and man's cleverly made fables? A book for dopes who look for hope. The world has bought the lie, the world has been hoodwinked by the greatest conspiracy in history. The prism of the Word for today, as every day, is very important, do take time to read and listen.

Here's an added bonus for the enemy. Mankind believed God in the beginning. There was no way that he or she was going to believe otherwise. They knew Him and they had a relationship and fellowship with Him. But the first parents of our human race believed the lie that there was something better than God, the knowledge of good and evil. So, the human race became infected by a disease; the deadliest disease in the history of the world in which every single person is born with. And how did the human race become infected? It happened on the day that Satan cast doubt on the Word of God. Did God really say that? The disease caught hold and we lost touch with real reality and began to believe that we are the gods of the world, never mind Greek myths. We are the gods of our own destiny, rejecting Creation's amazing Architect for the lie and running with the arch enemy and architect of ruin and hopelessness and death.

We bought it hook, line, and sinker. The remedy for man's malady is found in the Word of God. The desire of the enemy to kick God out of race, the human race, and make His Book out to be a laughingstock. Yet, it has not worked because many have been born again into a living hope. You shall know the truth and the truth shall set you free. Note the prism readings for today. Please take the time to read them. Eye-openers here for those who truly desire to see and to not only hear but listen.

DAY ELEVEN

HIGH HOPES AND GREAT EXPECTATIONS

The prism of the Word: Isaiah 14.12-17, Ezekiel 28.11-19, Matthew 12.15-21, and Ephesians 2.1-19.

The genius of Dave Gilmore, Polly Sampson,
and Pink Floyd – High hopes ...

The genius Dave Gilmore of Pink Floyd fame wrote many amazing songs. The final song of Pink Floyd's penultimate album is entitled *High Hopes*. The lyrics were written by Dave and Polly. For some reason I listened to Pink Floyd a lot when studying psychology with Open University. It was at a time when I was taking a good, long, hard look at life and its meaning and basically questioning everything. It was Alfred Lord Tennyson who wrote in his poem *In memoriam,*

'There lives more faith in honest doubt,
Believe me, Than in half the creeds.'

One was clear that one's faith needed to come under the microscope to see if it would stand up to intense scrutiny. We should not be afraid of such introspection and analysis. Gilmore's lyrics resonated with me at a time when I was trying to look at life and was that possible without God. Did I have a blind belief or a reasonable faith? Here are the incredible lyrics:

Beyond the horizon of the place we lived when we were
young
In a world of magnets and miracles
Our thoughts strayed constantly and without boundary
The ringing of the division bell had begun

Along the Long Road and on down the Causeway
Do they still meet there by the Cut?

There was a ragged band that followed in our footsteps
Running before time took our dreams away
Leaving the myriad small creatures trying to tie us to the
ground
To a life consumed by slow decay

The grass was greener
The light was brighter
When friends surrounded
The nights of wonder

Looking beyond the embers of bridges glowing behind us
To a glimpse of how green it was on the other side
Steps taken forwards but sleepwalking back again
Dragged by the force of some inner tide
At a higher altitude with flag unfurled
We reached the dizzy heights of that dreamed-of world

Encumbered forever by desire and ambition
There's a hunger still unsatisfied
Our weary eyes still stray to the horizon
Though down this road we've been so many times

The grass was greener
The light was brighter
The taste was sweeter
The nights of wonder
With friends surrounded
The dawn mist glowing
The water flowing
The endless river
Forever and ever

These powerful lyrics seem to suggest a whole myriad of concepts: childhood innocence, hope, expectations, disappointment, retrospection, nostalgia, regret, and the end of things, and the end of us as the endless river of time runs its course. It is indeed a powerful lyric and, in many ways, a true picture of life, that is, without God in it. As I write, Dave Gilmore is said to be a professed atheist. The process of time is likened to a river. It flows and eventually our beginning starts a process of decay, and we have an end. The river can only flow one way and the clock is ticking that will eventually and inexorably take our dreams away. The start of the river may be glorious and serene through the innocence of childhood eyes, but despite our best efforts, the river flows, taking us further from the beginning. We are growing older but are never really at peace within ourselves in our troubled and divided world. It's about how we are never really able to fully achieve all our desires and ambitions. Even if we were able to do so, time takes them all away.

As children we had high hopes and we somehow envisaged life being better than how it turned out to be. Even the things that turn out right are never what we expected them to be. Life goes on and on as each generation comes and goes and it's all seemingly endless – for ever and ever and in the final analysis it all seems utterly meaningless. There is a persuasive sadness in it all because high hopes are dashed in time's inevitable ebb and flow and we all eventually go the way of all humanity – death. The searching words are made even more poignant with the powerful haunting musical accompaniment and the ringing of the division bell. The bell tolls for us all eventually.

The Apostle Peter has much to say about life and the ticking clock and its inevitable ebb and flow too, but its endless and seemingly meaninglessness, as expressed in the song *High Hopes,* is surprisingly absent because of the hope he expresses in Jesus who lived in time as a human being and who experienced death. He was born as a baby in the flow of time, grew up into manhood, and died at the age of thirty-three. The end? The Bible states categorical from cover to cover that this was not the end. Jesus rose from the dead. We call it resurrection. He is the Source and the Giver of Eternal Hope.

It fascinates me that we live in a world that craves heroes. We clapped on Thursday evenings at our front doors for the NHS heroes in the Covid pandemic. We can't wait for the next Marvel movie. Captain America is the hero of many. My daughter wanted the Marvel Encyclopaedia for her 13th birthday. The characters and details are incredible. We need heroes. Yet it seems that Jesus, the greatest hero of all, is excluded from the select hero club; well, the probable reason being because He's God and we don't want to get involved with God because that's too heavy, and anyway, everyone says it's fantasy too. Is it really? We had better be sure of that as forever is forever and it's a big eternity, if it's true after all. Get ready to be ready. If you want the Bible gallery of heroes of the faith you need to read Hebrews 11.

Yes, predictive prophecy in the Old Testament told us Captain Salvation would defeat death by actually dying and rising again. Peter and his fellow Apostles tell us they were eyewitnesses of the risen Christ. They lived for Him for years afterward and most of them died a martyr's death for the honour of His Name. In fact, John, the son of Zededee and brother of James, was the only disciple to die a natural death. He had been banished by the Roman Emperor Domitian to the Isle of Patmos where he penned the book of Revelation, the last book of the Bible. John was the only one of the band of disciples who did not meet a martyr's death.

Peter, who did meet a martyr's death, first met Jesus in 27 AD. In 30 AD he denied Jesus and yet, after restored hope, in that same year he went on to become a church leader after Pentecost. Then for another 37 years he was a dealer in hope and preached the hope of the good news of the Gospel. His letters were written between 64–67 AD and in 67 AD he was executed at Rome, crucified upside down according to tradition. Paul may have been executed the same year. Peter and Paul died as they lived, in the possession of a sure and steadfast hope – a living eternal hope. They were not afraid to die because of their faith in their risen glorified Lord.

The Bible declares that those who trust and own Jesus Christ as Saviour and Lord will come into possession of the same sure-fire hope. The Lord becomes our close and personal Saviour and Friend. As Lord of eternity, He promises us eternal life and gives us here and now eternal hope. In conquering death, Jesus is now living in the power of an endless life, and as such is able to give us a living hope in time and beyond time– it's an eternal hope. High Hopes! And so Peter can write, *'Praise be to the God and Father of our Lord Jesus Christ! In his great mercy he has given us new birth into a living hope through the resurrection of Jesus Christ from the dead* (1 Peter 1.3).

And we can live with great confidence, expectation, and a robust optimism. You only have to read through Peter to see that this is a unique message and a unique hope. Here is what Peter says about life and living in the first chapter.

These first recipients of the letter, as we have already noted, were living as 'foreigners' scattered to the four winds (1). Life was not offering many high hopes in a hopeless place. But they were actually living with high hopes, high expectations, because they have been born again into a living hope transcending life in all its circumstances and even time itself (1.3). They could now live with a specific purpose to please God in everything they did (1.13). In fact, they were to live in reverent fear of God as temporary residents (1.17). The word 'fear' means reverential trust. They were living with high hopes because they had been ransomed from an empty, vain life (1.18) and this was actually planned before time and life on earth had begun (1.20). They were now living with their faith and trust and hope in God because God raised Christ from the dead. Now they were called to live a life of love (1.21). And as for that river of time flowing, Peter says you have been born again, not to a life that would quickly end, but to a new life that will last forever because it comes from the eternal living word of God (1.23).

Peter does what Dave Gilmore did, he acknowledges that this life is fading away and Peter does it by quoting from the Old Testament.

As the Scriptures say,
People are like grass;
Their beauty is like a flower of the field.

The grass withers and the flower fades.

But he adds this important bit:

But the Word of the Lord remains forever;

And that word is the good news that was preached to you.

When Dave Gilmore wrote the album *The Division Bell* in 1994, the question was asked, did Pink Floyd use drugs? One observer notes, *'The members of the band took a negative view of excessive drug use after Syd Barret lost his mind due to drug use. Pink Floyd as a band was always very experimental, a true and defining trait for musicians everywhere to emulate. However, they were great because they just were, not because of drugs.'*

Remember the scholarly critic who had difficulty with Peter and his fellow writers and could not handle what is written in the Book of Hope and suggested that they had been taking magic mushrooms? I met a guy some years ago when we volunteered together in the Samaritans who had experimented a lot with magic mushrooms, and he was having conversations with the furniture. Seriously! He could see the furniture with faces and a mouth speaking to him. The wardrobe had a lot to say, and it wasn't C.S. Lewis' wardrobe either.

Peter had found high hope not in a higher high but because of Him who is on High. However, getting back to our scholar, the message is the Book of Hope is for dopes too. Here is true hope, here is real solid reality hope. Perhaps our scholar was not so much on the magic mushrooms, but rather the effects of the hallucinogenic of unbelief induced by sin, from the fall of humanity on that day in the Garden, taking us all away from the reality of God. And as for the endless river, Jesus said, *'Anyone who believes in me may come and drink! For the Scriptures declare, "Rivers of living water will flow from his heart".'* (John 7.38)

That's high hope indeed. Peter sure is a dealer in hope, pointing us to the Giver of Hope and there's enough to go round for everyone one who believes, including would-be doubting scholars, the inteligencia ,and hope for dopes too. Is it possible to be so smart that it makes you really stupid? The wisdom of man is foolish in the light of the revealed and infinite wisdom of God.

DAY TWELVE

THE BIG PICTURE BEHIND TRUE HOPE

The prism of the Word: Isaiah 40.6-8), 1 Peter 1 (MSG), and Colossians 1.15-20, 3.1-4.

A Petrean masterclass in the axioms undergirding true hope

The big picture behind the true hope as presented in Peter's first letter takes the form of what is referred to as 'Doctrine.' This hope is undergirded by a number of intertwined doctrines or teachings. This hope is not a 'hanging by a thread' kind of hope, or hope for the best, prepare for the worst. It's not in the Humpty Dumpty categorization. This true hope is undergirded, and copper fastened by the Source of Hope, the God of eternity Himself. If you Google the word 'doctrine', the following comes up: *'The basic meaning of the term doctrine is "teaching." Christian doctrine, accordingly, is the attempt to state in intellectually responsible terms the message of the gospel and the content of the faith it elicits.'*

Peter does just that, the big fisherman from Galilee gives us a masterclass in the truth behind true biblical hope and there is a lot packed into the first chapter which is followed through and reiterated throughout the astounding letter. The word 'doctrine' to those not used to the terminology could be misguidedly viewed as something dry and abstract and not so easily grasped. When we say 'grasp', we mean to have cognizance of the concept, not the entirety of the content for that in itself is eternal and in our limited dimensions in time and indeed our limited categories for understanding, not completely comprehensible. That's okay. Astrophysicists do not reject the concept of space, they believe, even if it's so overwhelming and earthbound knowledge is very much severely limited.

We could opt for another word for doctrine and adopt the word 'axiom'. This word means a statement accepted as true as the basis for argument or inference, or an established rule or principle or a self-evident truth. What Peter sets forth are not just some bright, unfounded, airy-fairy ideas he had while sitting in the sun after an afternoon at the Roman baths. These axioms are not only from the beginning of time but from eternity. Peter wrote under the inspiration of God the Holy Spirit and that is why they are pertinent and relevant to every generation, including ours. It's relevant to each of us individually and personally today and every day.

We are using the word 'axiom' to state that these are the biblical truths upon which human beings are enabled to enter into the lasting possession of true hope. We are going to list these and give some explanation on each. Some narratives are longer than others and some are quite succinct. These are but some of the axioms that support the hope we have in Jesus Christ. This is quite a list though and shows Peter's in-depth knowledge and understanding as revealed by God Himself. At the same time the personality of Peter shines through and all who have delved into the contents of the letter agree that the writing and the use of language is most exceptional. Peter was quite an insightful and effective communicator. The usual suspects have questioned Petrean authorship on the basis of the eloquence of the Greek used and its masterful construction. This argument, however, ignores the similarities of the language of Peter as recorded by Dr. Luke in Acts. There is no reason to doubt his proficiency in Greek. After almost forty years since he had become a disciple of Jesus, one would think his abilities in various areas would be honed and upskilled.

Election (1.1)

Remember he was writing to a people who were under the jackboot of oppression and persecution? They were in urgent need of help and hope and encouragement. Indeed, this is the chief reason Peter wrote to them in the first place. In his closing greetings he states: *I have written and sent this short letter to you with the help of Silas, whom I commend to you as a faithful brother. My purpose in writing is to encourage you and assure you that what you are experiencing is truly part of God's grace for you. Stand firm in this grace* (1 Peter 5.12).

And in the opening verses Peter tells them something that is quite extraordinary and mind-blowing. He describes them as the 'elect'. This simply means that they are identified as God's chosen people. God the Father, who is sovereign, has elected them – chosen them to eternal salvation and eternal hope. The same applies to each generation who read these words. Believers are chosen to be included in God's family. This choice is not on the basis of what we have done or who we are but on the basis of God's eternal wisdom. The God who knew us and chose us in eternity past calls us to partake of His salvation from which flows innumerable blessings, not least true and eternal hope.

The axiom of election is taught throughout Scripture and it's one of those mysteries that can easily tie us up in knots. We are not meant to understand it all. Who are we to put God under a microscope for analysis, or try to see Him through a telescope to comprehend the ins and outs of all His work and will and eternal governance? But let's seek to consider this axiom in a balanced way so that we simultaneously keep in mind the axiom of election and the axiom of free will, even though these seem to be two seemingly incompatible concepts.

If we are trying to focus on election in our presentation of the Gospel of Hope before proclaiming the need for belief of the truth, we are putting the cart before the horse. Our responsibility is to believe, i.e., to exercise personal faith in the Lord Jesus, His life, His finished work on the cross, and His resurrection from the dead. It is our responsibility to exercise our free will and put our trust and faith in Him alone for salvation. It's not just a matter of belief as in an intellectual accent to the axion, it is about faith and trust in Jesus Christ as the only Saviour of sinners, and the Lord of our lives. The Bible does tell us that even the devils believe and tremble, but this is only an acknowledgement of God and His awesome reality.

Let us leave the electing to God and not get hung up on it. You are not God, He is. The gospel is for whosoever may come, and when we come to Him we find that we are chosen in Christ before the foundation of the world. Jesus put it this way,

'All that My Father gives Me will come to Me; and the one who comes to Me I will most certainly not cast out [I will never, never reject anyone who follows Me]' (John 6.37 AMP).

Foreknowledge (1.1)

God the Father is omniscient and knows the end from the beginning. This is one of the attributes of God. Being omniscient means He knows all things. This would have been reassuring to the original readers in spite of all they were facing. But the knowledge that God knows everything needs to be seen in the whole array of what has been called God's communicable attributes and His incommunicable ones. Not only is God omniscient but He is also omnipotent and omnipresent. His plans cannot be thwarted. It was Solomon, that wisest of men, who wrote *'Many plans occupy the mind of a man, but the LORD's purposes will prevail'* (Proverbs 19.21).

Our hope is centred in God who knows everything and who is over everything and who is with us in everything and who controls everything. He alone is the King of the universe, the Ruler of the nations.

Sanctification (1.2)

God the Holy Spirit sets people apart as His people and His holy nation (2.9). The word 'sanctification' used here means to be set apart, that is, set apart by the Holy Spirit for conversion from the old life, from the old ways, from sin and bondage into a new life, the salvation life, which Peter refers to a lot, is a life which is consecrated to God. A life filled with hope. This is true freedom and true hope which runs counterintuitively to the wisdom of the world. This is hope in all circumstances. Complete freedom in the perfect will of God. Sanctification is an ongoing process whereby the Holy Spirit works in our lives to make us more like our Lord and Master. Our hope is centred in God who gives us a new life, a life of eternal hope.

Trinity (1,1,2)

There is one God in three persons, God the Father, Son, and Holy Spirit. You will probably know the response of some or even many. One God but three persons? Some will scoff and tell us that this does not make sense. Mum has strong opinions and it's difficult to get a hearing when one does not agree. When I ask her to preface what she is saying with the words, *'in my opinion',* that does not go down well! But it is true. Just because something doesn't make sense to us does not mean it's wrong. The reality is that Scripture explicitly teaches this axiom. To even begin to contemplate this axiom we need to begin with the declaration in the Bible that God is transcendent. Well, to be God He would need to be transcendent. God calls Himself 'I AM.' And God has, as we have already recognised, particular attributes, some we get up to a point and some we cannot fathom. We are brought face to face with God and His incomprehensive complex identity. There is only one God and three distinct persons at the same time. We find this in Genesis 1.1-2. We are told that God created the heavens and the earth. Then we are told that the Spirit of God moved or hovered over the waters. God and the Spirit of God. When we come to John 1. 1-2, we are told that the Word was with God and the Word was God. All things were made by Him. He was in the beginning with God. Father, Son, and Holy Spirit.

Timothy Mackie and Jonathan Collins of the Bible Project use an analogy to try to help us. Tim says: *'We can't fully understand but perhaps we can better understand what cannot be fully understood.'*

It's a quote worth remembering in our seeking to understand this and other biblical truths, or axioms. The Bible Project uses an analogy of a 2D plane with an object with three dimensions passing through the 2D plane. We only see each as distinct, yet the three are one but not in a way that we are capable of understanding, nor does it fit into our limited categories of understanding.

Jesus's chosen title for Himself was Son of Man and we tend to think of His humanity – a man on earth, a distinct person. He prayed to His Father as a distinct person, God the Father. Yet, He was also the Lord with the distinct attributes of God. For example, the attributes of infinite wisdom are His. He is known as the Creator of the Universe. He is God, and He is, at the same time, the Son of God. The Pharisees sought to stone Him because He made Himself equal with God. Daniel saw Him as the Son of Man in glory on the Throne of God and being worshipped. God is one in three and three in one. Listen to the words of the prophet Daniel: *In my vision in the night I continued to watch, and I saw One like the Son of Man coming with the clouds of heaven. He approached the Ancient of Days and was led into His presence. He was given authority, glory, and sovereign power; all nations and peoples of every language worshipped him. His dominion is an everlasting dominion that will not pass away, and his kingdom is one that will never be destroyed* (Daniel 7.13,14).

Our hope is centred in the Triune God, His eternal Fatherhood, His eternal Sonship, and His eternal Spirit who makes truth known to us and guides us into all truth. We worship and serve one God and in so doing we are worshipping and serving the Father, the Son, and the Holy Spirit. Three distinct persons – one God. Some people who, *'in their opinion'*, do not accept the doctrine of the Trinity go on to say that Christians believe in three gods. This criticism is often levelled at the Christian faith by those who do not accept the deity of Jesus Christ. *'How can He be God and the Father be God, if He was praying to Him when on earth?'* The answer is simple, because there is one God and three distinct persons in the Godhead.

To reiterate, we simply don't have the capacity to grasp this axiom, but we accept its reality because it is biblical truth. This axiom permeates Scripture from Genesis to Revelation. Some critics point to the fact that the actual word 'Trinity' is not mentioned in the Bible, and for them that is sufficient grounds to deny the doctrine. The doctrine of the Trinity was first formulated among the early Christians and fathers of the Church as they attempted to understand the relationship between Jesus and God as presented in Scripture. The words 'The Trinity' are the English equivalent of the Latin word *Trinitas*, which was coined by the early Christian writer Tertullian. The word, which etymologically means something like 'the tripleness', is used to refer collectively to the Father, the Son, and the Holy Spirit. The doctrine of the Trinity means that there is one God who eternally exists as three distinct Persons – the Father, Son, and Holy Spirit. Stated differently, God is one in essence and three in person. These definitions express three crucial truths: (1) the Father, Son, and Holy Spirit are distinct Persons, (2) each Person is fully God, (3) there is only one God. we bow in worship and adoration before our God.

Regeneration (1.3)

God brings about new birth into a living hope. Believers are given a new, spiritual life that enables us to live in an entirely different dimension than the one our physical birth allowed. Regeneration means rebirth. Our hope is centred in God who has caused us to be born again into this living hope. This hope is not some kind of wishful thinking but rather we have a dynamic confidence that does not come to an end when this earthly life does; rather we live on into and throughout eternity with God in His immediate presence.

Resurrection (1.3,21)

God the Father raised Jesus from the dead. We place our hope in the cross of Jesus Christ when He bore our sins, and we are born again to a living hope because God has raised Him from the dead. The resurrection of Jesus Christ is the righteous basis of our salvation, as well as the foundation of our living hope. As sinners we had no hope beyond the grave. The resurrection of Jesus is the Father's affirmation to Christ's cry from the cross, *'It is finished,'* meaning it is accomplished, it is complete.

Our hope is centred not on a dead Saviour, but in a living Saviour who conquered sin, death, the grave, and our arch enemy, and His resurrection is the guarantee of ours. The Gospel of Jesus Christ is good news. The early church fathers said that Mark, who wrote the second book of the New Testament, was closely associated with Peter and had written down much of Peter's preaching. We find that from Mark 8.31 onwards Jesus makes several clear predictions about His death. In doing so each time Jesus said that after three days He would rise from the dead. Jesus conquered death and in doing so he gives true hope to all who believe in Him, He gives us eternal life. He is the Author of eternal salvation. What a hope, a true hope to have in a troubled world.

Thine be the glory, living conquering Son,
endless is the victory thou o'er death hast won.

Heaven (1.3)
God is the God of Heaven. Our hope is centred on God who has reserved a place in heaven for us and who keeps an incorruptible inheritance for us in heaven, our ultimate destination.

Salvation (1.5,9,10)
God saves sinners. Our hope is centred in God who saves us

from the disease of sin and its consequences. It's power, punishment, and ultimately its very presence. Salvation means we have been saved, we are being saved and we shall be saved.

Eschatology (1.5)

God is in control of the future and has a plan that cannot be thwarted by anyone. Our hope is centred in God who has a plan for our lives and who is in control of our future, and we have an eschatological hope. We look for the return of Jesus Christ. He promised He would return. And one day every knee shall bow to Him, and every tongue will confess that Jesus Christ is Lord to the glory of God the Father.

Faith (1.7)

God is a faithful God and demands faith. Our hope is centred in the God who is faithful, and we exercise faith in Him alone for salvation. We commit to Him our past, our present, and our future.

Appropriation (1,7,8)

God is a God of invitation. Our hope is centred in the God who invites us to believe in Him and for us to appropriate the salvation He offers in His Son and all the axioms that accompany salvation.

Prophecy (1.10)

God is the God of prophecy and predicted the day of grace in the Old Testament. Our hope is centred in God who gave us His great and precious promises and predictions throughout the Old Testament, starting with Genesis 3.15, and which are also set forth in the New Testament for the rest of time and then for eternity.

Angels (1.12)
God is the God of Hosts, the God of the Angel Armies. Our hope is centred in the God of the Angel Armies who sends forth His Angels to serve those who will inherit salvation, and who will be His instruments in drawing time to an end.

Holiness (1.15,16)
God is a holy God. Our hope is centred in the God of holiness who demands for us to be holy, set apart to Him and for His service. We live and serve before an audience of One, God. God has instructed us to be holy for He is holy.

Redemption (1.18)
God is the Redeemer God. Our hope is centred in God who has purchased us at such a great price, even the sacrifice of His Son whose blood is redeeming blood.

Word (1.23)
God is synonymous with His word and Jesus is called the Word. We believe in God; we believe His Word; and we believe in Jesus who is the Word from all eternity.

These are just some of the axioms presented by Peter and which set this high and heavenly hope apart from all other hopes.

This is how the Message Bible paraphrases it nearing the close of 1 Peter chapter 1.

You call out to God for help and He helps – He's a good Father that way. But don't forget, he's also a responsible Father, and won't let you get by with sloppy living. Your life is a journey, you must travel with a deep consciousness of God. It cost God plenty to get you out of that dead-end, empty-headed life you grew up in. He paid with Christ's sacred blood, you know. He died like an unblemished, sacrificial lamb. And this was no afterthought. Even though it has only lately – at the end of the ages – become public knowledge, God always knew He was going to do this for you. It's because of this sacrificed Messiah, whom God then raised from the dead and glorified, that you trust God, that you know you have a future in God. Now that you've cleaned up your lives by following the truth, love one another as if your lives depended on it. Your new life is not like your old life. Your old birth came from mortal sperm; your new birth comes from God's living Word. Just think: a life conceived by God himself! That's why the prophet said,

'The old life is a grass life,

its beauty as short-lived as wildflowers;

Grass dries up, flowers wilt,

God's Word goes on and on forever.

This is the Word that conceived the new life in you'.

DAY THIRTEEN

BRINGING MEANING TO A MEANINGLESS LIFE

The prism of the Word: Matthew 3.13-17.

Jean Paul Sartre: Belief in God is bad faith, non-belief good faith?

I remember when studying at the Open University a fellow student who had a great interest in philosophy bought me a book called *'Being and Nothingness'* by Jean Paul Sartre. One felt honour-bound to read it, or at least try to. I must admit I was taken by the title, and I took to reading the book. And what did I find? Well, I found it difficult as it is not one of his most accessible works. But in my reading and research I did find this out about Sartre; he referred to belief in God as 'bad faith' and he was determined to believe in the non-existence of God as this was 'good faith,' in his eyes. Sartre was of the view that this led to complete human freedom and with it an awesome social responsibility. In *Being and nothingness*, he speaks of his aloneness in the world without any help and how the responsibilities he must take on in a world of nothingness weighed heavily upon him to the extent that he felt that *'To exist is nauseating.'* Life, according to Sartre, is one of useless passion. He is seen as the father of existentialism.

Tom Flanley, a Cambridge University Scholar who studied Sartre very closely and noted his excessive hatred for God, suggests he suffered from what is referred to as Excess Reverse Syndrome' (ERS). Basically, this means where there is excessive hatred, love is lurking somewhere. It means what we deny all the time is actually our subconscious belief fighting to come out as true faith. To deny is to accept unwittingly. Certainly, in the case of human relationships, we know that love can bring up everything unlike itself in the love/hate relationship.

Flanley's idea is quite fascinating, but one is not suggesting that this is the case in terms of Sartre and his hatred of God, it is an interesting hypothesis though. An intense hatred of belief in God does not necessarily mean ERS, indeed, given our nature and fallen condition, we have no desire to believe in God and if we do we tend to be more interested in living as practical atheists, wanting our will and our way. This is a simplistic overview of the human condition, and we shall revisit this later in our explorations, suffice to say at this point that a determined unbelief in a majestic Creator God who designed us and loves us leads us to seek for others gods that we think can satisfy our needs.

The book that claims to be the written Word of God, the Bible, points out that we actually have a God-shaped vacuum in our lives that only He can satisfy, a craving for that which humanity lost in the garden – fellowship with the living God. Like Sartre we try to fill this void with all sorts of gods of our own making. Today we have many gods that we worship, and most of the time we do it unwittingly; pleasure, money, riches, possessions, prestige, and power, to name but a few.

Sartre kept on passionately condemning the notion of God but it would seem that God resided in the crevices of his mind. For Sartre, his obsession with the 'non-existence' of God was such that his atheism bordered on militant atheism, akin to today's Richard Dawkins and Christopher Hitchens. Flanley's view is that this pathological negation of God was bound to recoil and re-blossom into equally strong faith in God. One does wonder if that's why he called for a priest just prior to his death. Dismayed by this development, his followers asked him what happened to him when death was at his doorstep. His reply was, *'In case...'*

Sartre's apparent and astonishing change of mind and heart was revealed by his friend Pierre Victor. Pierre spent much of his time with the dying Sartre and had in his lifetime been in a position to speak with him at length on many of his views. According to Victor, Sartre had a drastic change of mind about the existence of God and started gravitating toward Messianic Judaism. This is Sartre's before-death profession, according to Pierre Victor:

'I do not feel that I am the product of chance, a speck of dust in the universe, but someone who was expected, prepared, prefigured. In short, a being whom only a Creator could put here; and this idea of a creating hand refers to God.'

His disillusionment and disenchantment with life, and indeed his confusion about religion, led him to expound profusely his brand of atheistic existentialism but it seems it was a façade in the end. This turning to God, as recounted by Pierre, must have been a big shock to his many followers who saw him as the most prominent and able exponent in his field. Indeed, his lover, Simone de Beauvoir, his fellow atheistic existentialist, was so outraged that she said, *'How should one explain this senile act of a turncoat?'*

Was Sartre brought kicking and screaming into the Kingdom like C.S. Lewis? I don't know. Oh I do hope so, but what we do know is he acknowledged his Creator in a death-bed confession.

It's a pity he had not understood Ecclesiastes and the culmination of the author's search for hope and meaning in life and death and human existence.

Even the cleverest and most intellectual of minds may change their life-long and well-guarded belief systems when the cold hand of death is near. Sartre was no exception. But why wait until death when there is life to live with divine meaning and purpose?

There is a lot of 'positive' stuff in the school of positive psychology, I guess that's why they called it positive psychology. I have read my fair share of it over the years. One of the emphases in this field of study is called the 'power of purpose'. I had been musing recently and mulling hope and hopelessness over in my mind and this is what I wrote down in my pocket notebook: *'The potential breeding ground for hopelessness is purposelessness and meaninglessness; but purpose and meaning can harness hope.'*

Can we move from the hopeless heartbreak alleys of life filled with slow decay to the door of hope into the verdant pasture lands of hopefulness? (Micah 2.14 msg). The backdrop to Peter's letter, as we have already seen, was adversity and difficulty – the vicissitudes of life, but in the words of a popular song, 'They found hope in a hopeless place.' So can we. Let's begin to reframe the concept of meaning in the context of faith, and how faith in the living God brings a powerful purposefulness to our lives, giving us hope.

Peter, the dealer in hope, emphasises the biblical claims that life has only any real lasting meaning if God is in it. This is the God who gives us grace and peace. Peter tells his readers that it is God who has chosen us from eternity to be in His family and belong to Him and know Him. There is a calling on our lives to live a particular kind of life – a holy life. This is not the antithesis of freedom, this is true freedom, as we shall see as we explore further in the days to come. We can live life to the full because God has given us life to live with profound purpose and meaning. The Gospel proclaims the invitation to believe and trust and receive the hope of God in Christ and live purposely and meaningfully in the plan of God.

By the mercy of God we are given a living hope and a brand-new life and we have everything to live for. We can live with great expectations and can have the assurance of eternal life, not only in the future, but here and now. God is watching over us and our future too, and it's secure in Him, the true Source of our authentic Hope.

Yes, life can be tough, and our faith is tried and tested, but we can live victoriously in Jesus. We may falter and we may fail and we may even lose sight of our hope but He is the same yesterday, today, and forever and He will never fail us. We trust in His Word.

We have not seen Him but we do love Him. We trust Him. The certainty of salvation is in His hands, not ours.

It was long ago written down, the plan of the eternal King of the universe is etched in history and in the indelible and unalterable Word of the Living God. The promised Saviour was not plan B, it was plan A, and all of history is now divided between BC and AD. Our own personal existence and history is not a mistake as we live in the plan and will of God; this is true freedom.

With this freedom comes responsibility, but unlike Sartre, who felt utterly alone and that he had to do it all by himself, we are not alone. We are called to live in and for God now and not slip back into the old ways. Satisfying our own selfish desires ironically does not satisfy. We are left with the words of the song by the Rolling Stones ringing in our ears, *'I can't get no satisfaction.'* The Creator designed us, and He knows what we need, and it is in Him that we get the most out of a meaningful, purposeful, God-directed life; living in hope, even when we don't feel it sometimes. It is ours to appropriate by faith.

We can call on God for help, He is our Father. We are not alone.

We have been redeemed by the precious blood of Christ. And our past, present, and future are in Him. God has revealed Himself to the world in Jesus and we can know Him. The hope as expressed in the Bible is that the past is settled, the further is secure, and the present can be lived fully in the unfolding of the divine plan for our lives.

We can live a life of love. We had a natural birth and now we have a spiritual birth. This world fades and time marches on but we have an eternal hope, and we have eternal life through faith in Jesus Christ alone. And all this is on offer to you and me through the Gospel – the Good News of Jesus Christ. Take it, live it, and live purposefully and meaningfully knowing that you matter and your life matters. God has a plan for you. Don't miss it and don't leave it to the end, like Sartre, and you could be cutting it so fine that it could be just too late. Yes, a soul saved but a life lost to being and nothingness.

You may have watched the Father Brown Detective stories, and I must confess that I did not know until recently that Gilbert Keith (GK) Chesterton was their creator. One of his many famous quotes was, *'If there were no God, there would be no Atheists.'* It's a great quote and worth some thinking about as you consider the prism of the Word for today.

Chesterton also said: *'According to most philosophers, God in making the world enslaved it. According to Christianity, in making it, He set it free. God had written, not so much a poem, but rather a play; a play he had planned as perfect, but which had necessarily been left to human actors and stage-managers, who had since made a great mess of it.'*

We have the responsibility to humble ourselves before God and acknowledge the mess and seek His mercy, grace, and forgiveness and obtain a living hope that gives us new life and makes everything new and the promise of eternal life into the bargain.

DAY FOURTEEN

HOPE CHANGES EVERYTHING

The prism of the Word: John 10.10 and 1 Peter 1.13-25.

Ruby Wax, 'The world – breeding ground for despair' and a hope manual

I think it was when studying psychotherapy that I came across the quote that goes something like this: *'There are things a person will only admit to their closest friends, and there are things a person will only admit to themselves, and there are things that a person will not even admit to themselves.'*

And so, we could enter into the realm of defence mechanisms, a term first used by Sigmund Freud. One of the key defence mechanisms that we use is 'denial', as alluded to in our quote. It is as the term suggests, a defence, and so human beings can consciously deny that painful facts exist, and denial can be a way of escaping thoughts, feelings, and events that are just too real and too painful to cope with.

A prime example is found in grief or traumatic grief when the body and mind deny reality; a natural way of anaesthetising the self to get through the painful experience until eventually denial gives way to reality and acceptance. Sometimes, however, people will live on in pathological denial. As one trained in psychotherapy, a 'given' is not to ruthlessly take away a person's defence mechanism but to facilitate it in the process of the talking therapy and the working through of the pain and suffering so as to come to terms with the loss or whatever caused the defence in the first place. This is where post-traumatic growth can take place. Denial is an attempt to block out the painful experience as the mind and body adjust to the reality of what has happened.

The insightful therapist or counsellor will take care in dealing with such defences and in a way that allows the person, if they are deemed to have sufficient ego strength, to gradually come to accept the reality and to move from the pain of the past to a place of post-traumatic growth. For some, the experiences are so traumatic and so hidden, that to try and raise the Titanic would be unwise. Some have described this kind of denial as a form of self-deception, however, in the therapeutic context of trauma, this, in my mind, is not the case. It's a natural coping strategy.

Recently, a friend of mine suffered a loss and was finding it difficult. A book I used with people in my pastoral ministry days came to mind; it was called *Good Grief*, written by the late Rev Sydney Callaghan; an unusual title for a book. The idea is there can be good grief or bad grief. The book takes the reader through the denial on a journey in the following way:

It hasn't happened to me – the place of denial
It shouldn't have happened to me – the place of anger
Why did it happen to me – the place of questioning; and then,
It did happen to me – the place of acceptance

Blatant deceit is an altogether different matter. Peter moves his focus from the great axioms that undergirds the believer's living hope to the outworking of these in the practicalities of everyday living. In chapter two, one of the things he says we need to get rid of is, yes, you've guessed it, 'deceit.' Deceit in this particular context is the act of causing someone to accept as true or valid what is false or invalid. It is the act or practice of deceiving: i.e., deception. And we can deceive ourselves. The Greek word that Peter uses for deceit is the word 'dolos', meaning trickery, and using bait to allure with the notion of a hook. It has the idea of 'decoy' behind it; guile, subtlety, and wily craft. Not a nice word and not a nice thing to do, nor to be on the receiving end of such trickery.

'Therefore, rid yourselves of all malice and all deceit, hypocrisy, envy, and slander of every kind' (2.1).

The Message Bible paraphrase talks about cleaning the house and making a clean sweep of malice and pretence, envy and hurtful talk.

'Therefore'; the conjunctive adverb is used by Peter to show the cause i.e., the intervention of the God of hope in our lives, as set out in chapter one, and the effect; the meaning and purposefulness and immense difference it makes to living in a relationship with God and pleasing Him. This is true freedom. When we come into possession of this living hope it has profound implications for the way we live and there are things to get rid of.

The best-selling author Ruby Wax acknowledges that the world is a breeding ground for despair and suggests that her book is a manual for those who seek a way out of all the frenzy of modern living. The author goes on to say that her manual offers a shelter from the constant hurriedness of stress and depression that humans experience. It is written from an evolutionary perspective, noting that life is really an illusion. What interested me was the fact that this is seen as a manual for living in the world today. The good thing is that people like

Ruby, who have experienced the depths of despair and hopelessness, with the best of intentions, use their personal experiences of struggle and pain to try to offer help to others and give them some hope. On a human level there is a lot of self-help stuff out there to help people get through each day. Doctors are now prescribing self-help books to encourage people to understand and develop good coping strategies as opposed to maladaptive ones. Some of it is good as far as it goes. And some of it is not good at all. We need discernment.

When we turn to the Bible, it makes big bold claims, indeed it claims to be the Designer's manual for living and the hope for all humanity. It boldly declares that it is the God-given manual for us humans living on the earth. So many people dismiss it and use the same old ancient arguments that have rolled effortlessly off the tongues of the sceptics for centuries.

'It's just a book and it can mean anything you want it to mean and it's full of contradictions anyhow.'

The reality is that the Bible has a simple message – the Gospel of Jesus Christ. Salvation is found in Him alone, His life, death, burial, and resurrection. But this inspired book has infinite treasures that are not given to the reader lightly or easily. They are spiritually discerned. There is only one true interpretation and God the Holy Spirit is the bookkeeper. I'm using the term 'bookkeeper' to describe the one who reveals and unfolds the Word to those who will read and listen and hear and heed.

A reading of the words of Jesus Himself tells us that the understanding of what is written is not given automatically to anyone. Check out Luke 8.10, 9.43-45, and 10.21. This plays out in a world where even the most intelligent of people can dismiss the Bible. This is not surprising given that it's a Book that needs to be treated with respect and the acknowledgement that the Divine Author needs to reveal its meaning. Spiritual discernment is required. And yet, its message is so simple that a child can grasp it; such is its uniqueness and the unparalleled nature of its divine composition.

This vineyard does not yield fruit to those who treat it carelessly and then expect to pluck choice ripe grapes. Its yield must be carefully cultivated and so, with the Word, in the presence of the Divine Master Teacher and Revealer of Truth. Jesus bestows his blessing only to those who respond carefully and respectfully to the Word of God and his will as expressed therein (Luke 11.28).

Jesus taught in parables. One of the best known of these is the Parable of the Sower. Even the disciples did not understand its meaning until they asked Jesus and then He explained it. It is well worth a mention here. This is a basic synopsis of the parable and its meaning. It is also referred to as the Parable of the Soils. There are four types of soil or ground, and they are:

- Wayside
- Rocky ground
- Thorny ground
- Good ground

Jesus said the seed is the Word of God and the ground is the human heart. The seed that falls on the wayside is quickly snatched away by the enemy. The seed that falls on the rocky ground is received with joy, but then the attractions and distractions of the world and the trials of life mean the seed is forgotten and cannot take root. The same with the thorny ground, the seed does not take root because it is choked with the cares, riches, and pleasures of this life. Then we have the good ground which represents the open and receptive heart.

Those who hear the Word with a noble and good heart keep it and bear good fruit. Check out Luke 8.4-15.

Jesus does indicate that not everyone who reads will understand it. That depends on the heart. Thus, the Bible may sound and seem to be somewhat ambiguous to some, and to others clothed in majestic mystery. In some places it may not sound like it making any sense and it may even be counterintuitive to the rational sceptical world and casual reader; be that as it may, this does not diminish it. We will elaborate further in another essay when we meet the plough boy.

The guys at The 'Bible Project do amazing work in their videos and podcasts and use the title 'My strange Bible', and it does sound strange in parts. I am using this word carefully because it is only strange to those who are ignorant. The 'ignoramus' reads it and declares *'it's just a book'* and concludes *'it does not make sense, I have read it and it's not what it's cracked up to be.'*

Such a stance only serves to substantiate the argument that it stands as revealed Truth, but only to those who have the credentials to understand it. We are not speaking here of a group of spiritual elites or a modern-day Gnosticism, but rather the childlike. We hear what Jesus said in a prayer to the Father.

At that same time Jesus was filled with the joy of the Holy Spirit, and he said, "O Father, Lord of heaven and earth, thank you for hiding these things from those who think themselves wise and clever, and for revealing them to the childlike. Yes, Father, it pleased you to do it this way" (Luke 10.21).

What Jesus is saying is that those who consider themselves too wise and having too much understanding and knowledge are afflicted with judicial blindness; they are left in the dark. Having refused the light, the light is withheld from them. The context is one of titanic unbelief on the part of the religious leaders of the day. On the other hand, for those who are humble and acknowledge their lack of wisdom and understanding, they receive His revelation and become acquainted with the One *'in whom are hidden all the treasures of wisdom and knowledge'* (Colossians 2.3).

No one can take up the Bible and read it without it having an impact. It will do one of three things. Either the reader will come to believe, choose not to believe, or try to sit on the fence of indecision with the higher critics. Here is what the Bible says:

> But the natural [unbelieving] person does not accept the things [the teachings and revelations] of the Spirit of God, for they are foolishness [absurd and illogical] to them; and they are incapable of understanding them, because they are spiritually discerned and appreciated, [and they are unqualified to judge spiritual matters] (1 Corinthians 2.14).

Dr Vance Havner (1901–1986), a dynamic and tireless revivalist preacher, preached all over America for 70 years. This is what he said about a man or woman trying to explain God's revelation, as set out in the Scriptures, to one who chooses not to believe.

'He might as well try to describe a sunset to a blind man or discuss nuclear physics with a monument in the city park. The natural man cannot receive such things. One might as well try to catch sunbeams with a fishhook as to lay hold on God's revelation unassisted by the Holy Spirit. Unless one is born of the Spirit and taught by Him, all this is utterly foreign to him. Being a PhD does not help, for in this realm it could mean 'phenomenal Dud'.

And yet it is in this realm – the spiritual realm – God has set up a highway of truth, God's highway and the way of holiness, even *'wayfaring men, though fools, shall not err therein'* (Isa 35.8). And thus, we find that the honest, humble, seeking soul who reads the Word of God has tremendous insight and knows a great deal more of the truth and what God has revealed, than do some of the so-called learned in the halls of academia, the phenomenal duds. And some phenomenal duds who are humble, honest, seeking souls get it too. And you don't have to freeze your brain to believe. Some people with the greatest brains have believed and used their intelligence to great advantage in the Kingdom. You don't relinquish your intelligence to believe, but if you think you are too smart or too clever or of too superior intelligence to believe, then it will not make sense, and we cannot enter into the place of saving faith until we remove the gods that cling to the thrones of our lives. We must take the humble place before God and exercise simple childlike faith in Jesus as Saviour and Lord of our lives.

We also find that no one can expect to understand God's word and God's ways, who seeks to know out of mere curiosity, nor those who think that when they have discovered them it is left to themselves to walk in them or not, just as they please. The Word of God says: *'My hands have made both heaven and earth; they and everything in them are mine. I, the LORD, have spoken! I will bless those who have humble and contrite hearts, who tremble at my word'* (Isaiah 66.2).

Here God graciously classifies the poor, and those of a contrite spirit, with those that tremble at His word.

Oh, that the learned who are sitting in judgement on God's word and on what He has taught, would quietly weigh this message. The humble gladly receive what God says, they may

116

even come with honest doubt but that does not lead them to call the scriptures in question because of preconceived notions and hardened attitudes. God blesses their contrite, confiding faith; whereas the learned may have what they call advanced views to maintain, and are too often full of high thoughts, and with years of honing their ability to test everything to the nth, as they think, and are thus not in a right spirit to be taught anything.

We read: *'Jesus called a little child to him and put the child among them. Then he said, "I tell you the truth, unless you turn from your sins and become like little children, you will never get into the Kingdom of Heaven. So anyone who becomes as humble as this little child is the greatest in the Kingdom of Heaven"* (Matthew 18.2-4).

How contrary is this to what we see around us and to what is the tendency to be intentionally or unintentionally influenced by the spirit of the age. To be as a little child! To believe, unhesitatingly, everything that God tells us in His word! This is the way to be taught by the Holy Spirit. Oh, to be more like Mary, to sit at the Lord's feet, and just to drink in all the gracious words that proceed out of His mouth! And then to study all that He has caused to be written, believing it *all* to be inspired by God, and find it profitable for doctrine, for reproof, for correction, for instruction in righteousness; that we, as the people of God, may be perfect, thoroughly furnished unto all good works.

'All Scripture is inspired by God and is useful to teach us what is true and to make us realise what is wrong in our lives. It corrects us when we are wrong and teaches us to do what is right. God uses it to prepare and equip his people to do every good work' (2 Timothy 3.16,17).

That being the case, we would need to consult it and we need to heed it. We need to be real and face up to it and stop trying to deceive ourselves, it is our only hope. He is our only hope! And hope changes everything, including the way we live. It offers us transformation from death to life, from purposelessness to purposefulness, from meaninglessness to biblical mindfulness, from being a nobody to being a somebody – special to God and included in His eternal plan.

I thought I had bought my favourite ground Italian coffee and it was actually coffee beans. I then decided to buy a grinder for the purpose. It would not work. It was dead and I, as a rule, do not read instruction manuals. That's so rich coming from me, given the encouragement for us all to read and obey God's instruction manual; that's different of course. The truth is, for years I didn't, but I would read anything else until I came to an end of myself and realised there is a better way, the only way, to hear the Word of the Lord.

Anyway, back to the coffee grinder – I tried to work it out myself. Guess what? I needed to read the instructions. It worked and I enjoyed my first experience of wondrous Italian coffee that I had ground myself. The Designer of the universe who made you and me and has given us a set of instructions, a manual of hope and how to live. A manual of true eternal hope. But we deceive ourselves and think we know better and the last thing we will do is read the instructions. Get rid of the self-deceit! His manual is a must! Here's what the manual says about deceit.

But blessed is the one who trusts in the Lord,
whose confidence is in him.
They will be like a tree planted by the water
that sends out its roots by the stream.

It does not fear when heat comes;
its leaves are always green.
It has no worries in a year of drought
and never fails to bear fruit.
The heart is deceitful above all things
and beyond cure.
Who can understand it?
I the Lord search the heart
and examine the mind,
to reward each person according to their conduct,
according to what their deeds deserve (Jeremiah 17.7-10).

'If we say that we have no sin, we deceive ourselves, and the truth is not in us. If we confess our sins, he is faithful and righteous to forgive us our sins, and to cleanse us from all unrighteousness' (1 John 1.8,9).
'And the great dragon was thrown down, that ancient serpent, who is called the devil and Satan, the deceiver of the whole world – he was thrown down to the earth, and his angels were thrown down with him (Revelation 12.9).

It's time to get into the Hope manual and say with the Psalmist David; *'Guide me in your truth and teach me, for you are God my Saviour, and my hope is in you all day long* (Psalm 25:5).

DAY FIFTEEN

THE ELIXIR OF LIFE

The prism of the Word: 1 Timothy chapter 2

Emma F Bevan, the broken cisterns of life and a well of hope

Human beings have always been fascinated with the notion of the elixir of life. It has featured in fairy tales and folk tales as a magical potion offering immortality and freedom from disease for the person that drinks it. The concept is found to date way back into many ancient cultures. The earliest is said to be found in some ancient texts in Mesopotamia. The world is still searching for this elusive and mysterious elixir of life. In ancient China, the Emperors also craved it and funded physicians and alchemists to seek it out. In ancient India, the belief in this much sought-after potion was viewed as being more akin to gods and deities in their polytheistic belief system.

Any consideration of the idea of the hope of immortality will invariably lead to the Bible since the Bible is the story of paradise lost and paradise regained. This led to legends about a mysterious object that could confer immortality, and the Holy Grail is the much sought-after object. This is said to be a miraculous cup which Jesus drank at the last supper. Anyone who drinks from the same cup will live forever in perfect health. Remember *Indiana Jones and the Last Crusade* and the quest for the holy grail?

Peter has already told us in his opening chapter of his first letter what the true biblical reality is. Eternal life, immortality, is not found in a holy grail or a philosopher's stone or anything of that nature. The hope of eternal life is found in Jesus Christ alone who defeated sin and death and rose again from the dead. His resurrection is the guarantee of ours. Those who frame the biblical account of hope and immortality in the same vein as the aforementioned cultures of myth and legend need to think again and give serious consideration to what is being revealed.

Mankind has looked everywhere for the secret ingredient to longevity and everlasting life and continues to do so, but to no avail. Here's the thing: have you ever looked and looked for something you thought was lost only to find out that you were looking in the wrong place? It's there, right under your nose. That is what mankind has been doing for ages, looking in the wrong place for a cure for all ills. And given that the arch enemy is hell bent on throwing in all kinds of illusions to take us on the wrong path, it's not surprising that people are lost and bewildered. Yet the answer has been as close as the nearest book shop and in some cases as close as the nearest bookshelf. The remedy or cure is found in the Word of God, the real, the genuine, and the original elixir of life. Peter tells his readers, who have found this true hope in God, that they should desire – long for – crave – the pure spiritual milk of the Word of God that they may grow and be nurtured in respect of the salvation they have found (1 Peter 2.2). This is eternal redemption.

The writer to the Hebrews refers to this when he says: *'Not with the blood of goats and calves, but with His own blood He entered the Most Holy Place once for all, having obtained eternal redemption'* (Hebrews 9.12).

Eternal life is found in Jesus Christ, but we must appropriate that work of salvation to our souls by exercising faith in Him.

Dust that Bible down and start reading. It was Jesus Himself who said; *'But whoever drinks the water I give them will never thirst. Indeed, the water I give them will become in them a spring of water welling up to eternal life'* (John 4.14).

He was addressing a woman at a well on a hot day who had left a trail of broken relationships in her wake. This poor, lost, and shame-based soul was out in the hot noon sun to get some water. Perhaps this was the time of the day she could avoid seeing anyone because she felt such toxic shame. And just in case we want to get on our uppity horse and think we are better than her, think again because we have broken the greatest and most important relationship of all – the relationship with God.

God's Word is the elixir of life, but we have to drink it in. Believing in water but not drinking it will not assuage our thirst but lead to certain death. If we want to possess eternal life, then we must appropriate the Word of God to ourselves. We need to accept the good news of the Gospel of Jesus Christ. The world is full of broken thirsty people and broken cisterns and empty wells.

Emma F Bevan (1827–1909) is reputed to have written the hymn *None but Christ,* which refers to our broken cisterns and the source of true satisfaction. Emma Frances Shuttleworth was born in Oxford in 1827. Her father, Philip Nicholas Shuttleworth, was Warden of New College, Cambridge. In 1842 he became Bishop of Chichester, but died two years later, leaving her fatherless at seventeen. As a girl, Emma was taught by a German governess, and became interested in Gothic art and mediaeval Christianity. Later on, she was much attached to the family of Baron von Bunsen, at one time Prussian ambassador to England, whose scholarly attainments largely influenced her study of German literature.

In 1856 she married Robert Cooper Lee Bevan, a banker. She published several books including books on hymns translated from German. It has been said that the greatest service Emma rendered to the Church was the translating of great German hymns into the English language. Emma wrote and published a number of volumes including several hymns which were chiefly her translations from German Pietists of the Middle Ages. Emma rejoiced in what she referred to as: *'The distinctness of the truth of the Gospel and the present possession and enjoyment of eternal life; and its glorious hope, peace and joy.'*

The translations of Mrs Bevan has exercised a deep influence upon the hearts of those who have read her works of poetry. Whilst most of her works were translations, the following Hymn has been attributed to her, and entitled *None but Christ.* These are the words:

O Christ, in Thee my soul hath found,
And found in Thee alone,
The peace, the joy I sought so long,
The bliss till now unknown.
Refrain
Now none but Christ can satisfy,
None other name for me!
There's love, and life, and lasting joy,
Lord Jesus, found in Thee.
I sighed for rest and happiness,
I yearned for them, not Thee;
But, while I passed my Saviour by,
His love laid hold on me.
Refrain
I tried the broken cisterns, Lord,

But, ah, the waters failed;
Even as I stooped to drink, they fled,
And mocked me as I wailed.
Refrain
The pleasures lost I sadly mourned,
But never wept for Thee,
Till grace the sightless eyes received,
Thy loveliness to see.
Refrain

The words of the Old Testament come to mind and perhaps these were her inspiration: *'For My people have committed two evils: They have forsaken Me, the Fountain of Living Waters, and hewn themselves cisterns – broken cisterns that can hold no water'* (Jeremiah 2.13).

And when you come to Christ you find true satisfaction at the well of salvation. We need to drink in His Word to grow up in our faith and understand the things of God from the true elixir of life, the Living Word of the Living God.

Abraham found the answer in ancient days. He was told by God to get out of Mesopotamia, the very place that was searching for the elixir of life, and head for the promised land. He left a flourishing civilization, where he was well educated, to follow God, the true God, leaving His family behind, who worshipped false gods. Ur and Haran were significant places of the moon-worship cult. The elixir of life was not found there, it was false and fake. God told Abraham not to be afraid but to trust Him, obey His word, and He would be His shield and His exceeding great reward. God revealed more and more of Himself to Abraham. He learned that God is the Almighty God, El Shaddai, and He told him to walk before Him and be obedient to His word. He found the elixir of life. To the watching world they probably thought Abraham had given leave of his senses. But he had put his faith in God, and we read in the letter to the Romans, *'Against all hope, Abraham in hope believed and so became the father of many nations, just as it had been said to him, "So shall your offspring be"'* (Romans 4.18).

When we come into the New Testament, we find the Sadducees arguing with Jesus about the resurrection. Jesus said that God is not the God of the dead but the God of the living.

Jesus replied, "Are you not in error because you do not know the Scriptures or the power of God? When the dead rise, they will neither marry nor be given in marriage; they will be like the angels in heaven. Now about the dead rising – have you not read in the Book of Moses, in the account of the burning bush, how God said to him, 'I am the God of Abraham, the God of Isaac, and the God of Jacob'? He is not the God of the dead, but of the living. You are badly mistaken!" (Mark 12.24-27)

And so, Peter encourages his readers to embrace God's salvation and get into God's Word and grow into the fullest experience and knowledge of their salvation. Here is the true soul-satisfying food and soul-quenching drink. Let us be done with the junk food of our own personal Mesopotamia – get out and get rid! Once you get a taste of the elixir of life, you will want more for here you are in the possession of eternal hope and everlasting life.

DAY SIXTEEN

THE EVERLASTING TEMPLE OF HOPE

The prism of the Word: John 4

Alexander the Great and the desire for world mastery

Alexander, king of Macedon (356–323 BC), better known as Alexander the Great, died in his early thirties having won many victories in battle. He was the King of Macedonia for less than thirteen years. He is regarded as one of the greatest military generals the world has ever seen. His Empire was vast, stretching from Macedonia to Egypt and from Greece all the way to part of India. There is a famous saying about Alexander the Great that goes along the lines of *'He wept, for there were no more worlds to conquer'.*

However, any classical scholar worth their salt would not entertain such a quote as it cannot be found in ancient antiquity. In fact, those who know are of the view that the more accurate version of events is the exact opposite. Indeed, it is noted in antiquity that Alexander wept having heard a lecture by Anaxarchus, a Greek philosopher who accompanied him to the East and whom he highly esteemed. When Alexander heard him speak on an *'infinite number of worlds',* he wept because he thought it a tragedy that there were an infinite number of worlds, but he could not even be the master of one.

The world is replete with empire builders, ancient and modern. And yet we are all building something in our own way,

SHORT ESSAYS ON FINDING HOPE IN OUR FRAGILE WORLD

and in our own personal world. We hope for a better life and all the ingredients for a better quality of life, and we make plans and seek to become masters of our world. Yet, whatever we achieve, we end up like Alexander because whatever we are building and however great our achievements, and however great our desire is to build more, we have to eventually leave it all behind. Jesus said, *'For what will it profit a man if he gains the whole world, and loses his own soul? Or what will a man give in exchange for his soul?* (Mark 8.35,36)

But what if we were involved in a building that has an everlasting foundation and which is of such a nature that it will never perish or fade but glow in the brightness of glory and majesty of Jesus Christ forever because it's built by God? That is exactly what Peter tells us in 1 Peter chapter 2. If you want to be involved in something that will last forever and be part of this everlasting kingdom, then get reading what Peter has to say. I have called it a temple, the temple of hope. Be part of the temple of hope.

Peter tells his readers that those who come to Christ are coming to the One who is the living 'Cornerstone' of God's temple. Even though He was rejected by the religious leaders and teachers of the law, God chose the Messiah for this great honour. The religionists were more concerned about their own earthly temple, which was eventually destroyed, as had been predicted by Jesus.

The cornerstone imagery is about the first stone set in the construction of a masonry foundation. As the first stone to be laid, it becomes the reference point for all other stones laid subsequently. Everything finds its definition in this one piece – the cornerstone. That's how we know what is straight and true and right. That's how we know if we are on the right track.

That's how we know if we are deviating from the original and intended Divine plan. The cornerstone reveals this, and Jesus Christ is the Cornerstone.

Jesse Campbell, Editor of Explore the Bible, Lifeway, writes: *'As that first stone provides the very definition and basis of what is right and wrong, what is true and what is false, so Jesus defines our reality. He is more than a Sunday Saviour or an occasional companion. He is the lens through which we filter everything else. He is the Cornerstone of our worldview, and the cross of Jesus is the reference point to make sure our interpretation of the events surrounding us are in line with what is good and right.'*

To be born again into a living hope means that we are described as living stones that God is building into His spiritual temple. And what is more, we are called holy priests through our Mediator between God and men to offer spiritual sacrifices that please God. This is the true church, it's not a physical building, this is the church that Jesus promised to build, and the gates of hell will not prevail against it. The church is the people, the people of God. It's not about religion and religious denominations, it's about a spiritual temple made up of those who are born again to a living hope. We are part of God's plan, and we build for Him and our purpose is to serve Him, not ourselves. This is true freedom; this is eternal life.

Peter quotes from the Old Testament Scriptures and he does so from Isaiah 28.16. *'Therefore, this is what the Sovereign LORD says: "Look! I am placing a foundation stone in Jerusalem, a firm and tested stone. It is a precious cornerstone that is safe to build on. Whoever believes need never be shaken."'*

We place our hope in the Cornerstone, the Chief Cornerstone, Jesus Christ. He is our only hope for pardon from sin and for eternal life. Now the interesting thing about this quote is that Peter is not the only one who quoted it. Jesus refers to the ignorance of the religious leaders at that time. The Parable of the Landowner precedes these words. Basically, the vinedressers decided to reject the son and heir and throw him out and kill him. This was a direct reference to and an indictment of the religious leaders of the day who had already decided to kill Jesus and were plotting his death from early on in His public ministry. Jesus asked the chief priests and elders what they thought the son's father, and owner of the vineyard, would do. They said that he would destroy the wicked and lease the vineyard to other vinedressers who would produce fruit in their seasons.

Then Jesus asked them, 'Didn't you ever read this in the Scriptures?

The stone that the builders rejected has now become the cornerstone.

This is the Lord's doing and it is wonderful to see.

I tell you; the Kingdom of God will be taken away from you and given to a nation that will produce the proper fruit. Anyone who stumbles over that stone will be broken to pieces, and it will crush anyone it falls on' (Matthew 21.42-44).

They then sought to lay hold on Him and kill Him, but they were afraid of the multitudes who took Jesus for a prophet. The meaning of the quotation from Psalm 118.22 is that those who are broken in repentance as a result of falling upon Christ are forgiven and receive salvation. If a person refuses to repent, this will result in judgement. The stone will fall on them. Paul, in his teachings, refers to the same concept of the Cornerstone.

'So now you Gentiles are no longer strangers and foreigners. You are citizens along with all of God's holy people. You are members of God's family. Together, we are his house, built on

the foundation of the apostles and the prophets. And the cornerstone is Christ Jesus himself. We are carefully joined together in Him, becoming a holy temple for the Lord. Through him you Gentiles are also being made part of this dwelling where God lives by his Spirit' (Ephesians 2.19-22).

Peter goes on to tell us that those who have trusted Christ recognise the honour that God the Father has given to Him. Jesus was rejected at His first advent, and today He is still rejected by many, but to those who believe He is our Cornerstone, and He is the Stumbling Stone to those who reject Him.

Christ alone, cornerstone
Weak made strong in the Saviour's love
Through the storm
He is Lord, Lord of all
He is Lord, Lord of all

Peter says that those who stumble are those who have not obeyed God's Word, the elixir of life, and will meet the fate that was planned for them. This is not a world of chance. God has a plan; a redemptive plan, and we are either a part of it or we are not. To reject Christ, our only Hope is to then suffer the eternal consequences of such a decision and meet the end planned for those who reject the Cornerstone.

'But you are not like that' (2.9) Peter says to his believing readers.

Here is our true Hope in a hopeless, meaningless world. God is our God, and he has chosen us, we are a chosen people, we are royal priests of the King of Kings and Lord of Lords. We are a holy nation; we are God's every own possession. Here's another of those prismatic moments in the Scripture writings – as a result of all that God has done, is doing, and is going to do, we can show others the goodness of God, for He called us out of darkness into His wonderful light. We have found our true identity and it is found in God and He has given us abundant mercy. Now that's hope, the Temple of Hope. In a recent conversation with my oldest son, we were discussing the concept of identity. Our observations were that for many their identity is defined by their job, their possessions, power positions, and building personal empires; shaky ground indeed to build one's identity upon. No wonder people get lost and lose hope. We find our true identity in the Lord.

Like Alexander the Great, another died in His early thirties and He too wept but not over a lost kingdom or a lost empire, for He is the King of Kings and Lord of Lords and one day all the Kingdoms of the world will become the Kingdoms of our Lord Jesus Christ. Jesus wept over lost people.

> 'And when he drew near and saw the city, He wept over it, saying, "Would that you, even you, had known on this day the things that make for peace! But now they are hidden from your eyes. For the days will come upon you, when your enemies will set up a barricade around you and surround you and hem you in on every side and tear you down to the ground, you and your children within you. And they will not leave one stone upon another in you, because you did not know The time of your visitation"' (Luke 19.41-43).

Today is the Day of Grace and the Day of Hope. It is our time of visitation, and we dare not miss it. Go for it. You have been chosen by God for a high calling. You have been called from nothing to something – from rejected to accepted (2.10), from hopelessness to hope, from having no identity to finding your true identity. Give Hope a home in your heart and be part of God's great architectural cathedral – God's great Temple.

DAY SEVENTEEN

THE HOPE THAT BRINGS PERFECT FREEDOM

The prism of the Word: 1 Peter 2

Sir William Wilberforce and the abolition of slavery

In the latter part of the 18th century, William Wilberforce led a protracted campaign to end slavery. It was not an easy battle to fight as there was much opposition to his abolitionist movement from those who wanted the slave trade to continue, not least for the money they were making. Undeterred, Wilberforce continued his campaign and in 1789 he gave a three-hour speech against slavery in the London Parliament. Then, in 1791, Wilberforce presented the House of Commons with another Bill to abolish the slave trade. On this occasion he had the support of the Prime Minister, William Pitt the Younger, but the Bill failed in its passage as it was rejected by 163 votes to 88. Thereafter, every year between 1789 and 1806, Wilberforce presented a Bill for the abolition of the slave trade. He was not going to give up. In 1804, the House of Commons voted in favour of abolition, but Wilberforce's Bill was alas rejected by the House of Lords.

In the year 1806, Wilberforce's friend James Stephen proposed a Bill that would ban British ships from carrying slaves to the French colonies. This was a clever move as the pro-slavery MPs didn't give cognizance to the significance of the Bill and were happy to allow it to pass. The upshot of this decision was that it literally halted two-thirds of the slave trade and made it unprofitable. In the glorious year of 1807, after eighteen long years of campaigning, the battle was eventually won, and Parliament abolished the slave trade. Slaves were free! Freedom! Free at last.

Today you can visit the birthplace of William Wilberforce. The museum tells the story of the transatlantic slave trade and its abolition as well as dealing with contemporary slavery. Galleries also offer a fascinating glimpse into West African culture. You can take a virtual tour on the internet. Given that my oldest son teaches in Hull, it's been a place that we have visited on numerous occasions and there is always something new to see. Here are just two of Wilberforce's great quotes:

'To live our lives and miss that great purpose we were designed to accomplish is truly a sin. It is inconceivable that we could be bored in a world with so much wrong to tackle, so much ignorance to reach and so much misery we could alleviate.'

'It is the true duty of every man to promote the happiness of his fellow creatures to the utmost of his power.'

Like Peter, Wilberforce was a dealer in hope. The words of Peter fit well with the life of William Wilberforce when he tells us what God's will is for believers in Jesus Christ; to live honourable lives and silence the foolish accusations made against us. We are free but we are not to use our freedom as an excuse to do evil. Then Peter tells us something amazing about the hope that can be obtained in Christ; it is in being God's slave. Here's the quote: *'For it is God's will that by doing good you should silence the ignorant talk of foolish people. Live as free people, but do not use your freedom as a cover-up for evil; live as God's slaves'* (1 Peter

2.15,16).

To put our hope in God brings true freedom. Remember the constraints and persecution his first readers were under? And yet they had true freedom. Peter tells us that this freedom is found in being God's 'slave.' (2,16). That seems a bit odd though, free but a slave to God. What does he mean? It means to exercise our freedom by serving God. Jesus as the Redeemer sets us free from sin and its power and, by the mercy of God the Father, we are born again into a living hope where we find perfect freedom in God, in knowing God, in loving God, in living for God, and in serving and worshipping God.

The word for servant or slave is *doulos* and means 'to belong to'. It is literally 'bond-slave' but it is used with the utmost dignity in the Bible to describe those who bow the knee to the Lordship of Jesus Christ and live under His authority as His devoted followers. He is both Master and Friend. This is true freedom and it's the freedom that we enjoy because of Christ our Hope. The word *doulos*, in a metaphoric sense, means one who gives himself up wholly to another's will.

Do you want to live with true hope and in real freedom? Here is what Jesus Himself said about the futility of gaining the world in the context of following Him:

Then Jesus told his disciples, "If anyone would come after me, let him deny himself and take up his cross and follow me. For whoever would save his life will lose it, but whoever loses his life for my sake will find it. For what will it profit a man if he gains the whole world and forfeits his soul? Or what shall a man give in return for his soul?" (Matthew 16.24-26)

This life of freedom means living as temporary residents and foreigners (2.11) in this world. This world is not our home. We are to keep away from worldly desires – that is not the path to freedom – that is the road to enslavement. God turns human wisdom on its head. The world says the highest freedom lies in being true to oneself, indulging your ego and defying the expectations of others, and for some that is denying what God expects. Being true to God is true freedom. Live an exemplary life before God and in a world of unbelievers. Live to honour Him, the Creator and the Judge of all the world, and show respect to everyone in the freedom that God gives us.

'Be a good citizen – make the Master proud. Don't indulge your ego at the expense of your soul. Revere God and respect all' (2.13-17 MSG).

DAY EIGHTEEN

THE DAY THEY TRIED TO KILL HOPE

The prism of the word: John 8.31-36, and Galatians 5.1-13.

*Józef Paczynsk the barber of the Auschwitz-Birkenau
extermination camp*

Auschwitz-Birkenau was Nazi Germany's largest concentration and extermination camp, the largest mass murder site in history. As the most lethal of the Nazi extermination camps, Auschwitz has become the emblematic site of the 'final solution', a virtual synonym for the Holocaust. Between 1.5 and 2 million people died at Auschwitz; 90 percent of them were Jews. Rudolf Höss was the camp commander of Auschwitz who introduced the use of the pesticide Zyklon B to the killing process, thereby allowing Auschwitz to murder 2,000 people every hour. Watching millions of innocent human beings dissolve in the gas chambers, burn in the crematoriums, and their teeth melted into gold bars, Höss had the audacity to write poetry about the 'beauty' of Auschwitz.

He was tracked down by Hanns Alexander, a German Jew who had fled Berlin in the 1930s. Höss was arrested by the Allied military police in 1946 and handed over to the Polish authorities. Höss had also murdered thousands of Polish people. In 1947 Höss was tried and sentenced to death. He was returned to Auschwitz to be hanged on a one-person gallows built outside the entrance to the gas chamber. This is the confession of Rudolf Höss, commandant of Auschwitz and Auschwitz-Birkenau, (catalogue reference WO 309/217) Transcript.

Statement made voluntarily at Gaol by Rudolf HOESS (Höss) former commandant of Auschwitz Concentration Camp on 16th day of March 1946.

'I personally arranged, on orders received from Himmler in May 1941, the gassing of two million persons between June/July 1941 and the end of 1943 during which time I was commandant of Auschwitz.'

Signed Rudolf Hoess

Fr. Cdt. R. Auschwitz-Birkenau

Witnessed this 16th day of March 1946 at (-) Gaol, Germany

Countersigned: – J. [unknown]

A political Prisoner, Józef Paczynski, prisoner number 121, became the personal barber to camp commander Rudolf Höss. For much of the second world war, Paczynski was led to Höss's home and ordered to cut the hair of one of the worst mass murderers in history. For decades afterwards he was repeatedly asked why he did not use his tools to slit the throat of the man responsible for some two million deaths at Auschwitz-Birkenau. His answer:

'It would not have stopped the killing but would have meant certain death for himself and many others. I thought about it, but when I realised what the consequences would be, I simply could not do it.'

Paczynski outlived his torturer and died in Kraków. Höss died in 1947 at the age of forty-five. Józef Paczynski lived on, keeping his hopes alive for another sixty-eight years, and died at the ripe old age of ninety-five. He is buried in the Rakowicki Cemetery, Kraków, in Poland. A newspaper had this heading for his obituary; *'Hope dies last.'*

In 2017 a film was nominated for best live-action short at the Oscars and at BAFTA It was called *'Hope dies last.'* It's only several minutes long. A malnourished, Polish prisoner waits in a well-appointed room. A cart with a shaving brush, foam, and a razor-blade stands nearby, ready to be used. Then an official enters the room. Without a word, the man seats himself, and then the prisoner begins to groom him with meticulous care, despite his nerves, and the razor-blade closely shaves the hairs on the official's neck. One slip and the prisoner could kill him, but he also may be killed before he even gets the chance. Höss never ever spoke to Paczynski the entire four years he served the Auschwitz commander.

One film critic writes, *'What if Paczynski had killed Höss? And ultimately, would it have affected anything? Did the possibility of changing his fate – even if he never took it – enable him to hold on? Such enormous questions are unanswerable, but they haunt nevertheless – much like this remarkably lucid, powerful short film.'*

Why would anyone want to kill off hope, the hope of millions? It's really beyond human comprehension. Even with some understanding of the total depravity of humanity and the fallen human nature, it's still hard to comprehend. Then there is the arch enemy of humanity and hope, Satan the deceiver, who desires to kill the hope of every person on the planet. The reality is that Höss and his fellow murderers could not kill hope. That's impossible. Hope rises from the very grave of every innocent victim to cry freedom and victory. As I write today, Ukraine, a sovereign nation, fights for freedom in the face of genocide dished out by the bloodied hands of the evil dictator, Putin. Hope rises as the bombs fall, a nation that keeps hope alive, national freedom and hope on display in all its glory.

But what if the Eternal Source of Hope was to live on earth and offer eternal hope to the hopeless? What if the Source of Life itself was to come into the world and offer eternal hope to those who believe in Him? Then the arch enemy would want to kill Him off. That would make perfect sense, and using human instruments to do it, and being the religious leaders, scribes, and Pharisees of their day would also add a twist of devilish irony. That is exactly what Peter accused the Pharisees of doing. The prism of the word for today explains all this. Peter says:

You killed the Prince of Life. Jesus Christ who went about doing good was killed and died the most horrible death known to mankind – death by crucifixion. You nailed Him to a cross and killed Him. But they could not kill hope and they could not kill life because God released Him from the horrors of death and raised Him back to life for death could not keep Him in its grip (Acts 2.24).

Peter's words pierced their hearts. God's prearranged plan allowed them to do what they did because Jesus was the perfect sacrifice for our sins, and He purchased eternal redemption for us. The crowd asked Peter what they should do, and this is his reply.

Peter replied, "Each of you must repent of your sins and turn to God and be baptized in the name of Jesus Christ for the forgiveness of your sins. Then you will receive the gift of the Holy Spirit. This promise is to you, to your children, and to those far away – all who have been called by the Lord our God." Then Peter continued preaching for a long time, strongly urging all his listeners, "Save yourselves from this crooked generation!" Those who believed what Peter said were baptized and added to the church that day – about 3,000 in all (Acts 2.38-41).

Towards the end of the second chapter of his first letter, Peter tells us that Jesus was sinless. He was not a deceiver. He did not retaliate when they insulted Him. He did not threaten to take revenge. He left His case in the hands of God. Then Peter takes us into the depths of the significance of the crucifixion by telling us that Jesus personally carried our sins in His own body on the cross; that by His wounds we are healed. And now we can live in real hope because the Source of Hope died for us hopeless sinners and rose again to give us the gift of eternal life and eternal hope. And if we turn to Him in repentance and put our trust in Him, He forgives all our sins, and we can live with a confident hope that is guaranteed because our hope is in Him alone.

The Lord Jesus also gives us the power to overcome sin and to live for what is right. We who have wandered away in wrong paths as a result of our own selfish and proud wills can be forgiven. In obeying the Gospel, we can return to the Shepherd and Guardian of our souls. That's the reason we can have this hope because He becomes our Shepherd and Guardian. If you haven't done so already, make Him yours today – return to Him – He is our only Hope. The Hope that will never die. Hope never dies if it's found in Jesus Christ. You can't kill off this hope! Not even all the hordes of godless demonic murderers or hell itself can kill this hope. Jesus lives. Put your hope in Jesus Christ.

DAY NINETEEN

HOPE, HARMONY, AND HOME

The prism of the Word: Acts 2.22-47, 3.12-26, 1 Peter
2.22-25

Relational, inspirational, and transformational living

This hope which is available to every individual on earth
because of what Jesus has accomplished has very practical and
interpersonal implications. Thus, in the third chapter of First
Peter, we find references to how people of hope relate to one
another. This is not a hope insurance policy that is activated
upon death. This is a living hope that we have right now. It is an
inspirational and transformative hope. The reality is that we
have no guarantees in life, we live with hopes of being here and
living long but we have no certainty we will be here tomorrow,
or even breathe in the next five minutes. We live in the world
hopefully but can be in the possession of a sure-fire lasting hope
by faith in Christ that will remain as long as God lasts; and that is
an eternal hope.

If we have our hope in God, then this is transformative in this
respect. We have our faith in God and believe He is in control,
and we trust Him. Whatever happens, we have this eternal
hope that enables us to live with complete confidence every
day. We have a peace that passes all understanding because
God gives us His grace and His peace. We have His living eternal
Word to give us reassurance and to guide and direct us through

life's journey. And we have eternal salvation in His Son Jesus Christ and His Eternal Spirit lives in us. The writer in Hebrews says: *'Now faith is confidence in what we hope for and assurance about what we do not see'* (Hebrews 11.1).

So, faith means we have this hope, it is a confident hope, and we have assurance about what we do not see. We can live each day in this confident hope. It makes a difference to everyday living because we have God in our lives, and He wants us to be like Him. This hope gives us a meaning and a purpose every day and will bring harmony into our lives and our way of being. It is a relational, inspirational, and transformational hope. If it does not manifest itself in this way, then we have not understood this sure and steadfast hope. Being in a relationship with the God of hope brings us into the realms of redemptive freedom and we are enabled by His power to live for Him, according to His plan for our lives as individuals, and fulfil the purpose we were designed for, living in the will of God and as part of His overarching, unshakeable, and eternal plan.

So, our homes and our interactions and our relationships are to be of a specific nature. Brothers and sisters in the family of God, family life, wives and husbands can live in harmony and are to live harmonious lives. Hope leads to harmony, harmonious homes, harmonious living, because we are in harmony with God our Saviour and Lord. We can't really talk about having such hope if you are not treating others right. This kind of hope manifests itself in a life well lived to the glory of God and showing love to others.

The arch enemy thought he had struck gold in the garden of Eden. Mankind would now bow to his will and worship him. For some that is the way they decide to go and they became satanists. For everyone else, we have turned to our own way and followed our own will. This means there are billions of 'wills' in the world. Selfish wills, self-worship and arrogant wills – and so, in a hopeless world that has rejected the God of hope and replaced Him with the god of self and a zillion other gods, total disharmony reigns across the globe and this is the road to hell. Just look at the chaotic world of abuse, violence, war, death, and destruction. It's a horrible picture and it arises out of the selfish, sinful will of men and women who want their own way and will stop at nothing to get it. But for those who repent and turn to God, harmony is restored. Harmony with the living God is restored and we can seek to live in harmony with those around us. But we still have a fallen nature, and we need to work at it in terms of leading that harmonious life we were created for.

In the book of the prophet Isaiah, we read these words;

But He was wounded for our transgressions,
He was bruised for our iniquities;
The chastisement for our peace was upon Him,
And by His stripes we are healed.
All we like sheep have gone astray;
We have turned, every one, to his own way;
And the Lord has laid on Him the iniquity of us all
(Isaiah 53.5,6).

Peter gives us a particular perspective of the sheep going astray in his letter. Here is what he says: *Who Himself bore our sins in His own body on the tree, that we, having died to sins, might live for righteousness – by whose stripes you were healed. For you were like sheep going astray, but have now returned to the Shepherd and Overseer of your souls* (1 Peter 2.24,25).

We were like sheep going astray but now we have returned

to the Shepherd who died to take away our sins and who lives to give us this living hope and wisely provides for all that we need. He is also our *'Episkopos'* – our Guardian and Protector, the one who watches over us, the Bishop of our souls.

Then, in 1 Peter chapter 3, Peter gives us all the good stuff that can happen in our lives when the God of Hope and Harmony comes in. We are called to please God by leading godly lives so that even if we open our mouths, we exhibit godliness. This is about living pure and reverent lives before our Shepherd and Overseer. It is not about what we wear or our outward appearance, it's about being clothed in the beauty that comes from within. Having a gentle and quiet spirit that Peter says is so precious to God is required. Peter speaks particularly to wives in the opening verses of chapter three, but men are to do the same by honouring their wives and having the same spirit. And then he says we are all to be of the same mind, whoever we are or whatever we are (3.8). Peter gives an equality to women in a world where women were despised, he describes them as *'equal partners in this new hope-filled life'* (1 Peter 3.7).

True beauty is holiness and trusting God and accepting His authority in all aspects of life. We are to live lives of honour, treating each other with dignity and understanding. We are all equals with different roles. If we live right, our prayers to God will not be hindered. If we live in disharmony with others, how then can we say we are living in harmony with the Lord? God wants unity, not disunity. He wants harmony in our world, not disharmony. He wants harmony in our homes because His home is the place of perfect heavenly harmony, basking in the light of the unity and harmony of the Godhead, Father, Son, and Holy Spirit. The world would be a different place if we turned to God; it would be the antithesis of what we see today. Just look around you and the counterfeits, the fakes, the too-good-to-be-true secular formulas, false Messiahs who are inspired by the Devil himself. True harmony and wholeness are found in the living God of sure and steadfast hope.

We are to love. We are to be tender-hearted. We are to keep a humble attitude. We are not to repay evil for evil and we are not to retaliate when we are insulted. We are to do the very opposite and pay them back with a blessing. This is the calling of all those who have this living hope. This is what God calls us to do and to be – a blessing. *'That is what God has called you to do, and he will grant you his blessing'* (3.9b). Then Peter quotes from the Old Testament:

For the Scriptures say,
"If you want to enjoy life
and see many happy days,
keep your tongue from speaking evil
 and your lips from telling lies.
Turn away from evil and do good.
Search for peace, and work to maintain it.
The eyes of the Lord watch over those who do right,
and his ears are open to their prayers.
But the Lord turns his face
 against those who do evil." (Psalm 34.12-16)

Paul reminds us the principle here is the quality of life. God is concerned about our quality of life in all its dimensions.

'These things will last forever – faith, hope, and love – and the greatest of these is love' (1 Corinthians 13.13).

DAY TWENTY

RATING SCALES OF HOPE (PART 1)

The prism of the Word: Psalm 34, 1 Corinthians 13, and 1 Peter 3.

The Warrick and Edinburgh Mental Wellbeing Scale (WEMWBS)

It's somewhat easy to be hopeful when all is going well. However, even the absence of difficulty and troubles does not automatically mean the presence of hope. An American professor that I met some years ago, and who was instrumental in the introduction of a popular wellbeing scale, showed from research that most people are not flourishing in life but rather 'languishing' in the mundaneness and mediocrity of everyday existence. That was a decade ago and the world has become an even more sinister and fearful place with pandemics, wars, and economic crises.

Yet Peter tells us that it is possible to live a flourishing life in the great ordinary everyday as well as in troublesome times. Nothing is seen as mundane or mediocre, even in uncertain times, if God is in it and we live and do everything to His glory. And real hope can be born out of adversity and not conspicuous by its absence in the heat of the daily battles of life and living.

The fact is we all need hope. Hopes of peace and wellbeing. It may mean we hope for a better day, a better life, a better standard of living, or the hope we will get the next meal. Hope for suitable accommodation. Hope to overcome sickness and illness.

Hope to rebuild that broken relationship. Hope for a job or a better job, more money, hope for achievement and success and recognition and appreciation. In the midst of a war-torn world, it could simply be the hope to actually survive and build a better and safer world.

In the mental health field, the recovery ethos has taken off and is now well embedded in the mental health and wellbeing arena. Governments now produce wellbeing policies and scales and see mental health in terms of mental capital. In my part of the world, Northern Ireland, Health Trusts have Recovery Colleges, and one of the key components in the recovery journey is hope. It's all about giving people hope, because to be without hope is certainly not conducive to good mental wellbeing and can lead to a dark place where life is languishing and seen as being totally meaningless with nothing to offer. When there is no light at the end of the tunnel, some will even go so far as to end it all and take their own life, in what is now called 'completing' suicide. One of the main reasons for people in this impasse is believing there to be no hope for the future. An immediate solution is sought to end the psychological torment and meta pain they are experiencing. This is what is referred to as a constriction of thinking. If this kicks in, an immediate solution to life's problems is needed in the 'now' and in that critical moment they see death as their only way out. It's a dangerous moment. When someone who has been very depressed suddenly becomes calm and even seems happy, alarm bells should ring because they may have already made the final decision – the final solution. Yet seeking help can actually make the difference. This is where the role of the Samaritans has been so important in offering a listening ear so the person is heard. This can mean the difference between life and death.

The Irish Institute of Suicidology found in their research that one in six people said they had at some point in their lives had suicidal thoughts. In the mental health field this is termed 'suicidal ideation'. We all need hope, and we commend those who seek to bring hope to those who need it most, and we all need it. There is a sure and steadfast hope that not only encompasses our everyday ephemeral hopes, expectations, and dreams but enlarges them and imbues them with supernatural power and eternal dimensions. This is Divine hope – it is hope in Almighty God and derives from His nature and essence; it will last as long as God lasts.

This true hope, when embedded in our souls, hearts, and minds, has the potential to make a vast difference to our outlook on life. One uses the word 'potential' because whilst we have true hope as a present possession by virtue of Christ's cross work and the appropriation of that finished work by faith, we can live in a place of preoccupation with our worries and our fears. Hope can seem a distant memory; and yet the hope that God gives does not evaporate in the vicissitudes of life, or in the ebb and flow of our emotions; it is still there, even if we have lost an acute awareness of it. We may not feel it, but faith comes by hearing the Word of God. We need to feed our minds on the word of God and get good sustenance from the Divine Hope Manual. The mind matters. What we put into it is of vital importance.

The claims of the Bible's sure and steadfast hope supersede all other ephemeral hopes and remains intact and strong, even when life is falling apart, and even when that life is ebbing away, as invariably we all must eventually fly away. It's a sure-fire eternal hope. The writer of Hebrews speaks of God's infallible purpose and His promises which bring hope. God has bound Himself to an oath so that those who receive His promise could be perfectly sure that He would never change His mind. We read: *'God has given His promise and His oath. These two things are immutable because it is impossible for God to lie. Therefore, we who have fled to Him for refuge can have great confidence as we hold to the hope that lies before us. This hope we have as anchor of the soul, both sure and steadfast'* (Hebrews 6.18,19).

Our spiritual wellbeing is predicated on the awesomeness of Divine Sovereignty. In terms of human responsibility, our part is simply to flee to Him for refuge and trust in Him alone for salvation. Herein is hope, this sure and steadfast hope is secured. So, what does having this hope mean?

We are going to employ a wellbeing scale to help us answer this question. It is normally used so that people can check out their mental wellbeing online by completing what is called the Warrick and Edinburgh Mental Wellbeing Scale (WEMWBS). It has fourteen questions. The emphasis is on emotions but also includes mental functions. The wellbeing scale can indicate how hopeful we are and at the end it will score our responses. It's easy to do online for a mental wellbeing check-up. Peter did not use a rating scale, but he mentions hope specifically for the third time in his letter in 3.15b.

'But if someone asks about your hope as a believer, always be ready to explain it. But do this in a gentle and respectful way' (1 Peter 3.15b).

Let's take the WEMWBS and see what we come up with from the Bible, from a believer's perspective. The responses given are a way of trying to explain the hope that we have.

Statement 1. I've been feeling positive about the future
My feelings are changeable so I can't depend on them but, because my faith is in God and His Word, I can trust in His

promises. The Bible is not just an old leather-backed book from antiquity, it is the living Word of the Living God, something which, as we have already noted from the dealer in hope, is imperishable forever (1 Peter 1.23-25).

Here is another quote from Hebrews: *'Let us hold unswervingly to the hope we profess, for He who promised is faithful'* (Hebrews 10.23).

I know that my future is in God's hands, and He will be with me throughout my entire lifetime and then bring me at last to my heavenly home. Therefore, I am positive about the future. God has given me a sure and steadfast hope for the future.

Jesus said, *'The Spirit alone gives eternal life. Human effort accomplishes nothing. And the very words I have spoken to you are spirit and life'* (John 6.63).

Statement 2. I've been feeling useful

Because my life belongs to God, and seeking to live in obedience to Him, I believe that God has a plan for my life and that he has assigned me my tasks. Therefore, I do believe I am useful, and my life has meaning in Him. It is my hope that when I see Him, He will be pleased with my life and my service for Him.

The Bible tells me: *'Whatever you do, work at it with all your heart, as working for the Lord, not for human masters, since you know that you will receive an inheritance from the Lord as a reward. It is the Lord Christ you are serving'* (Colossians 3.23,24).

Statement 3. I've been feeling relaxed

I am prone to stress, anxiety, and worry and it's hard to relax sometimes. I can find myself not in a place of relaxation but in a state of 'stresslaxation', a new buzzword for trying to relax but can't because I am working on stuff in my head and can't switch off from what is making me stressed. It's very real in the world today. Isn't it ironic, being stressed out by relaxation? It's the idea that downtime makes anxiety worse. But when I pray and ask God for His help, He gives me hope each day and I can rest in Him and He gives a peace that passes all understanding. Putting my complete trust and hope in God is, for me, the way to relax and rest. This is what Paul said in one of his letters.

'Be anxious for nothing, but in everything by prayer and supplication, with thanksgiving, let your requests be made known to God; and the peace of God, which surpasses all understanding, will guard your hearts and minds through Christ Jesus' (Philippians 4.6,7).

So here is something to seek to live out each day; to be anxious about nothing, and that seems impossible sometimes, but to pray about everything and anything to transform the negativity into positivity. So, the believer is encouraged to be anxious for nothing and pray about everything, knowing that God can do anything (Jeremiah 32.26).

The words of Jesus come to mind: *'Peace I leave with you; my peace I give you. I do not give to you as the world gives. Do not let your hearts be troubled and do not be afraid'* (John 14.27).

Statement 4. I've been feeling interested in other people
The right answer is yes, I am very interested in other people because I am told to love my neighbour as myself and this I seek to do and share my hope in Christ with them. The love that God has for me incentivises me to show love to others, even my enemies. And yet at times I could see people far enough and I am happy in my little study with my books. Writing is a way of sharing. I do engage with people and involvement in the church

is a great way to build relationships. Good relationships at work are also very important and connexity with family is crucial. Being a good neighbour and looking out for others is also imperative. The quote comes to mind about people and one can identify with it sometimes; *'I have only one nerve left, and you are on it.'* I'm learning patience too from the Good Book. Again, the 'Life Book' gives direction on this: *'Don't look out only for your own interests, but take an interest in others, too'* (Philippians 2.4).

Statement 5. I've had energy to spare

Life can be stressful, and the demands of life can become too much and at times I feel wrecked, exhausted. We can work long hours without a break to pay the bills and be able to eat. However, avoiding burnout is very important. I have learned to put my hope in God's Word and His promises. He gives power to the faint, and they that wait upon the Lord shall renew their strength. Because God is my hope, I can rely on him to strengthen me for the journey. This powerful and encouraging Scripture comes to mind.

> *But those who hope in the Lord*
> *will renew their strength.*
> *They will soar on wings like eagles;*
> *they will run and not grow weary,*
> *they will walk and not be faint* (Isaiah 40.31).

Statement 6. I've been dealing with problems well

There was a time when I would have tried to muddle through on my own because I thought I knew better than God. I wanted to do things my own way, but I now know better. The Bible has shown me that I am not meant to even attempt to step out on my own, but God is with me to help me by the Holy Spirit, to seek to deal with my problems. I can bring everything to God in prayer, knowing He has promised to direct me. I can ask for His wisdom and His mind on how to deal with each and every situation. His Word inspires hope that I can work through my problems with His help, support, and His presence. The Scriptures come to encourage and comfort. Peter, the dealer in hope, refers to this: *'Give all your worries and cares to God, for he cares about you'* (1 Peter 5.7).

Statement 7. I've been thinking clearly

I have learned that there is a battle for the mind, my mind. What I feed it on will determine my thoughts and preoccupations. The Word of God is my constant companion and I read it every day. This gives me a focus. It us what one secular writer has called the 'deep work'. God's word helps me to concentrate and to think clearly. Deep work requires a distraction-free environment. I can apply this to my work each day when I am pulled in all directions. In terms of my spiritual life, I find that spending time with God each morning is a key priority daily. I call it coffee with God. This clears my head and sets me up for the day. There are so many voices clamouring to be heard; when I hear God's voice in His Word, He gives me clarity of thought and I can be hopeful that I can have the mind of Christ on all aspects of my life and in important decisions. This gives me hope as my mind is renewed daily in His presence.

We are now halfway through our rating scale and will continue the next seven statements in the following short essay.

DAY TWENTY-ONE

RATING SCALES OF HOPE (PART 2)

The prism of the Word: Proverbs 3.1-35, Isaiah 40.12-31, and Philippians 4.6-7.

Self-acceptance, love, confidence, and joyfulness

Statement 8. I've been feeling good about myself

I am more inclined to give a negative statement about myself rather than a positive one. There are times I feel good about myself and there are times when I don't. Before I put my trust in the Lord, I seldom ever felt good about myself, but He has taught me how to see myself as He sees me, and that has given me a totally different perspective.

Being aware that God loves me and that He has forgiven me all my sins and has accepted me, and that I am of immense value to Him, means I can feel better about myself, and some days even feel good about myself. His word tells me I am precious and unique, and Jesus taught me to love my neighbour as myself; so I have learned there is a self-love that is healthy. Jesus teaches me to accept me, and He is the Lord of my life so I can learn from Him. Peter does say (3.15) I am to worship Christ as Lord of my Life and live in obedience to Him. This means that because He has accepted me, I am able to accept myself. He actually calls us His workmanship or masterpiece (Ephesians 2.10) so He's working in me and on me. And He can work through me too.

'For we are God's masterpiece (workmanship), He has created us anew in Christ Jesus, so we can do the good things he planned for us long ago' (Ephesians 2.10).

Statement 9: I've been feeling closer to other people

Peter reminds us of the teaching of Jesus (1 Peter 3.8), we are to love each other and be tender-hearted. The church community is a place where we can have fellowship with like-minded people. We are to bless people and not to retaliate or insult them because this is what God has called us to do. There is a bond between us in the church fellowship. We pray for one another. We support one another. The feeling of closeness can come and go. The time when I feel closest to my brothers and sisters is when we have our communion service, and we remember the Lord's death and eat the bread and drink the wine together. There is a sense of oneness and closeness as the Lord is in the midst, blessing His people.

'And let us not neglect our meeting together, as some people do, but encourage one another, especially now that the day of his return is drawing near' (Hebrews 10.25).

Statement 10. I've been feeling confident

Some people are more confident than others. It is important for us to cultivate confidence but also be careful with it so as not to be over self-confident. Being a believer gives me confidence. In Christ we find our true confidence. *'For I can do everything through Christ, who gives me strength'* (Philippians 4.13). Jesus told His disciples, *'Without Me you can do nothing'* (John 15.5).

There is a healthy self-confidence in the faith walk. We plan effectively for a task, or a project, and we feel confident that we will succeed. The student prepares well for the exam and is confident of doing well. The source of our confidence is a bit like the source of hope. The Bible says that God should be the source of our confidence and not ourselves. We need to have a dependency on God to find real confidence. The preacher in the Proverbs tells us, in the context of our trusting in God, that *'The Lord will be your confidence and will keep your foot from being caught'* (Proverbs 3.26).

King David was a great warrior and fought many battles in his lifetime. Yet he tells us plainly: *'Though a mighty army encamp against me, my heart will not fear: though war rise against me, yet I will be confident'* (Psalm 27.3).

David gives the reason for his confidence that the Lord is his fortress (Psalm 27.2). He has learned to wait patiently on the Lord, who is his hope and his confidence.

Do I feel confident? Well, the answer is the Lord gives me the confidence that I need. Feelings come and go, and fear can creep in, but faith holds on to the promise that the Lord is my confidence, and my dependence is on Him. In the challenges of life, it can be easy to lose confidence. How many of us have felt like giving up? The Bible comes to encourage us again and again. For example, the writer to the Hebrews writes: *'So do not throw away this confident trust in the Lord. Remember the great reward it brings you! Patient endurance is what you need now, so that you will continue to do God's will. Then you will receive all that He has promised'* (Hebrews 10.35,36).

Statement 11: I've been able to make up my own mind about things

There are so many influences in the world today vying for my attention and trying to persuade me to do this or that. It can be difficult to make up my mind. Am I making the right decision?

Am I on the right path? Small and big decisions are part of life and, to make up my own mind, I need wisdom and understanding. This is where my relationship with God comes in. Since Jesus is the Lord of my life, I need to seek His mind on what I should do. I've had what I thought to be some great plans but when they have not been in His plan, I have sometimes made up my mind that I know better and that's led to failure and mistakes and roads that became cul-de-sacs. I have learned to seek the mind of God and the will of God and that's the best way to make up my mind. Having my mind set on the revealed will of God in Scripture and His path of wisdom leads to what can be termed *'spontaneous godliness.'*

The renewal of my mind is the essential means of transformation from the inside out. Our minds have a mindset, and this needs renewal on a regular basis (Ephesians 4.23). My mind needs a reset through the new birth to bring me into alignment with God and His Word. I am to love the Lord with all my mind (Matthew 22.37).

Paul describes the transformation of mind in this way: *Therefore, I urge you, brothers and sisters, in view of God's mercy, to offer your bodies as a living sacrifice, holy and pleasing to God – this is your true and proper worship. Do not conform to the pattern of this world but be transformed by the renewing of your mind. Then you will be able to test and approve what God's will is – his good, pleasing, and perfect will* (Romans 12.1,2).

Statement 12. I've been feeling loved

Again, our statement mentions feelings. Feelings come and go. Sometimes I feel loved and sometimes I don't. No matter how I am feeling, I know that the Bible teaches me that God loves me so very much; indeed, it is a love that is beyond our understanding, the God of the universe has time for each individual and loves each individual completely. We can read much about this love in the letter of First John.

'This is love: not that we loved God, but that he loved us and sent his Son as an atoning sacrifice for our sins' (1 John 4.10).

'We love because He first loved us' (1 John 4.19).

Jeremiah tells us: 'The LORD appeared to us in the past, saying: "I have loved you with an everlasting love; I have drawn you with unfailing kindness"' (Jeremiah 31.3).

'The Son of God loved me and gave Himself for me' (Galatians 2.20).

Divine love is beyond measure. Human love is needed too, and the church shows love to me by their care and support.

Statement 13: I've been interested in new things

I love learning about the world and the universe. The universe and its immensity fascinates me, as does the way it works and how the earth can sustain life because of its strategic location to the sun and the other planets in our solar system. It is God's creation grandly designed and working like clockwork. I love most of all learning new things in the Bible. It is inexhaustible and God shows me new things every day as I read it and meditate on it. The Bible also tells us about the future and the renewed cosmos where hope reigns.

'He will wipe every tear from their eyes. There will be no more death or mourning or crying or pain, for the old order of things has passed away' (Revelation 21.4).

My prayer is: 'Open my eyes that I may see wonderful things in your law' (Psalm 119.18).

Statement 14: I've been feeling cheerful

People say 'cheer up!' It's probably the last thing we should say to someone who is struggling. When life is tough it can be hard to remain positive. We have the blues, and we feel down. Yet, the Bible commands us to rejoice in the Lord (Philippians 4.4). He is not only our Source of Hope, but also our source of Joy. Joy has been described as a consciously chosen way of thinking. *'The Joy of the Lord is your strength'* (Nehemiah 8.10). Being cheerful in the Lord, yes. Feeling cheerful all the time? That's another matter. We are told in Scripture to rejoice always (Philippians 3.1, 4.4).

Peter tells us to rejoice: *'There is wonderful joy ahead'* (1.6).

'You rejoice with a glorious, inexpressible joy' (1.8).

'Rejoice in your trials for they make you partners with Christ in His sufferings' (4.13).

That's a way of attempting to describe the Christian hope using the WEMWBS rating scale. Don't forget to check out your mental wellbeing online too. But let us not forget to check out our spiritual wellbeing by reading the Word of God, listening to His voice, and experiencing the wonderful Hope He had given to us in His Son.

DAY TWENTY-TWO

THE SAFE HAVEN OF HOPE

The prism of the Word: Psalm 27, Matthew 22.37-39,
Philippians 4, and Revelation 21.

RMS Titanic, RMS Carpathia, and the rescue mission

The *Titanic* Visitor Centre is a must-see in Belfast, the capital city of
my home country. The souvenir shop has many keepsakes, and
you can purchase some great T-shirts. One T-shirt has a message
on it that is typical of Northern Ireland humour, and it reads, *'She
was all right when she left here'*; a reference, of course, to the
Titanic that was built in the Belfast shipyard, Harland and Wolffe.
Another T-shirt has the message, *'Built by Ulster men, sunk by an
English man'*, a reference to the Captain of the *Titanic*, Captain
Edward Smith, who was an Englishman.

The RMS *Titanic* was operated by the White Star Line and
could carry over 3,300 people; 2,435 passengers and 900 crew.
But there were only enough lifeboats for a third of the people
on board. In fact, there were 20 lifeboats which had capacity for
1,178 people. 1,523 people were lost on that fateful night, 815
passengers and 688 crew. It was her maiden voyage and,
because she carried mail, her name was given the prefix 'RMS' –
Royal Mail Steam Ship. She had two sister ships; one was called
the *Olympic* and the other was called *Britannic*. *Britannic* was
sunk by a mine in February 1916. *Olympic* had a long career and
retired in 1935. She was a troop ship during the first world war

and was called 'Old Reliable.'

Unlike Old Reliable, The RMS *Titanic* sank in two hours and forty minutes with a massive loss of life on the 15th April 1912. It is believed that the last survivor to leave the ship was Charles Joughin, the head baker. Joughin was asleep when the ship hit the iceberg. In the succeeding hours he managed to order his bakers to bring bread to the lifeboats, help women and children to safety, at times by force as they were scared to leave the *Titanic*. Charles survived by treading water for about two hours before encountering a lifeboat, and eventually being rescued by the RMS *Carpathia*.

RMS *Carpathia* was operating as a cruise ship at the time, under the command of Captain Arthur H. Rostron. When the distress call came through about the *Titanic*, the ship's crew quickly sprang into action. Their actions saved countless lives. The *Carpathia* passed six icebergs on its way to the *Titanic*. Captain Rostron is said to have bowed his head and whispered a quiet prayer during the high-speed, high-risk journey of sixty miles. Thinking back on the daring rescue, Rostron, who was a man of faith, reflected: *'I can only conclude another hand than mine was on the helm.'*

As RMS *Carpathia* approached the site of the sinking at 4 a.m. on April 15th, Rostron ordered green starburst rockets to be launched to alert the survivors. They then began the rescue operation that lasted some four hours. By 8:15 a.m., the Carpathia had rescued 712 survivors. Despite being dangerously over capacity, they set sail for New York, arriving on April 18th where they were greeted by thousands of people. 712 souls had been rescued and were now in the safe haven of hope. RMS *Carpathia* was the only ship to respond to the *Titanic*'s distress signal.

The *Carpathia*'s crew received medals from the survivors for their efforts. Crew members were given bronze medals and officers were handed silver, while Captain Rostron received a silver cup and gold medal. Rostron was later knighted by King George V and was invited to the White House by President Taft who presented him with a Congressional Gold Medal – the highest honour the United States Congress offers.

You could say that this was the rescue mission story that Hollywood missed!

And today there is another story that not only most of Hollywood has missed, but many in the world have missed too, or don't even give it a passing thought; the greatest rescue mission of all time. Paul tells his readers the ultimate story of the rescue mission to bring hope to a lost and perishing world.

'For He has rescued us from the kingdom of darkness and transferred us into the Kingdom of His dear Son, in whom we have redemption, the forgiveness of sins' (Colossians 1.13,14).

He rescued us

The word for 'rescued' is a Greek word (*rhuomai*) pronounced *rhoo-om-ahee*. It means 'to draw or pull to oneself'; to rescue – to snatch up – to be drawn up by a deliverer. It is the same word that is used in the Lord's prayer, *'... deliver us from evil.'* It means, 'Lord, Deliver me to Yourself and for Yourself.' That is, "Lord, deliver me out of my (personal) troubles and bring me to You and for Yourself.'

One Greek scholar says it has the concept of snatching out for oneself. Another scholar builds on the idea to draw out, noting that it implies removing someone in the midst of the presence of danger or oppression and delivering them right out of and into the arms of rescuer.

Imagine being in the cold icy waters of the North Atlantic Ocean. The temperature was approximately 2.2 degrees Celsius when the *Titanic* was sinking. Imagine a firm friendly hand reaching out to you to draw you up into the safety of the rescue vessel. As we contemplate the cross-work of our Lord, we become aware of the nail-pierced hand reaching down to us to rescue us and we can say with Paul, *'For He has rescued us from the kingdom of darkness and transferred us into the Kingdom of His dear Son, in whom we have redemption, the forgiveness of sins'* (Colossians 1.13,14).

He has transferred us into the Kingdom of His Dear son

The word for transferred, *methistémi* (pronounced *meth-is'-tay-mee*), means 'to be moved from one place to another'. We have been taken right out of the kingdom of darkness and brought into the Kingdom of His dear Son.

Into the Kingdom of His dear Son

Into the *basileia* (pronounced *bas-il-i'-ah*) denoting God's kingdom, God's sovereignty, God's royal power. Here we have the Kingship, the sovereignty, the authority, the rule, and the saving power of Jesus Christ our Lord, the one who came to rescue sinful humanity. To rescue us.

That's the Gospel story. We were the ones in need of rescue. We were the ones who were perishing in our sins, but the captain of our salvation came to rescue us from sin, to save us and to bring us salvation so that he could bring us safely home to God, the only haven of Hope for fallen humanity. For you and for me!

'In bringing many sons and daughters to glory, it was fitting that God, for whom and through whom everything exists, should make the captain of their salvation perfect through what he

suffered' (Hebrews 2.10).

Jesus was the perfect sacrifice for sins, and He has made a way for us to be right with God if we put our trust in Him.

Peter in his second letter speaks of another Big Boat.

And God did not spare the ancient world – except for Noah and the seven others in his family. Noah, a preacher of righteousness, warned the world of God's righteous judgement. So God protected Noah when he destroyed the world of ungodly people with a vast flood (2 Peter 2.5).

What is our hope in? Who is our Hope in? There is one true Hope, the God of Hope. There is only one way of Hope.

Peter's fellow apostle, Paul, says:

In those days you were without Christ. You were excluded from citizenship among the people of Israel, and you did not know the covenant promises God had made to them. You lived in this world without God and without hope (Ephesians 2.12).

There you have it. Without Christ, without God, and without Hope. But God, in His foreordained and eternal plan, planned the plan of redemption and we can be rescued, brought back, redeemed as Peter has alluded to in the opening chapter of First Peter.

For you know that God paid a ransom to save you from the empty life you inherited from your ancestors. And it was not paid with mere gold or silver, which lose their value. It was the precious blood of Christ, the sinless, spotless Lamb of God. God chose him as your ransom long before the world began, but now in these last days he has been revealed for your sake. Through Christ you have come to trust in God. And you have placed your faith and hope in God because he raised Christ from the dead and gave him great glory (1 Peter 1.18-21).

We do well to repeat the words again: *'For He has rescued us from the kingdom of darkness and transferred us into the Kingdom of his dear Son',* and the writer goes on to say, *'In whom we have redemption, through His blood, the forgiveness of sins'* (Colossians 1.13,14).

'Christ suffered for our sins once for all time. He never sinned, but he died for sinners to bring you safely home to God. He suffered physical death, but he was raised to life in the Spirit' (1 Peter 3.18)

The rescue is complete, sins can be forgiven, they can be gone. Saved from the penalty of sin, saved from the power of sin and one day from the presence of sin.

Hollywood may have missed it; the world may miss it. Don't you miss it!

DAY TWENTY-THREE

SLIPPING THE SURLY BONDS OF EARTH

The prism of the Word: 1 Peter 3.18-22.

John Gillespie Magee: 'High Flight'

On the 28th January 1986 the Challenger Space Shuttle broke up after 73 seconds in flight with the tragic loss of seven souls. Ronald Regan captured the moment with a speech of historical significance and ended with these memorable words: *'We will never forget them, nor the last time we saw them this morning as they prepared for their journey and waved goodbye, and slipped the surly bonds of earth to touch the face of God.'*

Powerful and fitting words from the President, filled with emotion and so poetic, even in the pathos. And there is the hope that they touched *'the face of God.'* The poetic language is a way of describing being in the eternal presence of God. Is there really such a hope?

Commentators have noted that what Ronald Regan said on that fateful day was without doubt an indirect quote from a poem by John Gillespie Magee, entitled *High Flight*. Magee was a World War II Royal Canadian Air Force fighter pilot and war poet. Tragically he was killed in an accidental mid-air collision over England in 1941. This is the poem that made him famous.

Oh! I have slipped the surly bonds of Earth
And danced the skies on laughter-silvered wings.
Sunward I've climbed, and joined the tumbling mirth

Of sun-split clouds, – and done a hundred things
You have not dreamed of – wheeled and soared and swung
High in the sunlit silence. Hov'ring there,
I've chased the shouting wind along, and flung
My eager craft through footless halls of air . . .
Up, up the long, delirious burning blue
I've topped the wind-swept heights with easy grace
Where never lark, or ever eagle flew –
And, while with silent, lifting mind I've trod
The high untrespassed sanctity of space,
Put out my hand, and touched the face of God.

You could, as some have, go into a comprehensive analysis of the poem but suffice to say for our purposes the poem is expressing the spiritual nature of the poet's lofty and expressive musings. He describes the sensations of being separated from the earth and flying in parts of the sky that even birds such as the high-flying eagle have not even entered into. The experience is all in all a spiritual one that brings him near to God. As he moves effortlessly through the *'high untrespassed sanctity of space'*, he relishes the wondrous freedom and total exhilaration of these moments. He concludes with the famous line, *'Put out my hand, and touched the face of God.'* This final line is the perfect summary of what the rest of the poem is trying to depict.

Flight, for the poet, is leaving everyday life behind and entering into a new realm, one that is closer to Heaven than earth. The experience is profoundly spiritual, bringing him nearer to the God of the universe. But is it possible to have such an experience here and now? Can we find a hope of such a spiritual dimension that we can live in the great every day with an unshakable hope in the face of the greatest adversity? Is there such a hope that it springs eternal? According to Peter, we live in God now and when we slip the surly bonds of earth, we shall touch the face of God; we will live in His immediate presence forever. This is the true Hope, and it is the certain hope of every believer. It is sure and it is certain.

As we gleaned yesterday from Peter, it is worth repeating again and again: *'Christ suffered for sins once for all time. He never sinned, but He died for sinners to bring you safely home to God. He suffered physical death but was raised to life in the Spirit'* (1 Peter 3.18).

Paul, Peter's fellow dealer in hope, reminds his readers that we look forward to the blessed hope, the glorious appearance of the Great God and our Saviour Jesus Christ. There was a first advent and there will be the sequel. It is sure and it is certain.

For the grace of God has been revealed, bringing salvation to all people. And we are instructed to turn from godless living and sinful pleasures. We should live in this evil world with wisdom, righteousness, and devotion to God, while we look forward to the blessed hope, the glorious appearing on that wonderful day when the glory of our great God and Saviour, Jesus Christ, will be revealed. He gave his life to free us from every kind of sin, to cleanse us, and to make us his very own people, totally committed to doing good deeds. You must teach these things and encourage the believers to do them. You have the authority to correct them when necessary, so don't let anyone disregard what you say (Titus 1.11-15).

In his letter to the Colossian church, Paul's theme is the supremacy of Jesus Christ. It is because of His deity His death reconciles those who believe in Him to the Creator. This takes the believer into a new dimension. Take the words of John Gillespie Magee:

I've topped the wind-swept heights with easy grace
Where never lark, or ever eagle flew –
And, while with silent, lifting mind I've trod
The high untrespassed sanctity of space,
Put out my hand, and touched the face of God.

The believer whose hope is in God is enabled to live in a spiritual world where intimacy with God is possible; God can be known, and we can be in a personal relationship with Him. Such an experience is spiritually discerned and is only possible by being born again into this living hope (1 Peter 1.3-9). This is not some new-age form of mystic Gnosticism for a select few; rather this is open to all those who put their faith and trust in Jesus Christ as Saviour and Lord. When we bow the knee to Him alone, then we can soar to heights of bliss that the natural person just cannot do. Paul puts this unique kind of 'high flight' in this way:

Living the new life
Since you have been raised to new life with Christ, set your sights on the realities of heaven, where Christ sits in the place of honour at God's right hand. Think about the things of heaven, not the things of earth. For you died to this life, and your real life is hidden with Christ in God. And when Christ, who is your life, is revealed to the whole world, you will share in all his glory (Colossians 3.1-4).

This is not some kind of obscurantist escapist mentality from the reality of living in the here and now and dealing with life and all its varied vicissitudes. To find out more about this, C.S. Lewis gives his take in tomorrow's exploration of hope with the interesting comment about 'eternal harp playing.'

The prequel or prerequisite to the awesome potentiality of

living in the spiritual dimension is found earlier in the first chapter of the letter to the Colossians.

Freedom from rules and new life in Christ

And now, just as you accepted Christ Jesus as your Lord, you must continue to follow him. Let your roots grow down into him, and let your lives be built on him. Then your faith will grow strong in the truth you were taught, and you will overflow with thankfulness.

Don't let anyone capture you with empty philosophies and high-sounding nonsense that come from human thinking and from the spiritual powers of this world, rather than from Christ. For in Christ lives all the fullness of God in a human body. So you also are complete through your union with Christ, who is the head over every ruler and authority (Colossians 2.6-10).

DAY TWENTY-FOUR

HOPE AND ETERNAL HARP-PLAYING

The prism of the Word: Titus 1.11-15, Colossians chapters
1 and 2.

C.S. Lewis: Mere Christianity

We will keep the mystery and the suspense going for a few
moments on the significance of eternal harp-playing; in the
meantime, it would be remiss of me not to include something on
hope from the great thinker and writer, C.S. Lewis. The
importance of hope is highlighted in his book, *Mere Christianity*,
where he says:

*Hope is one of the Theological virtues. This means that a
continual looking forward to the eternal world is not (as some
modern people think) a form of escapism or wishful thinking, but
one of the things a Christian is meant to do. It does not mean
that we are to leave the present world as it is. If you read
history, you will find that the Christians who did most for the
present world were just those who thought most of the next.*

He bases his thoughts on those famous words of Apostle
Paul to the church at Corinth. *'Three things will last forever –
faith, hope, and love – and the greatest of these is love'* (1
Corinthians 13.1-13).

His argument for the Christian's hope of heaven is based on
the evidence of centuries of godly Christian activity, from the
apostles who set on fire the conversion of the Roman Empire, to

those who built up the Middle Ages, right through to the evangelicals who abolished the slave trade. Those who were so active in changing the world for good, and for God, and making a vast difference to the place they left behind, were those who did so precisely because their minds were occupied with Heaven.

Lewis then argues that Christians have become ineffective in the world and the reason is we have ceased to think of the other world. *'Aim at Heaven and you will get earth "thrown in": aim at earth and you will get neither.'*

The rule he suggests is that to change this world we need to focus on the next. Take the example of health:

But something like it can be seen at work in other matters. Health is a great blessing, but the moment you make health one of your main, direct objects you start becoming a crank and imagining there is something wrong with you. You are only likely to get health provided you want other things more – food, games, work, fun, open air. In the same way, we shall never save civilization as long as civilization is our main object. We must learn to want something else even more.

Lewis then suggests that most of us find it very difficult to want Heaven at all, except insofar as Heaven means meeting again with our friends who have died. It reminds me of the statement *'everyone wants to go to Heaven, but nobody wants to die'.*

Lewis' answer to this problem is for us to be aware of the way we have been trained; he says: *Our whole education tends to fix our minds on this world. Another reason is that when the real want for Heaven is present in us, we do not recognize it. Most people, if they had really learned to look into their own hearts, would know that they do want, and want acutely, something that cannot be had in this world. There are all sorts of things in this world that offer to give it to you, but they never quite keep their promise.*

The advertising industry is a global industry employed to market products so we will want them and go out of our way to get them. Slogans are used to catch our eye and hook us in. The latest must-have gadgets are in big demand; people queue up for hours to get their hands on them. One of the oldest and most recognised brands in the world is Coca Cola. It's amazing to see the various slogans used to advertise the product from as far back as 1886. It is a remarkable story of over one hundred and twenty-five years in the evolution of marketing this iconic brand. For the author the most memorable slogans include:

Things go better with Coca Cola (1963)

It's the real thing (1969)

Have a Coke and a smile (1979)

Coke is it! (1982)

You can't beat the real thing (1990)

Taste the feeling (2016)

Real magic (2022)

That's probably enough free advertising for Coca Cola; but you get the point. You can't beat it! You have the real thing if you get it! It will make you smile, and you will feel the happiness it brings into your life. This is where life is at, so you need it and you dare not miss it. That's advertising and marketing for you, and it works. In 2021, the Coca-Cola company's net operating revenues worldwide amounted to around 38.66 billion U.S. dollars. That's the power of advertising. Who would have thought that from May 8, 1886, when Dr John Pemberton sold the first glass of Coca-Cola at Jacobs' Pharmacy in downtown Atlanta, we would be where we are today. He was serving nine drinks per day in its first year; Coca-Cola, the new refreshment destined for a global market. More than 1.9 billion servings of these drinks are sold in more than 200 countries each day. The truth is, Coca-Cola was a failure when it started. Dr John Pemberton, the founder of Coca-Cola, likely netted about $50 dollars in his first year. A colossal failure when you consider that he spent $70 on advertising. There is a lesson here in itself.

The reality is that C.S. Lewis is right when it comes down to what we really need and what gives true satisfaction; *'There are all sorts of things in this world that offer to give it to you, but they never quite keep their promise.'*

If we are to market true hope, I wonder what slogans we could come up with. *True hope in a troubled world,* could be a start.

Lewis challenges us about our being tethered to this world:

Sadly, many of us are so tethered to this world and the things it offers that we scarcely take thought of the world to come. Yet it is precisely by reflecting often on the joys, beauties, and satisfactions of eternal life in the world to come that we find a hope that empowers us to live fully for Christ today.

Paul put this thinking in this way to the church of Colossae, which we came across in yesterday's essay, and it is worth repeating again.

If then you have been raised with Christ, seek the things that are above, where Christ is seated at the right hand of God. Set your minds on things that are above, not on things that are on earth. For you have died, and your life is hidden with Christ in God. When Christ who is your life appears, then you also will appear with him in glory (Colossians 3:1-4).

Oh yes, I almost forgot – the eternal harp-playing. So, what on earth has hope got to do with harp-playing? I must admit that I had not thought of harp-playing in connection with hope until I read C.S. Lewis. In his chapter on Hope, Lewis makes fun of those who reject the Christian idea of Heaven because *'They don't want to spend eternity playing harps.'* The answer to such people, he says, *'is that if they cannot understand books written for grown-ups, they should not talk about them.'*

Let us aim for Heaven and get earth thrown in as well. The prism of the Word today perhaps needs some explanation. One of the ways of getting into Scripture is not only to read it, but to listen to it being read. Download the YouVersion Bible App and you can listen to different translations. Today I had a long car journey. So, I got First Peter on the Apple Play in the car and was able to listen to the first letter of Peter a number of times on my journey as I kept replaying it. Why not try it today, in the context of what C.S. Lewis is talking about – the focus on Heaven will change earth for the better. Go through the letter of Peter and listen out for the connection between the Christian's hope and our future in Heaven and the implications for living in the world.

Which world are we living for? To live for the next will greatly impact how we live here. Eternal harp-playing may indeed be the harpist's idea of Heaven, but it's not mine really. Why not check out in a study what the Bible does say about Heaven. You will be surprised, amazed, transformed, and incentivised to bring, by the power of the Holy Spirit, the influence of Heaven to bear on earth. Why not start with the Lord's prayer, rather the Disciple's prayer.

Our Father, which art in Heaven, hallowed be thy Name, Thy Kingdom come, Thy will be done in earth, as it is in Heaven … (Matthew 6.10-13).

DAY TWENTY-FIVE

HOPE IN A SUFFERING WORLD (PART 1)

The prism of the Word: 1 Peter chapters 1-5

The dealer in hope tackles the difficulty of suffering

When Mike Tyson was asked by a reporter whether he was worried about Evander Holyfield and his fight plan, he answered, *'Everyone has a plan until they get punched in the mouth.'*

Sun Rzu, in the Ark of War, said, *'Victorious warriors win first and then go to war, while defeated warriors go to war first then seek to win'.*

We too have our plans which can be upended in the hard knocks of life. Peter's first letter mentions the 'punches' in terms of suffering over fifteen times in five short chapters. In fact, this letter of hope from Peter, the Dealer in Hope, does not flinch away from the reality of suffering. The Thompson Chain Reference Bible takes the angle, remembering our concept of the prism, that the central theme of first Peter is victory over suffering as exemplified by Christ. Thus, Thompson combines the two things indicating hope in the form of victory in suffering, with Christ as our great example.

Suffering comes in different forms and in different ways. The suffering Peter refers to, however, is of a particular nature, namely suffering as a direct result of one's faith, suffering as a Christian. We will deal with suffering again in our short essays, but for our purpose today we are thinking specifically of what

Peter had to say on the subject of persecution and suffering because of one's faith. We will go through the letter highlighting what Peter said.

1.6. Peter talks about believers being grieved by various trials, and yet he says that we are to rejoice. He is adamant that believers are to be joyful in trials because of the wonderful joy that lies ahead. Overcoming trials, and he does say fiery trials, will prove and reinforce the genuineness of our faith which is far more precious than mere gold. When our faith remains strong, because we trust in God, this will bring great praise and honour and glory to Jesus Christ on the day that He is revealed to the world.

This sounds easier said than done. The point he is also making is that we are not alone in our trials and difficulties. The God of Heaven is not only transcendent, He is also immanent. He is with us in every situation, even though we cannot always expect skies of blue and to ride on the crest of the wave. He is with us. We can be sure that He is faithful, and He will see us through. Not all things are good, but God is always good, and He will make a way for us. One day every wrong will be made right for ever and we can rejoice in Him, even in adversity and those tough days in life's rollercoaster. To be a follower of Jesus is to be on the victorious side and we can live victoriously in Christ.

1.10. Peter refers to our Saviour the Lord Jesus Christ, whose sufferings were predicted in the Old Testament. He is seen as the suffering Messiah. But not only were His sufferings predicated, the glories that should follow are also predicted.

'He is a Man of sorrows and acquainted with grief' (Isaiah 53.6) and He is the honoured and victorious One who *'poured out His life unto death, who was counted among the rebels, and bore the sins of many and made intercession for the rebels – the*

transgressors – us! (Isaiah 53.12)

2.4,7. Peter goes further in his references to Christ in the context of suffering when he says that Jesus was rejected but He has become the Cornerstone. Our Lord was disowned and rejected by the Nation of Israel, but He was the Chosen One and precious. Those who suffer for Christ will also be rejected in some way or another, but we are precious to God, and we have been chosen by Him. Peter is encouraging us to see beyond the visible. Things are not what they seem because God is the God of history and our history is in His hands and we are on the victorious side because Jesus is our Champion, our Victor over sin and death.

2.12. Abuse comes in many forms, including verbal abuse. Even if we are persecuted in this way, we are not to retaliate but to sow good deeds and glorify God. 2.18. Again, Peter talks about being treated unjustly. We are encouraged to endure sorrow when suffering unjustly with all the ridicule and mockery that goes with being a follower of Jesus. They ridiculed the Master, and they will do the same to the disciple. We are to be mindful of God in the midst of these trials. He is mindful of us, He is in control, and His plans cannot be thwarted. God is pleased when we stand strong in our faith and patiently endure unjust treatment. It's a fight between good and evil, and it's an unseen war which can manifest itself in ridicule and persecution.

2.23, Peter tells us more about the example of Christ. He was reviled, insulted, but He did not retaliate. He did not threaten revenge when He suffered. Instead, He left His case in the hands of God the Father. He entrusted Himself to Him that judges justly. Then, in verse 24, Peter tells us that we who rejected Him are the very ones He died for to deal with our sins and to bring in a new era, the era of grace, when we can live for righteousness and die to sin.

1.3.8,9. Suffering in this world for Christ should not deter us from doing what is right. We must do the right thing! It may be counterintuitive to the way of the world, a world of the 'counterpunch' retaliation mentality. We are in the Kingdom of God and that means a counter-cultural way of living. Let's remember that,

A lie doesn't become truth,
Wrong doesn't become right,
And evil doesn't become good,
Just because it's accepted by the majority.

We are marching to the beat of a different drum and hope is our watchword. The Rev. Dr Martin Luther King Jr. said, *'We must accept finite disappointment, but never lose infinite hope.'* Tough times don't last.

Followers of Jesus who suffer for righteousness' sake will be rewarded by God.

1 Peter 3.13. We are not to worry and not to be afraid of threats. Peter was going to be killed for his faith not long after he wrote his two letters. He was not bothered in the least because he had entrusted himself completely to his Lord and he knew that Jesus was with him and that he had nothing to fear from anyone.

Our priority too is to worship Christ as Lord with our lives and be ready with dignity and respect, to give a reason to everyone for the hope that we have in the midst of suffering and persecution. We are to bless our enemies and not retaliate, and we will receive God's blessing. We are not to repay evil for evil or abuse for abuse. The hallmark of the followers of Jesus is love for everyone, including our enemies. This can only be accomplished by God's grace.

3.18. *'Christ suffered once for sins, and He did so to bring us to God.'* He was put to death for us, but he rose from the dead and He lives and rules and reigns. He said not to fear those who can kill the body. We are secure in Christ for time and for eternity and Jesus has already won the victory for us.

1.41. Christ suffered physically. He suffered pain. Peter tells his readers to have the same mind and be ready to suffer for Christ even if it means physical pain. Persecution of believers has ensued over the centuries and today the most persecuted group in the world are those who follow Jesus as Lord and Saviour.

As I write and you read, there are Christians in the world right now being put to death for their faith. North Korea, Afghanistan, and Somalia are among the most dangerous places in the world if you are a believer.

In 2020 a staggering 260 million Christians in the top 50 countries on the World Watch List face high or extreme levels of persecution for their faith. In the previous year, it was 245 million.

In 2019, 2,983 Christians were killed for their faith. That figure is shocking and upsetting, but it is fewer than the number of believers reported killed in 2018 (4,305) or 2017 (3,066). This is largely due to fewer murders in Nigeria which remains far and away the country where Christians are most likely to be killed for their faith.

Peter says suffering for Christ shows that we have died to sin. Suffering for Christ intensifies our desire to glorify Him and incentivises us to do the will of God.

4.4. We may be maligned and marginalised because we don't run with the world anymore. It's one of the reasons Christians are persecuted. We can be misunderstood and misrepresented but

Christ will hold us fast and those who slander us will have to face God one day. God is the Judge who stands ready to judge the living and the dead.

'Will not the Judge of all the earth do right?' (Genesis 18.25)

Peter notes: *'For the time has come for judgement, and it must begin with God's household. And if judgement begins with us, what terrible fate awaits those who have never obeyed God's Good News?'* (1 Peter 4.17)

4.12-19. Peter says it's normal to suffer for Christ in this world. Those who follow Christ should not be surprised at the fiery trials they face. Such trials make us partners with Christ. We have the privilege of sharing in His sufferings. And we will have that wonderful joy of seeing His glory when He is revealed to the world. We are not to be ashamed but glorify God in the Name of Jesus Christ.

'Let those who suffer according to God's will entrust themselves to our faithful Creator while doing good. Trials are to make us better, not bitter.' Peter was a witness of the sufferings of Christ (5.1).

He says that we too will share in His glory. We are to live in the will of God and God allows the mystery of suffering to purify His Bride, the Church.

5.8. The enemy wants to devour us, and he will use others to try and do just that. The whole family of believers are going through the same thing all over the world.

5.10. Peter gives hope to his fellow suffering believers, suffering because they name the Name of Jesus Christ as Saviour and Lord. Trials and tribulations will not last forever. Listen to his words in verse 10.

'In his kindness, God called you to share in his eternal glory by means of Christ Jesus. So after you have suffered a little

while, he will restore, support, and strengthen you, and he will place you on a firm foundation."

Don't give up. Be strong in the faith. God has your back and we are on the victory side. Shine your light. The darkness won't like it. Some will hate it and hate you and persecute you, but our Lord and Master said *'I have told you these things, so that in me you may have peace. In this world you will have trouble. But take heart! I have overcome the world'* (John 6.33).

'All power to Him forever – To Him be the dominion for ever and ever. Amen' (1 Peter 5.11).

'May the God of hope fill you with all joy and peace as you trust in him, so that you may overflow with hope by the power of the Holy Spirit' (Romans 15.13).

DAY TWENTY-SIX

HOPE IN A SUFFERING WORLD (PART 2)

The prism of the Word: 1 Peter 2.21-25

Immortal hope in mortal frames, eternal hope in transient lives

We have already noted that Peter does not flinch away from the reality of suffering, yet he believes in hope, even in a suffering world. So how does he reconcile these two concepts? The age-old question that is often posed and has been a major problem in a world of suffering in every generation is *How can a good God allow or even permit suffering in the world?*

Why doesn't He do something about it? And then this leads to many different postulations such as; that's if He exists at all, or, if He does He has left the world scene and retreated. He has left the world to its own devices and either ignores it or watches indifferently from a safe distance; or He watches with compassion but there is not much He can do about it.

And what about the murderous and wicked deeds that occur daily in a troubled world? What about all the wars and the brutality and the slaughter of the innocents? Then there is sickness, disease, and death to contend with. Where is God? That probably sums up most of the issues raised by people. So, it seems God has a lot to answer for, or does He? The attitude of many is 'get Him into the dock, try Him, make Him suffer, and kill Him off.' God has already been killed off in the minds and hearts of many in the world today.

And now for a simple answer to all this. The reality is there is not a simple answer. And pious quotes will not cut it. But perhaps we can find some of the answers, but not all of them, to these age-old questions. We will seek to explore some of the answers as we continue on our quest in this essay on suffering. Then, in subsequent essays, we will continue to unravel some of these complex issues with the information we have been given, some of which may not be common knowledge.

At this point we can say from the biblical perspective that we can learn about governance and the way the world worked at the beginning, and the way it became. The biblical account of the beginning informs us of a perfect universe with one will, God's will. Then there were two; Satan sinned through pride. Mankind began in a perfect world and a perfect environment. God gave the governance responsibilities of the world to mankind. That is an important point to grasp.

God set the rules, or we could use the term TOR – 'terms of reference' – as an analogy to help us understand. The TOR of humanity was set right at the beginning. As a manager in the mental health arena for many years, one has been involved in setting up many working groups. At the outset the TOR is set in place and is made clear to all involved. The name of the group is established, and the TOR sets out such components as reporting, authority, purpose, roles, responsibilities, and expectations.

Humanity with our federal heads, Adam and Eve, as our representatives were given the TOR, with the various components. The governance, management, and administrative responsibilities of the world were given to them and to us. In Genesis chapters one and two we can read about these. For example: *'Then God blessed them and said, "Be fruitful and multiply. Fill the earth and govern it. Reign over the fish in the* sea, the birds in the sky, and all the animals that scurry along the ground"' (Genesis 1.28.).

This means that control and dominion of self and the world was given to mankind to fulfil the perfect will of God and serve the good purposes and wellbeing of everyone and all of creation. It was a world of complete harmony and absolute perfection; it could not have been any better. But!

Then our first parents sinned, and decay and death were some of the catastrophic results of such a decision. Spiritual death, i.e., separation from God, was the greatest catastrophe of all. It is not without significance that the first person born into a fallen world became a murderer. From the One perfect Will of God there grew millions and then billions of wills. A haywire world has ensued ever since. Many of the problems in our world are of our own making. It's what mankind chose. It's what we chose. We need to take personal responsibility. And each individual, including world leaders, despots, and dictators, will give an account to God. We will come back to these deep and challenging issues in due course.

As for sickness and disease, whilst a lot of it has been attributable to us and the world we have created, there are still unanswered mysteries as to the suffering of the innocents and sickness in little children who suffer terminal illnesses, and we are at a loss to comprehend it. People sometimes say, *'If I were God, I would take it all away in a flash.'*

We cannot shy away from these seemingly insurmountable problems. My cousin has just been diagnosed with pancreatic cancer and given six weeks to live. Tell me about God in this context, people say. You can't tell me this is the direct or directive will of God, but God has permitted it, and this could be described as the permissive will of God. Dying and death became part of the human condition. But does God really understand it? What does it actually mean to suffer and to die? And what about the children that were killed, those innocent children when the wicked king, Herod the Great, King of Judea, ordered their killing, after the magi were warned not to go back and tell him where Jesus was born. We have always lived in a cruel and unjust world.

We know that Jesus died at the age of thirty-three. We know He suffered, and we know He died a horrible, horrendous, ignominious death. It was the religious leaders of the day who orchestrated his death. And yet we all had our part in the killing of God incarnate on the tree at Calvary and He bore our griefs and carried our sorrows. The sovereign God is the suffering God and is with us in our human vulnerability and mortal condition. He came to give us immortal hope in our mortal frames, eternal hope in our transient lives. He came to save us and give us eternal life; that life which was lost in the first garden of the world.

Pastors know more than most the reality of suffering and, in the course of their pastoral ministries, meet many suffering people. Having served in pastoral ministry for over fifteen years, one can testify to having personally witnessed all kinds of suffering. One recalls sitting in the hospital with those who were breathing their last, leaving distraught families behind, or waiting with a family as their loved one is undergoing lifesaving surgery and the chances of recovery are slim. I remember when a dear lady lay dying and then came what they called in the countryside 'the death rattle.' We had prayed and she had been anointed with oil and much prayer had gone up and still she died. People seriously injured in farm accidents, killed in fatal road traffic accidents, and then one had to conduct their funerals. I remember going to a pastor at a new church and for the first six months I was conducting one if not two funerals a week: deaths – some expected and some totally unexpected. What do you say to a grieving mother who has lost her only son in an RTA? What do you say to lovely godly people who have just been diagnosed with a terminal illness and are given months to live? What do you say to a young man and a young woman who tell you they have been sexually abused as children and are outraged at the audacity of God for allowing it? How could He? What do you say? There are no words, just being with them in their pain and feeling the burden of human pain and suffering and sobbing in soul silence and knowing and not knowing. And don't ever say, *'I know exactly how you feel'*.

Because you don't, even if you have been through a similar experience, everyone is totally unique. It's like depression – it has a thousand faces, and everyone's condition is unique. We can talk about a cluster of commonalities and that can be useful for the clinicians but not for the victim in the midst of their suffering.

Then there is the woman who tells us during pastoral care of a stillborn baby forty years ago and tells of the unresolved grief and guilt she has carried all those years. Then there is the young man who is blown up by an IRA bomb and he is in hospital fighting for his life and needing major surgery to remove a piece of shrapnel from his brain. It's a world of suffering and more. And where is God? He's a young man with a young family and the kids are asking, will Daddy be ok? And you don't know the answer and you don't know what to say. And when someone asks the honest question, where is God? Where is your loving God? Platitudes are not going to cut it! The raw pain and hurt and the cry of the soul for the answers cannot be masked with pious platitudes and quoting verses.

And I don't know the answers to it all and I can't know. This is because I am not God. This is not a cop-out at this juncture because as we proceed in the following days, we are going to seek to give some reasons for the hope that we have in the face of disease, sickness, evil, and death. But it's not my place to defend God. I am sure He is more than capable to answer the questions of the sincere seeker with a genuine desire to know. Ask Him!

Consider the book of Job as a good place to start. He is not obligated to answer anyone, and yet He answered Job. Job discovered that we are accountable to Him. He is not accountable to us. As for those who use these postulations to have a go at God and condemn Him; a silent Heaven may be all they will encounter, unless they seek God and ask Him personally to show them. And we will never fully know until time is no more and eternity has begun for every last human being on earth. One of the greatest dilemmas for many is what seems to be a silent heaven. However, given that the Bible is God's manual for living, we need to ask what the Bible says about suffering since this is how God speaks to each generation in the day of grace.

For many of those whom I got to know and who had endured the most grievous of trials and the most intense suffering, there was a hope that I had never seen before. There was joy in pain, there was a deep calm and a sense of God's presence that I had never witnessed before. People who loved and trusted God, even more in the midst of the most intense, prolonged, and outrageous suffering. God was their hope in the storm, He was their light in the darkness and He was their comfort in their grief. This was not some stoical response; this was knowing God and His sustaining presence and grace in the midst of it all.

One cannot record the inarticulate speech of these profound experiences. Unbelievable, astounding, incomprehensible as the mysteries of the living God were unfolding before my very eyes in the lives of people who had total faith and complete confidence in God and an intimacy with Him that He was there in the suffering and suffering with them. God was near. It was palpable. This cannot be explained. It can't be in time; it will be in eternity.

How could this be? How could they believe in God? How could they trust Him? How could they love Him? How could they have such hope when there was no hope in the natural sense. The answer: they had an eternal hope. And this was not some kind of spiritual defence mechanism. This was not some kind of crutch that they were using to limp through the crisis. No! It's as if God was right there in them, with them, beside them, suffering with them, and He was their stay and strength. He was and He is. He is God with us, Emmanuel. How so? This hope is real! We will continue tomorrow in the subject of hope in suffering and seek some answers from Scripture. In the meantime... don't forget the prism of the word for today.

DAY TWENTY-SEVEN

HOPE IN A SUFFERING WORLD (PART 3)

The prism of the Word: 2 Corinthians 1.3,4

And of course there is the book of Job to get into as well. Watch out
for Job's friends and God's response. The first time you read it, you
may well say 'I need to read that again and again and again to get it.'
Well, see how you get on.

John Milton: Paradise Lost – Paradise Regained

'I would make it alright, right now, if I were in charge!'
What if we could, in one moment of time, make everything
right? Indeed, who would not want to do so? That can be the
cry of the human heart that is breaking. It can also be the shout
of defiance from the angry person who waves their fist at God.
But what if we could change everything so that in an instant the
world would be a perfect world? No more suffering, no more
sickness, no more sorrow, and no more death. No more evil, no
more abuse, no more hurt, and no more uncertainty. The world
becomes perfect. No more ageing, no more degeneration, and
no more corruption. From the dystopian to the utopian. And
you answer, 'What planet are you living on because there is no
planet utopia?' But surely it is our heart's desire, that if not
now, one day all will be made right! That's obviously impossible,
humanly speaking. Think about it, every wrong and every
injustice made right, and every sickness banished from

humanity. *'Dream on'*, you say.

What we need to realise is that there was a time in the history of the world when none of the aforementioned things existed. There was a perfect world. Humanity lived in a perfect world. Everything was right! No sin, no sickness, and no death.

The enemy of humanity, true to form, has introduced many conspiracy stories to tickle our ears so that most people jeer or dismiss or reject, or just laugh at the biblical account of the reality of what happened. God made the world, and it was perfect. He made Mankind – Adam and Eve – and He placed them in a perfect world in a perfect environment and everything, including them, was absolute perfection. We don't know how long it was perfect for, but it was. Adam and Eve were destined to live forever – they had immortality. They didn't need to seek out the elixir of life, they already had it. They had the real thing; it was the real deal. They had it made. This means there was no sorrow of any description. And they did not age; no deterioration, no need for Botox to make the wrinkles fade, and no such thing as sorrow and death. It was foreign to them. In Adam, the federal head of all humanity, and his wife Eve, we had perfection.

God did make it clear to our first parents that there was one thing they were not to do. You know the Biblical account of the forbidden fruit. Mankind had loads of choices, but this was a choice they were not to entertain because in the day they would disobey God they would surely die. It was crystal clear, enjoy a perfect world, live forever, and enjoy the perfect company of one another and enjoy the wondrous company of the Creator, God Himself. Live in the land of paradise where there is perfect harmony, peace, and rest, in the will of God.

The day came, however, when a highly intelligent and captivating non-human creature entered the garden in disguise.

He was malevolence personified and had other diabolical and deadly plans for mankind. But it was all dressed up in what seemed to be an advancement in wisdom and superior knowledge, the possibility of knowing good and evil. And into the bargain, it would seem, that God was not the real deal – He was withholding something that they should not be without and now here was the golden opportunity to take it for themselves and actually have it all and more. Sound familiar? It's the lie that's still peddled today – God is a killjoy! – when in fact it's the very antithesis of such.

We now know only too well what the enemy's plans were: death, pain, suffering, and sorrow, and all the rest that goes with it. Eve was deceived, Adam was not. Adam deliberately, consciously, and in the cold light of day took the fruit and he ate it and in a moment, in an instant, it all changed and sin had entered the world. Spiritual death hit them in an instant. The relationship with the Eternal God was broken. The greatest tragedy in the universe occurred because from God flowed all good, and still does, but now sin and evil had entered.

Now would flow all kinds of evil and death. However, because mankind was made in the image of God, there would always be good in the world. Just think of how many good people you know and how many evil people you know. We still have good in the world. People can do some amazingly good things to help their fellow human beings. This is because we are made in the image of God, but living alongside the good is evil. Now man and woman had the propensity for unimaginable evil.

History shouts it out loud of man's inhumanity to man – the dystopian, the architect of which is Satan himself, where people are dehumanised and left wretched, fearful, and terrorised; the result of the fall of mankind. Mankind's governance of the world, given by God before the fall, is now one of both blessed goodness and despicable evil. Mankind now governs the world with the knowledge of good and evil.

Mankind, from that very second, began to age and eventually Adam and Eve would die physically, and the mark of death was placed upon every son and daughter of Adam. You don't believe this? Check the obituary column in your local paper. And yet to this day, and every day, the same plot is played out. You can have it all – more wisdom and knowledge that God wants to withhold. He's a killjoy, that's if he ever existed. Go for it, take it and enjoy it – the forbidden fruit, but sin when it is conceived brings forth death.

Now here is a very important thing for us to grasp. We can blame God for allowing it. We can blame the devil and we can blame Adam and Eve, but the reality is that Adam made a decision that each of us would have made. Adam embodied all the qualities of being a perfect man. He knew that he was made perfect and placed in a perfect world and he had a wisdom and a knowledge and a completely fulfilled life where God would actually walk with him in the garden. He had a perfect relationship with God, but even with all that he blew it. He blew it big time. And as our federal head he made the decision that you and I make every day. We choose our own way. The reality is that we are all responsible for every sinful problem in the world today. It's time for personal responsibility. It was my sin that nailed Jesus to the tree. We are responsible.

Please don't misunderstand me and please don't misrepresent what I am trying to say here. Innocent people suffer in the world today. A person goes for a run and an evil individual attacks and kills them. The evil-doer is guilty of the awful crime and the villain needs to be apprehended and punished. Their victim is innocent. Justice needs to be done. A person suffers illness, not necessarily because of their own personal sin, rather it's because of the sin disease that we all have and hence we will all die physically. None of us are getting out of here alive.

My dear mentor and pastor, one of the loveliest and kindest and most godly of men, a man with a great big heart and love for others, died a year ago at the age of 58 after a year-long and painful battle with cancer. I can't explain that. I cannot tell why God allowed it, but He did. You can't tell me God took him out because he was deserving of such suffering and death. These are things we cannot understand with our fallen and limited knowledge and understanding; but one thing is sure, it all stemmed from that decision in the garden, and we are all affected and our world and everything in it is in a state of deterioration and eventual death.

But Pastor David died in the possession of eternal life and eternal hope. He is not dead; he went to be with the Lord of Glory to enter the perfection of heaven. And one day there will be a new earth wherein dwells righteousness.

Do you think all the suffering and pain in the world does not weigh heavily on the heart of God? It is not that He is doing nothing, it is not that He is a bystander who is weak and weary. God is active in the world. If He were not, then the evils and what we see around us today are nothing compared to a world where there is no God. It happened in the days of Noah, and people say, *'You can't seriously believe that God destroyed the world with a flood. And how could He destroy everyone if He is a God of love?'* The Genesis record tells us that: *'The LORD saw how great the wickedness of the human race had become on the earth, and that every inclination of the thoughts of the human heart was only evil all the time'* (Genesis 6.5).

To get the impact, here are the ways a number of versions seek to express the original Hebrew.

'Everything they thought or imagined was consistently and totally evil.'

'Every intention of the thoughts of his heart was only evil continually.'

The world can be a bad place, but we are not at this point yet. God will have His day and on that day, all will be revealed and every wrong made right and it will be a day of Divine justice and retribution. It will be a day of salvation and eternal hope for many but for others a day of despair and that will not end. On that day, Jesus shall reign and every knee will bow and every tongue that ever gave utterance will confess that Jesus Christ is Lord. And the devil and his angels will be placed in the bottomless pit. And the universe will be perfect, and paradise will be restored. Sin will never happen again, nor all the horrible stuff that goes with it. The body is placed in mother earth until the day of resurrection because the dead will rise again from the grave. Every person who has ever died will be raised from death and will stand before the Judge. And for those whose hope is in Christ:

The mortal shall put on immortality and the corruption shall put on incorruption. And then shall be brought to pass the saying. "Death where is your sting, oh grave where is your victory?" Ours is the victory through our Lord Jesus Christ (1 Corinthians 15.55).

You may argue and say, *'Well I would not have done what Adam did. I would have said no to Satan.'* Adam and Eve stood at a tree and they disobeyed God, sin came in and so death passed upon all mankind because all have sinned. Move along on the pages of history and one day there was another tree, only on this occasion it held the body of a man, and His tree was a cross. He was the very God who walked in the garden with Adam, He is the very God who created the universe. And He is the very God who became a baby in Bethlehem. And He died in agony and pain! All the pains that the powers of hell could unleash on Him took hold of Him.

And what did that generation say to the one on the tree? '*We will not have this man to reign over us.*' God chose the cross, we chose sin and death. God chose to make a way back to Himself, but it meant that His Son, Jesus Christ, the Messiah, would become a man, live a perfect life, say no to the devil, live the only perfect life ever on planet earth and give His perfect life in death. What does the world do with the tree today? The tree that represents the finished work of Christ —His cross work, providing salvation and offering us eternal redemption. The world is still doing what Adam did. Choosing the forbidden fruit and not faith in Christ. Adam deliberately turned his back on God and eternal life. Are you?

But more than hell was unleashed on Christ? He took upon Himself every sin on that cross. Behold the Lamb of God that takes away the sin of the world. Milton sought to capture it:

Work Redemption for mankind, whose sins
Full weight must be transferr'd upon my head.

And Jesus took all the sickness and all the suffering of the world upon Himself. In those hours on the cross, every sin known to mankind, every pain and every sorrow ever experienced in the world by everyone from the first day to the last day of world history, was heaped on Him and then all the wrath of a holy God against sin and all its consequences was placed upon Jesus and we cannot even begin to comprehend what that could mean – it will take eternity and even then that it is too short for us to know what God did on that cross to bring us back. To give us eternal life, to give us what Adam gave up – immortality.

Jesus made a way back to God and a perfect universe and a perfect world is going to come into being again when He returns to planet earth and He places His feet on the Mount of Olives. There is no planet B, there is no plan B either. Because in eternity past God's plan was redemption and salvation through Christ. God is a God of love and in love He planned the plan of redemption. The violence against Christ was ours but the Love of God shines through, and love won the day.

The devil and his fallen angels must have rejoiced because Jesus was dead. That's it – it's over – the world will continue in its sorrow and sin and hopelessness, rolling on to destruction. The Devil is the king of mass destruction. In all destruction he is the originator of mass destruction. The King of life was dead. Long live evil and hell on earth for its poor souls would have been the sentiments of Satan and his fallen army of demons, as they rubbed their hands in glee. But on that Sunday morning, the third day, Jesus rose from the dead and he brought immortality and life to light through the gospel. Hell is defeated, the devil is defeated, sin and suffering and sickness and death are defeated and our relationship with God can be restored; we can have an eternal hope in our hearts today and have the eternal prospect of living perfectly where there is no death. Oh, how He loves us.

God is bringing the world to its conclusion. There is an intensification of sin and all that goes with it in these last of the last days. Why does God not intervene when people shout? He has, He did? He has spoken in His Son. What does God know about suffering personally? What does He not know about it? He experienced it all on the cross. God will make everything right and he will right every wrong. Each of us will give an account of ourselves to God. Every sinner, every abuser, every murderer, every self-righteous hypocrite will stand before God. We will all stand before God, and we can only be saved by the Christ who is called the second Adam.

'Just as everyone dies because we all belong to Adam, everyone who belongs to Christ will be given new life' (1 Corinthians 15.22).

Get ready to be ready. There's a way back to God right here and right now. And today you stand at a tree – the cross of Cavalry. What will you choose? And it is only by the power of the Holy Spirit that anyone can be born again into this living hope. Chosen in Christ before the foundation of the world. As He calls you, heed His call. Reverent David used to say God has a plan for our life and often quoted Jeremiah. The Lord says, *'I know the plans I have for you, plans for good and not for evil. Plans to give you hope and a future'* (Jeremiah 29.11).

Jesus is our Hope. Put your faith in Him and His cross work and leave the rest to God. Live in his plan. Fulfil His purpose for your life and be assured that you have an eternal hope, eternal life, and immortality.

The greatest 'epic' poem in the English language was written by John Milton (1608-1674), *Paradise Lost* and *Paradise Regained*. *Paradise Lost* is twelve books long and *Paradise Regained* is four books long. The work has been deceived as a 'brief epic.' Here is a taster which eloquently described what we have been saying in this short essay about the cross work of Christ to redeem us.

Of Man's First Disobedience, and the Fruit
Of that Forbidden Tree, whose mortal taste
Brought Death into the World, and all our woe,

With loss of Eden, till one greater Man
Restore us, and regain the blissful Seat.

We hear the answer of heaven in *Paradise Regained*:
He now shall know I can produce a man
Of female Seed, far abler to resist
All his sollicitations, and at length
All his vast force, and drive him back to Hell,
Winning by Conquest what the first man lost
By fallacy surpriz'd. But first I mean
To exercise him in the Wilderness,
There he shall first lay down the rudiments
Of his great warfare, e're I send him forth
To conquer Sin and Death the two grand foes,
By Humiliation and strong Sufferance:
His weakness shall o'recome Satanic strength
And all the world, and mass of sinful flesh;
That all the Angels and Ætherial Powers,
They now, and men hereafter may discern,
From what consummate vertue I have chose
This perfect Man, by merit call'd my Son,
To earn Salvation for the Sons of men.
So spake the Eternal Father, and all Heaven
Admiring stood a space, then into Hymns
Burst forth, and in Celestial measures mov'd,
Circling the Throne and Singing, while the hand
Sung with the voice, and this the argument.
Victory and Triumph to the Son of God
Now entring his great duel, not of arms,
But to vanquish by wisdom hellish wiles.
The Father knows the Son; therefore secure

Ventures his filial Vertue, though untri'd,
Against whate're may tempt, whate're seduce,
Allure, or terrifie, or undermine.
Be frustrate all ye stratagems of Hell,
And devilish machinations come to nought.

DAY TWENTY-EIGHT

HOPE'S VICTORY IN THE JAWS OF DEATH

The prism of the Word: Genesis 3.1-15, 1 Peter 1.18, and 1 John 3.8.

But He was wounded ...

Nearly everyone will experience an open wound at some point in their lives, but the level of severity will range significantly depending on the type and nature of the wound. A wound can be described as an injury that breaks the skin or other body tissue. Wounds can be open with broken skin and exposed body tissue or closed when there is damage to tissue under intact skin. Wounds can be caused in several different ways by a variety of different objects, be it one that is blunt or sharp, including projectiles. Wounds are classified into several categories dependent on the cause and resulting injury.

A contused wound refers to a blunt trauma wound, causing pressure damage to the skin and/or underlying tissues.

An incised wound is a clean, straight cut caused by a sharp edge (i.e., a knife). This type of wound tends to bleed heavily as multiple vessels may be cut directly across. Connecting structures such as ligaments and tendons may also be involved.

A lacerated wound is a messy-looking wound and is caused by a tearing or by a crushing force. This type of wound does not tend to bleed as much as incised wounds but often causes more damage to surrounding tissues.

An abrasion wound is a type of wound caused by a scraping force or friction. These tend not to be very deep but can often contain many foreign bodies such as dirt (i.e., after a fall on loose ground).

A puncture wound is a deep wound caused by a sharp, stabbing object (i.e., a nail). It may appear small from the outside but can cause a lot of damage to deep tissues.

An avulsion wound is a wound caused by a tearing force in which tissue is torn away from its normal position. This type of wound may bleed profusely depending on the size and location. The tissue is often completely detached.

So, you may ask, what on earth have these wounds got to do with hope, never mind hope's victory in the jaws of death? Well, they have everything to do with Hope. There are referred to as 'messainic prophecies' contained in the Old Testament, and when you read them you will begin to understand the reason for the aforementioned wounds. For example, Isaiah tells us about Jesus, the suffering Saviour: *'But He was wounded for our transgressions, He was bruised for our iniquities; The punishment that brought us peace was upon Him, And by His stripes we are healed'* (Isaiah 53.5).

The fact of the matter is that Jesus endured all these wounds as a result of the full-force gale and utter intensity of man's wrath in His crucifixion and death for you and me. Mankind's diabolical violence in all its ferociousness was unleashed on Jesus Christ, yet the cross displays the intensity of the love of God for us in the sacrifice of His beloved Son for our sins. However, if we were only to dwell on the physical sufferings of Christ, we would not get an in-depth understanding of His Divine cross-work.

There are not only the awful physical sufferings of Christ, as if that weren't enough, there are also the spiritual, psychological, and supernatural sufferings of Christ on the cross. God the Father placed the sin of the world upon His holy sinless Son and then, on top of all that, the Sinless Saviour, who became sin for us, took our punishment for our sins upon Himself. The full and complete wrath of a Holy God against sin fell on Him; Almighty vengeance fell on Him. God is a God of love, and it was love that planned salvation, the plan of the Godhead from eternity past. Planned by the Trinity, One God, where Jesus, the second person of the Godhead, co-equal and co-eternal with the Father, became sin, and He took our punishment so that we could go free and have eternal hope. This is the mystery and the meaning of the cross of our Lord Jesus Christ.

The complementarity of biblical truth explains the mystery to us in the Gospel of saving grace. It is the Gospel of hope for humanity. Here is one example from the second letter of Paul to the church at Corinth.

For God was in Christ, reconciling the world to Himself, no longer counting people's sins against them. And He gave us this wonderful message of reconciliation. So we are Christ's ambassadors; God is making His appeal through us. We speak for Christ when we plead, "Come back to God! For God made Christ, who never sinned, to be the offering for our sin, so that we could be made right with God through Christ" (2 Corinthians 5.19-21).

In John's record of the death of Christ, he tells us that Christ bowed His head and dismissed His spirit. To get the full force of the meaning we need to read through John's Gospel from the beginning. For He who died was from the beginning.

'So when Jesus had received the sour wine, He said, "It is finished!" and bowing His head, He gave up His spirit' (John 19.30).

The work was accomplished, and Jesus said, *'It is finished.'* The Greek word translated is *tetelestai*, an accounting term meaning 'paid in full'. Jesus is saying to us in this triumphant cry from the cross that the debt owed by humanity to our Creator God on account of Adam's sin is finally and forever dealt with. Jesus, in saying *'It is finished'*, declares that not only does He take away mankind's sin, but now He removes it as far as the east is to the west. As we look back to the cross, the Psalmist David looked forward to it and he wrote:

The Lord is compassionate and merciful,
slow to get angry and filled with unfailing love.
He will not constantly accuse us,
nor remain angry forever.
He does not punish us for all our sins;
He does not deal harshly with us, as we deserve.
For his unfailing love toward those who fear Him
is as great as the height of the heavens above the earth.
He has removed our sins as far from us
as the east is from the west.
The Lord is like a father to His children,
tender and compassionate to those who fear Him.
For he knows how weak we are;
He remembers we are only dust (Psalm 103. 8-14).

The cross work of Jesus, the Messiah, was the way in which He can remove our sins from us and give us hope. The work is finished, done, signed, and sealed because of the blood of Jesus. And our Saviour God offers us this true hope – eternal hope – eternal life. This is the only way; there is no other way. Jesus Himself, in answer to a question posed by Thomas, who asked, *'We have no idea where you are going, so how can we know the* way?', said, *'I am the way, the truth, and the life. No one can come to the Father except through me. If you had really known me, you would know who my Father is. From now on, you do know him and have seen him'* (John 14. 5-7).

In dismissing His spirit, Jesus did what no one on earth could ever do. No one has the power to dismiss their spirit. Only Jesus Christ the Son of God could do that. He could have done it earlier when He was being flogged and His back ripped in furrows with the Roman lash; but He didn't. It was not until He had borne and taken upon Himself every physical injury that is possible to the human frame, and then the full weight of sin, and every disease and sickness was placed upon Him; and then the fullness of the wrath of God against sin and all its horrible consequences fell upon Him. Having drained the cup of suffering to its bitterest and deepest dregs, He then stepped into death. When we say 'so and so' died, we really mean death took that person. Jesus actually died but death did not take Him. He stepped into death and that is entirely different. He said Himself:

And other sheep I have, which are not of this fold: them also I must bring, and they shall hear my voice: and they shall become one flock, one shepherd. Therefore My Father loves Me, because I lay down My life that I may take it again. No one takes it from Me, but I lay it down of Myself. I have power to lay it down, and I have power to take it again. This command I have received from My Father (John 10.16-18).

His death was a unique death in so many ways, but what we are emphasising here is that He stepped into death. There is also mystery here because the man who died on that tree was fully man, and fully God. It was Charles Wesley (1707–1788) who captured this in his hymn *'And can it be,'* in the second verse:

Tis mystery all! The Immortal dies!
Who can explore His strange design?
In vain the firstborn seraph tries
To sound the depths of love Divine!
'Tis mercy all! let earth adore,
Let angel minds inquire no more.
'Tis mercy all! let earth adore,
Let angel minds inquire no more.

When the soldier pierced Jesus' side, we learn from that puncture wound that He was already dead. Listen to the words of John:

Jesus knew that his mission was now finished, and to fulfil Scripture he said, 'I am thirsty.' A jar of sour wine was sitting there, so they soaked a sponge in it, put it on a hyssop branch, and held it up to his lips. When Jesus had tasted it, he said, 'It is finished!' Then he bowed his head and gave up his spirit.

It was the day of preparation, and the Jewish leaders didn't want the bodies hanging there the next day, which was the Sabbath (and a very special Sabbath, because it was Passover week). So they asked Pilate to hasten their deaths by ordering that their legs be broken. Then their bodies could be taken down. So the soldiers came and broke the legs of the two men crucified with Jesus.

But when they came to Jesus, they saw that he was already dead, so they didn't break his legs. One of the soldiers, however, pierced his side with a spear, and immediately blood and water flowed out.

This report is from an eyewitness giving an accurate account. He speaks the truth so that you also may continue to believe. These things happened in fulfilment of the Scriptures that say,

'Not one of his bones will be broken,' and 'They will look on the one they pierced' (John 19. 28-37).

John is very specific; he tells us that when the soldier pierced His side, immediately blood and water flowed out. There is a thin layer round the heart to protect it – it's called the pericardium and it is filled with fluid. If it had still been intact, water then blood would have flowed out. John tells us of the pericardium rupture due to the severe trauma and stress upon the loving heart of Jesus. The unimaginable burden of sin. He endured more than any man, more than anyone could endure, longer than anyone could endure, and then He stepped into death – His precious heart stopped beating. He died not *of* a broken heart but *with* a broken heart for you and me, and in stepping into death He did so in the knowledge that on the third day He would rise from the dead. The Bible says:

For God saved us and called us to live a holy life. He did this, not because we deserved it, but because that was his plan from before the beginning of time – to show us his grace through Christ Jesus. But it has now been revealed through the appearing of our Saviour, Christ Jesus, who has destroyed death and has brought life and immortality to light through the gospel (1 Timothy 1,9,10).

And the following references also makes it crystal clear:

'But we see Jesus, who was made a little lower than the angels for the suffering of death, crowned with glory and honour; that He by the grace of God should taste death for every man' (Hebrews 2.9).

'Because God's children are human beings – made of flesh and blood – the Son also became flesh and blood. For only as a human being could he die, and only by dying could he break the

power of the devil, who had the power of death' (Hebrews 2.14).

'He who sins is of the devil, for the devil has sinned from the beginning. For this purpose the Son of God was manifested, that He might destroy the works of the devil' (1 John 3.8).

Peter tells us that Jesus, our Hope, our Living Hope, suffered for us and He was victorious in sacrificial death, over sin and death and the grave and His bodily resurrection proves it. This is the guarantee of our true hope.

'Christ suffered for our sins once for all time. He never sinned, but he died for sinners to bring you safely home to God. He suffered physical death, but he was raised to life in the Spirit' (1 Peter 3.18)

It was a physical, bodily resurrection by the power of the Holy Spirit. At the very end of the Acts of the Apostles, Dr Luke records Paul's confinement in Rome. Paul was permitted to have his own private lodgings, though he was guarded by a soldier (Acts 28.16). It was not long until Paul had extended invitations to the local Jewish leaders, and in fact within three says he met them in his lodgings and his purpose was as follows, in his own words: *'I asked you to come here today so we could get acquainted and so I could explain to you that I am bound with chains because I believe that the Hope of Israel – the Messiah – has already come.'*

They rejected the Messiah, Paul said they had hardened their hearts against Jesus and so he wanted them to know that this salvation from God has also been offered to the gentiles and they will accept it (Acts 28.27,28). Have you?

Remember that mighty message preached by Peter on the day of Pentecost?

But God knew what would happen, and his prearranged plan was carried out when Jesus was betrayed. With the help of lawless Gentiles, you nailed him to a cross and killed him. God raised him up, losing the pangs of death, because it was not possible for him to be held by it (Acts 2.23,24).

Jesus' cry from the cross, *'It is finished'*, was a shout of victory in the very jaws of death. Our hope is in the Christ of the cross, His cross work and resurrection.

The synoptic Gospels tell us of something of immense significance when Jesus died. Matthew, in his record, tells us that when Jesus yielded up His Spirit *'At that moment the curtain of the temple was torn in two from top to bottom'* (Matthew 27.51).

The Temple had two veils or curtains, the first was in front of the holy place and the other separated the holy place from the most holy place. It was this second veil that was torn, The veil was four inches thick and it was said that even horses tied to each side could not pull it apart. The rending of the veil demonstrated that God had opened up the way of access to Himself through His Son. Only God could have torn the veil from the top to the bottom. Alfred Edersheim, in his book *The Life and Times of Jesus the Messiah*, wrote:

The Veils before the Most Holy Place were 60 feet long, and 30 feet wide, of the thickness of the palm of the hand, and wrought in 72 squares, which were joined together; and these Veils were so heavy, that, in the exaggerated language of the time, it needed 300 priests to manipulate each. If the Veil was at all such as is described in the Talmud, it could not have been rent in twain by a mere earthquake or the fall of the lintel, although its composition in squares fastened together might explain how the rent might be as described in the Gospel.

'By his death, Jesus opened a new and life-giving way through the curtain into the Most Holy Place' (Hebrews 10.20)

It is up to us to appropriate what Christ had done and receive His salvation as a free gift and live for Him as our Lord and Saviour with a hope that is unending.

'For the wages of sin is death, but the free gift of God is eternal life through Christ Jesus our Lord' (Roman 6.23).

DAY TWENTY-NINE

NAILING THIS HOPE ONCE AND FOR ALL

The prism of the Word: John 19.28-37, Hebrews 6.19, and 10.19-22.

The Cornerstone

Today we want to nail this hope once and for all. We could say that Jesus really did nail it on that cross on Golgotha's rugged hill. Paul tells us that *'Having cancelled the charge of our legal indebtedness, which stood against us and condemned us; He has taken it away, nailing it to the cross'* (Colossians 2.14).

The Bible teaches it was our sin and its penalty that was taken away. Jesus Christ was nailed to the cross, and by giving His life, the record of our debt – the wages of sin we have earned – can be wiped out.

We have already noted that Thompson, in the Thompson Chain Reference Bible, had suggested that the central theme of First Peter is victory *over* suffering as exemplified by Christ. We could also refer to victory *in* suffering as exemplified by Christ, and similarly, victory *by* suffering as exemplified by Christ, and victory *through* suffering as exemplified by Christ. So here are all the relevant references in First Peter to the sufferings of Christ.

The sufferings predicted
The Old Testament prophets looked forward to the coming of the Messiah, the Saviour of the world. They were really keen to know

all about this salvation for the world that would come through Christ as they predicted what they had been told in advance; Christ would indeed suffer, and then great glory would follow after His death and resurrection (1.10). The Angel armies of heaven who sang at His birth were also keen to watch all that was happening on earth in relation to the Suffering Messiah (1.11.).

The ransom paid

Then Peter refers to the fact that God paid the ransom to save us, and this redemption was not purchased with gold or silver, which will eventually lose their value, but with the precious blood of Christ. He was the sinless, spotless Lamb of God and He suffered and died to redeem us out of the slave market of sin and the empty life that goes with it, so we could be born again and brought into a right relationship with God (1.18,19). This was no plan B on God's part, but Christ was the Lamb chosen as our ransom long before the world began. It was always the one and only unthwarted plan of the Sovereign God of the universe for the world.

The Cornerstone placed

Peter refers to Jesus as the Cornerstone whom God the Father has given the place of honour and worship. He is the Living Stone of God's temple and, having suffered in our place, He is now in the place of prominence and pre-eminence. Those who trust in Him and His sufferings are brought into this spiritual temple, recognising the honour that belongs to Him. Through His mediation we can offer sacrifices of praise to God and those who trust in Him will never be disgraced (2.4-10). For those who reject Him, He is the Rock that will make them stumble and fall because they have not obeyed God's Word about Him as our Saviour and

Ransom, Redeemer, Cornerstone, and Lord.

Christ suffered for us

We are told that Christ suffered for us. All the sufferings that we have already mentioned, and we are only scratching the surface, was for us. He did it for us. And He personally carried our sins in His own body on the tree (2.24). By His wounds we are healed (2.25). And God who has called us to do good has called us to follow in His steps. We are to follow Him, the One who is our Hope.

Who are we following? We are all followers of something or someone. Whose steps are we seeking to walk in? We are to walk in His steps (2.21-25).

'To this you were called, because Christ suffered for you, leaving you an example, that you should follow in his steps' (2.21).

Christ suffered for our sins once for all time (3.18). He died for sinners to bring us home to God. He suffered physical death but was raised to life in the Spirit. Again, Peter reiterates that Christ suffered physical pain for us (4.1). In our trials we are partners with Christ in His sufferings (4.13). Peter was a witness of the sufferings of Christ (5.1). And because Jesus took our place, we must put our faith and trust and hope in Him. God in His kindness has called us to share in His eternal glory by means of Jesus Christ, His only Son.

Peter nails it and we need to as well. We need to ensure that our Hope is in Him alone for salvation.

Get into the Bible, our Hope manual, trace the story of hope. Look into the Old Testament prophecies of the coming of the Messiah. Start right from the fountainhead of all prophecy in

Genesis 3.15.

The ransom paid
Trace the unfolding drama of redemption throughout the Bible. Meditate on the ransom price and the cost of our redemption, and worship at His feet.

The Cornerstone placed
Look up the Old Testament prophecies of the predictions of the Cornerstone.

In our place
We need to realise what this means. Jesus came for you and for me. He came to be born and He was born to die for us so that we might be born again and that we might never die. Now here's a thought to mediate upon today: *He took my place and died for me.*

'The Son of God loved me and gave Himself for me' (Galatians 2.20)

It's time to nail it once and for all and put your faith and trust in Him. If we have already done so, it's time to seek to know Him more.

DAY THIRTY

CHOCOLATE, GALAXIES, AND A BIG SPACE TELESCOPE

The prism of the Word: 1 Peter 1.18-24, 2.4-6.

Where did we come from?

A recent study suggests that there are around 700 quintillion planets in the universe, but only one like Earth. It's a revelation that's both beautiful and awesome, and also staggering. A quintillion is 1 followed by 18 zeros. And the chances of life beginning at all are 1 in a trillion trillion. A trillion is a million million. We are going to seek to answer the fundamental question; *So where did we come from?*

We need to get our thinking caps on, so here we go.

The history of chocolate is said to have begun in Mesoamerica (now Central America and Mexico), where it's believed the ancient Olmec civilization first cultivated cacao beans as early as 1750 BC. But the first evidence of cocoa as a drink comes from the Mayan people in 900 AD. They were Mesoamerican Indians occupying a nearly continuous territory in southern Mexico, Guatemala, and northern Belize.

Fast forward to 1810 and the Galaxy milk chocolate brand was made and launched by Mars Incorporated. Galaxy Chocolate covered a large range of products, including the Milky Way which was marketed as *'The sweet you can eat between meals without ruining your appetite.'* It was first launched in the USA in 1924 and in the UK in 1934. The UK version comprised of nugget and chocolate whereas the US version had caramel. In 1935, Forrest Mars Senior manufactured the world's first Mars bar in Slough, England, and there are different formulations of the Mars bar around the world with different ingredients to satisfy the tastes of different consumers.

Mars, Milky Way, Galaxy? So, what is it about? Chocolate bars and astronomical objects? The fact of the matter is that Mars and Milky Way are not directly related to anything heavenly, other than the taste apparently. Galaxy, however, was probably named with the astral in mind. The bar was launched in the UK in 1965 at the height of the space race as a direct competitor to Cadbury's chocolate. The starry name was very popular and slotted in very nicely alongside Mars and Milky Way.

If you haven't already gone to get a bar of chocolate, you are probably asking yourself by this stage, *'And what on earth has this got to do with where we came from?'* Bear with me, all will be revealed shortly, but there is, in the author's mind, a random connection between chocolate manufacture and the launch of the James Webb Space telescope on the 25th December 2021.

The James Webb Telescope succeeded the Hubble Telescope, and with a 6.5 metre mirror, was purpose-built for looking deeper into space and further back in time. At a cost £8.5 billion, with ten years in the planning and twenty years in the building, the James Webb Telescope (JWST) has led to great excitement coupled with anxiety at what it would unfold after its long journey into space.

The good news is that it opened perfectly and has commenced its mission in space. It took a month to reach its destination, a million miles from earth, four times the distance of the moon from the earth. Its mission is to try and find out about how galaxies were formed by showing the first stars to light up the universe. Its brilliant inventors tell us that it is a voyage back to the birth of the universe and goes in search of the edge of darkness, total and compete. One writer commenting on the mission said:

It's hard to imagine a time when all that existed was darkness, when you could travel in any direction for millions of miles and still see absolutely nothing ... it's the story of the dark ages that gripped the universe before the first star ignited and how the cosmos ultimately filled with light.

Those who presume to know about these things, the experts, are astrophysicists. An astrophysicist tries to understand the universe and its stars, planets, and galaxies. There are many Christians in this field who believe in the God of creation. But others with different viewpoints, and who do not believe; the ones you hear on the MSM (MainStream Media) tell us that the universe was formed by a 'big bang', which contained all the basic elements, hydrogen, helium and a smattering of lithium, required for the existence of all things. Then these basic elements had to be forged or manufactured in the stars to produce the carbon that makes up every living thing, and all the nitrogen for earth's atmosphere. The silicon in the rocks also had to be manufactured. All the atoms had to be constructed and made in the nuclear reactions that took place that made the stars shine, and in the mighty explosions that ended their very existence. The thinking of those 'in the know' is that: *'We are only here because the first stars and their descendants seeded the universe to make stuff.'* And that includes us. It's all an accident, according to this perspective.

We all make assumptions, every one of us, and when we

come to such vital matters as to the origin of the universe, and our own existence, we need to examine ourselves. An important point at this juncture is to be aware of the importance of what is termed self-reflexivity in our search for truth. Typically, reflexivity involves examining our own judgments and belief systems during the process. The goal of being reflexive is to identify any personal beliefs that may have incidentally affected us in our search. Self-reflexivity means we must be prepared to question our own assumptions. It is a very healthy thing for all of us to do. Have we been conditioned to believe something, or do we really believe it because we have really thought it through and come to that informed decision? This is true for both believers and unbelievers. The reality is both perspectives exercise 'faith,' but which is blind faith, and which is a reasonable faith, to believe in a Creator God or in chance? And what about the hope we are considering. Is it a real hope? It is a true hope? Is it a realistic hope? Is it a sure-fire hope? Is it a lasting hope? Is it a reasonable hope? Is it a rational hope? Or is it another Humpty Dumpty hope? We all need to decide.

Those on MSM are telling us that all the material came from the stars to make everything needed to ensure that our blue planet stands out uniquely in space. Yet it is the only known planet that supports life. It has all the elements necessary, including oxygen, water, and habitable temperature. Water and air are in the right proportion and the presence of life-supporting gas and balanced temperatures make earth a unique planet. It is fine tuned to support life. The fact is it is very finely tuned.

Earth has a solid surface with a predominately nitrogen atmosphere whereas the gas on other planets is mostly hydrogen, and Venus and Mars have mostly carbon dioxide in their atmospheres.

Astrophysicists also study exoplanets, that is, planets beyond our solar system, that orbit a star like the sun. 5,000 have been found and there are probably thousands more yet to be discovered. There are planets that are similar to earth, and yet a recent study has concluded that no exoplanet can sustain life as we know it on earth. The study was entitled *'Efficiency of the oxygenic photosynthesis on earth-like planets in the inhabitable zone.'*

Photosynthesis is the process used by plants, algae, and certain bacteria to turn sunlight, carbon dioxide (CO_2), and water into food and oxygen.

It was thought previously that the exoplanets were habitable. The researchers concentrated on understanding the conditions for oxygen-based photosynthesis that allows complex biospheres found on earth to flourish. One of the findings is that stars around half the temperature of the sun cannot sustain an Earth-like biosphere, for they fail to deliver enough energy in the correct wavelength range. The study went on to say that even if oxygenic photosynthesis were possible, such planets could not sustain a rich biosphere that is required like earth. The earth is finely tuned and points to masterly and intricate design.

Yet the experts on MSM tell us it's all an accident, the result of the 'big bang' and various multi-accidental events and the unbelievable manufacturing of the basic elements that by total chance produced millions upon millions of galaxies of chocolate! I mean, the universe! You get my drift; or drifter, if you know anything about the history of chocolate. What are the chances of smoothy silk Galaxy chocolate turning up in 1965 after a plethora of multi-accidental events?

And what are the chances of you being here? Of me being

here? The probability of you or I actually existing, never mind a galaxy or a star, and there are an estimated 100 thousand million stars in our Milky Way Galaxy alone (100 billion), the chances are reckoned to be 1 in 10 squared to the power of 2,685,000, that's 10 followed by 2,685,000 zeros. The odds of us being alive are basically zero.

For those of us who believe in God, we put our faith and trust in the Creator of the universe; we believe that we are His creation, and we came into being as a result of His omnipotence and His incredible design and purpose. It all points to Him. The Christian faith is a belief in the Creator God who knows us and wants us to know Him. He wants us to be in a personal relationship with Him. He wants to save us and empower us for living.

Victor Stenger was an American particle physicist, philosopher, author, and religious sceptic. Following a career as a research scientist in the field of particle physics, Stenger was associated with the New Atheism of Richard Dawkins and others. Here is an example of his counterpoint to those of us who believe in the personal God of creation:

The picture of the multiverse today starts with our own visible universe of 100 billion galaxies, each containing 100 billion stars, 13.8 billion years old ... Besides that we also have the eternal multiverse containing an unlimited number of other bubble universes of comparable size ... Surely, then, it is ludicrous to think that humanity ... is the special creation of a divinity that presides over this vast reality.

Note the reference to the multiverse – that means lots of universes, of which there is no evidence whatsoever. A reason for the theory of the multiverse is that for the earth to exist, vast universes had to go through loads of changes to then get it right in our universe, for a habitable earth. This argument falls into a black hole because the very notional idea of a multiverse will also require fine tuning. Their argument does not make sense.

As C.S. Lewis put it;

It is a profound mistake to imagine that Christianity ever intended to dissipate the bewilderment and even the terror, the sense of our own nothingness, which come upon us when we think about the nature of things. It comes to intensify them. Without such sensations there is no faith.

One former atheist who read C.S. Lewis' space trilogy says he took up his telescope and said: *'Again I wept. But this time for a very different reason: gratitude. Now I knew personally the God who had spun into being the trillion stars and countless planets of the Andromeda galaxy and the Milky Way.'*

To quote Lewis again: *'We may ignore, but we can nowhere evade the presence of God. The world is crowded with him. He walks everywhere incognito. And the incognito is not always hard to penetrate. The real labour is to remember, to attend … in fact to come awake. Still more, to remain awake.'*

TV scientist Professor Brian Cox takes the view that we are alone in our galaxy because the chance of complex life evolving is vanishingly small. Brian believes it needed extraordinary circumstances for human life to evolve, so he doesn't think it has been repeated elsewhere. He states: *'The biologists I know think that it was such a freak occurrence that anything got multicellular.'*

Note that this eminent physicist calls multicellular life *'a freak'.* But it's also true that the chances of single-celled life emerging by accident from lifeless chemicals are virtually zero. Add to that the calculation by mathematicians that there has not been enough time in the universe for life to have evolved, and it's clear that there is a big problem with the evolution story.

It is not unreasonable to deduce from the evolutionary perspective that it takes far more faith to believe that life started and developed by accident than it does to believe in a Creator. Andrew Halloway, a British freelance editor, writer, and publishing consultant, has had a long-term interest in the creation/evolution debate. He is the contributing editor of the publication *'The Delusion of Evolution.'* Halloway takes the view that superficially evolution can seem like a sound defence for atheism, but the deeper you look, the more you find that science confirms there must be a God.

Writing in the publication, on the views of Richard Dawkins, evolutionist and atheist, Andrew says the following:

Professor Richard Dawkins has spent his career attacking Christians for their 'blind faith', yet admits he can't prove his own beliefs. The world's best-known evolutionist and atheist, the scourge of those who believe in God, has declared that he holds a belief that isn't proved. Evolutionary biologist Richard Dawkins has sold millions of books promoting evolution as a fact, and toured universities ridiculing those who believe in a Creator because he says they have no proof of their belief. Yet Dawkins has admitted that he holds a belief that cannot be proved – evolution.

Responding to the question, *'What do you believe is true even though you cannot prove it?'* posed by a science website, Dawkins' answer was: *'I believe, but I cannot prove, that all life, all intelligence, all creativity and all 'design' anywhere in the universe is the direct or indirect product of Darwinian natural selection.'*

In an open letter to his daughter Juliet on her tenth birthday (published in his book *A Devil's Chaplain*), Dawkins advises her to accept only beliefs supported by evidence. *'Have you ever wondered how we know the things that we know?'* asks Dawkins.

The answer, he says, is evidence. Dawkins advises Juliet:

Next time somebody tells you something that sounds important, think to yourself: 'Is this the kind of thing that people probably know because of evidence? Or is it the kind of thing that people only believe because of tradition, authority, or revelation?' And next time somebody tells you that something is true, why not say to them: 'What kind of evidence is there for that?' And if they can't give you a good answer, I hope you'll think very carefully before you believe a word they say.'

So if Dawkins asked himself his own question, *'What kind of evidence is there for that?'* His answer when it comes to evolution as an explanation for all life is, *'There isn't enough evidence, I just believe it!'*

'Christians,' Halloway argues, *'believe in Christ not just on the basis of faith but also because of his bodily resurrection, witnessed by hundreds of people, many of whom laid down their lives rather than change their view. Believers also base their faith on their own personal experience of God, logical argument, and evidence from the Bible, history, archaeology, cosmology, and other sciences.'*

The Bible says *'Lift your eyes and look to the heavens: Who created all these? Do you not know? Have you not heard? The Lord is the everlasting God,* the Creator of the ends of the earth ...'* (Isaiah 40.26)

'For he commanded and they were created.' (Psalm 148.5).

In relation to the James Webb Space Telescope, what it all comes down to is the purpose of the mission which is about seeking to answer the basic, fundamental question we began with: *'Where do we come from?'*

God, in His Word, tells us where we came from.

And the vastness of the Universe and all the galaxies and stars also cry out *'In the beginning God created the heavens and the earth'* (Genesis 1.1.)

Eugene Petterson's amazing Message Bible is a paraphrase version, written in up-to-date, everyday language, and here is the rendering of Paul's words when dealing with the philosophies and anti-Christian belief systems of his day.

Watch out for people who try to dazzle you with big words and intellectual double-talk. They want to drag you off into endless arguments that never amount to anything. They spread their ideas through the empty traditions of human beings and the empty superstitions of spirit beings. But that's not the way of Christ. Everything of God gets expressed in him, so you can see and hear him clearly. You don't need a telescope, a microscope, or a horoscope to realise the fullness of Christ, and the emptiness of the universe without him. When you come to him, that fullness comes together for you, too. His power extends over everything (Colossians 2.8-10).

Such is the richness of the original Greek language, a comparison of various versions helps us to understand what is being said. The NLT puts the text in this way:

Don't let anyone capture you with empty philosophies and high-sounding nonsense that come from human thinking and from the spiritual powers of this world, rather than from Christ. For in Christ lives all the fullness of God in a human body. So you also are complete through your union with Christ, who is the head over every ruler and authority (Colossians 2. 8-10)

Without Him the vast universe is empty and meaningless, and so are we; but with Him we are complete.

DAY THIRTY-ONE

LOOK UP! DON'T LOOK UP!

The Prism of the Word: Isaiah 40.12-31 and Colossians chapter 2.

You cannot be serious!

One of the ways we can relax in our hectic world is to watch a film. We all have our favourites. My main bone of contention with films today is the use of bad language. Perhaps we should start a campaign, *'Great films don't need bad language to be great.'* Anyhow, recently I watched a film which was quite brilliant in spite of the bad reviews, and apart from the language at times, was very thought-provoking. One had thought it was a serious film, and it certainly has a serious theme, but it turned out to be quite comical in the way people responded to vital information as presented by the two main characters.

The film was called *Don't Look Up* (spoiler alert and bad language warning) and features an astronomer and his PhD student who discover a planet-killing comet hurtling towards earth. Having completed all the calculations, Dr Mindy and Kate Dibiasky contact the authorities to tell them that this comet would catastrophically impact earth in six months and 14 days. The evidence was 100% accurate; it was unavoidable and inevitable, and people really needed to know. How will they respond to such terrible news?

Eventually the astronomer and his student are invited to the

White House to brief the President. They have a very long wait because the President must deal with other 'more important' issues, such as scandalous accusations against her nominee to the Supreme Court, and then there are the Primaries to think about in three weeks' time. The astronomical two have to eventually stay in a hotel whilst the President plays politics, and in addition to her essential work schedule, a birthday party also takes priority. Eventually they get to meet the President and her sociopathic son who acts as her Chief of Staff. But they are not taking the news seriously. The dialogue goes something like this:

'How accurate is this information, because nothing can be 100% accurate?'

'Well, it's 98.7% accurate.'

'There you go, it's not 100% accurate, so you could actually be wrong.'

'No! A killer comet is going to hit earth in six months and 11 days and the earth will be destroyed.'

'Don't tell anyone, it will alarm them too much and we have the Primaries to think about in three weeks' time.'

The warnings go unheeded and so the intrepid two go on a media campaign to warn the world. They wait for the top news story on the main news to hear how the media have handled it. And guess what, the main story is about a relationship breakup of a famous celebrity, and then the dishing of the dirt on the nominee to the Supreme Court. Nothing about the big news story that the earth is going to end in six months' time.

When the PhD student tells it as it is, in stark language, she is branded as totally mad and out of touch with reality. She is hooded and taken away by the FBI to a secret location and coerced into signing an agreement not to tell the truth and not to access any social media. People go about their everyday business and the relationship breakup is the only show in town with some competition from the nominee to the Supreme Court. Eventually NASA confirms the findings but again they try to keep it under wraps.

The arch villain in the movie discovers the killer-comet has trillions of dollars' worth of valuable minerals and so he thwarts humankind's only hope to save the world. He then draws up his own elaborate plans as to how to extract these valuable assets from the killer-comet as it plunges to earth. Dr Mindy then tells the world how it really is, he too is hooded and taken away.

Two big campaigns are then underway. The *'Don't Look Up Campaign'* and the *'Look Up Campaign'*. The President is in her element at one of her big campaign meetings for the Primaires, whipping up the crowd and the crowd is heard chanting, *'Don't look up, don't look up.'* The cameras home in on one man in the audience and as he chants, he starts to look up, and as he does so, he sees it! There it is, the killer-comet, 9km wide, and he can plainly see its dust-tail in the sky. Eventually everyone looks up and everyone can see it. That's perhaps too much information but you need to watch the film to see the ending (again, language warning).

The film has a number of powerful messages. People ignored the message. People denied the message. People were more interested in frivolous things. People just went on with everyday life. People rubbished the messengers as being deluded, mad, and in urgent need of psychiatric treatment. People were easily led and didn't think for themselves. People left it too late.

In 1 Peter 5.1, Peter says that a day is coming when Jesus will come back again and be revealed to the entire world. It's not on the main news, it's not even taken seriously by most people. People who go on about it are deemed as fanatical and intellectually weak; quite mad really. And anyway, Peter wrote this in the first century, c63AD, and the event has not happened, and that was two thousand years ago. We will get to the seeming 'timelapse' shortly. The Redeemer who will redeem all of creation has not appeared, well, not yet.

The wise individual cannot ignore the fact that predictions about future events occupy about one quarter of the entire Bible. The teaching of the second coming of Jesus Christ is found in some 1,800 passages in the Bible, with 318 of these in the New Testament. So, we are not talking about some obscure reference to this event, the Bible is replete with it. Jesus Himself promised that He will come back again. According to the Bible there is a date in the Divine calendar and that day will without doubt arrive.

Paul tells us that God the Father has '*Fixed a day on which he will judge the world in righteousness by a man whom he has appointed; and of this he has given assurance to all by raising him from the dead*' (Acts 17.31).

Peter gives an amazing answer to the 'Don't look up' brigade; yes 2,000 years ago. Some of his narrative, one would think it was written yesterday. He also explains the seeming timelapse. A thousand years is like a day to the Lord. We see things from an earthly perspective. God sees time differently. Let's listen to the prophetic words of Scripture in the second letter of Peter.

But you must not forget this one thing, dear friends: A day is like a thousand years to the Lord, and a thousand years is like a day. The Lord isn't really being slow about his promise, as some people think. No, he is being patient for your sake. He does not want anyone to be destroyed but wants everyone to repent. But the day of the Lord will come as unexpectedly as a thief. Then the heavens will pass away with a terrible noise, and the very elements themselves will disappear in fire, and the earth and everything on it will be found to deserve judgement.

Since everything around us is going to be destroyed like this, what holy and godly lives you should live, looking forward to the day of God and hurrying it along. On that day, he will set the heavens on fire, and the elements will melt away in the flames. But we are looking forward to the new heavens and new earth he has promised, a world filled with God's righteousness.

And so, dear friends, while you are waiting for these things to happen, make every effort to be found living peaceful lives that are pure and blameless in his sight.

And remember, our Lord's patience gives people time to be saved. This is what our beloved brother Paul also wrote to you with the wisdom God gave him – speaking of these things in all of his letters. Some of his comments are hard to understand, and those who are ignorant and unstable have twisted his letters to mean something quite different, just as they do with other parts of Scripture. And this will result in their destruction.

Peter's final words in the Bible …

You already know these things, dear friends. So be on guard; then you will not be carried away by the errors of these wicked people and lose your own secure footing. Rather, you must grow in the grace and knowledge of our Lord and Saviour Jesus Christ.

All glory to him, both now and forever! Amen (2 Peter 3.8-18).

Jesus Himself told us about future events which are now all around us. You can read about this in the prism of the word for today. Jesus told us to take note: *'When you see these things begin to happen, look up, and lift up your heads, because your redemption is drawing near'* (Luke 21.28).

The sure and steadfast hope we need is found in Jesus Christ who has promised to come back again. It's time to look up with hope and confidence. Herein is true hope.

'Any doubts? The honest doubter searches for real hope and finds the light. The unbeliever is prepared to live in hopelessness and stumble in the dark.' (Author)

Jesus promised to come back again. He told his disciples and John as one of the expert eyewitnesses records the words of Jesus, *'And if I go and prepare a place for you, I will come again and receive you to Myself; that where I am, there you may be also'* (John 14.3).

Dr Luke also records for us the words of Jesus as a warning not to be predicting dates about His return.

He said to them: 'It is not for you to know the times or dates the Father has set by his own authority. But you will receive power when the Holy Spirit comes on you; and you will be my witnesses in Jerusalem, and in all Judea and Samaria, and to the ends of the earth' (Acts 1.7,8).

Then we are told what the angels said to the disciples.

After he said this, he was taken up before their very eyes, and a cloud hid him from their sight. They were looking intently up into the sky as he was going, when suddenly two men dressed in white stood beside them. 'Men of Galilee,' they said, 'why do you stand here looking into the sky? This same Jesus, who has been taken from you into heaven, will come back in the same way you have seen him go into heaven' (Acts 1.9-11).

Look up! Don't look up! Which camp are we in?

Let us get ready to be ready.

DAY THIRTY-TWO

HOPE SPRINGS ETERNAL

The prism of the Word: Luke 21 and Matthew 24

Marilyn Adamson and questioning faith in nothing behind it all

Tradition has it that Peter suffered death by being crucified upside down. His writings clearly indicate that contrary to what it seems this was not a senseless Roman death, and this was not the end of his hope. Peter and his fellow apostles saw the bigger picture; an eternal one with a bright, everlasting future. As we have traversed the path in our exploration of biblical hope, we have found that Peter expresses both the source and the nature of this hope. This is a certain hope. This is very different to what we do in the natural world – we hope in the face of uncertainty that all will be well. This biblical hope is distinctly different in that it is sure and steadfast, it's a sure-fire hope, This is what he has wrote:

'So prepare your minds for action and exercise self-control. Put all your hope in the gracious salvation that will come to you when Jesus Christ is revealed to the world' (1 Peter 1.13).

'Through Christ you have come to trust in God. And you have placed your faith and hope in God because he raised Christ from the dead and gave him great glory' (1 Peter 1.21).

Check out the prism of the day readings from 2 Corinthians. Death was the very vehicle that brought Peter and the other disciples into the full realisation of his hope in the person of Jesus

232

Christ. A sure and steadfast hope! Peter, who had obtained eternal hope and eternal life on earth, now entered into the fullness of it in the immediate presence of Christ, in the glories of Emanuel's land, Heaven. That is an awesome hope to have in a world drowning in hopelessness.

The day he met Christ on the earth was the day he found, encountered, and embraced true hope in the person of the Son of God, Son of Man, our Lord and Master, Saviour and Redeemer, Jesus Christ. For those who have the same encounter on earth today with the Living Christ and find Him to be their True Hope, if we die before Jesus comes again, we enter, like Peter, into the fullness of that hope in Heaven. Today you too can find true hope in Jesus Christ. Those who trust Him and follow Him in this life have eternal life and have found eternal hope. Hope springs eternal.

The phrase *'hope springs eternal'* comes from the poetic pen of Alexander Pope (1688-1744) when he coined the famous expression in his 1732 work, *An Essay on Man: Epistle I.*

Pope was a popular English writer who wrote many notable poems and other works during the 1700s. He expressed his Christian faith in his writing in *An Essay on Man* through what has been described as 'couplets of iambic pentameter.' This refers to two lines written so that they end in the same sound, or a rhyme.

The poem's four sections, known as epistles, present a philosophical argument for divinely designed order in the world. In light of God's good design for the world, the poem argues humans have a duty to focus on the good that exists – such as eternal hope – and to express that hope in a life well lived, a life lived for God. At the commencement of his work as he writes to Henry St. John, Lord Bolingbroke, these awesome words were penned:

> *Say first, of God above, or man below,*
> *What can we reason, but from what we know?*
> *Of man what see we, but his station here,*
> *From which to reason, or to which refer?*
> *Through worlds unnumber'd though the God be known,*
> *'Tis ours to trace him only in our own.*
> *He, who through vast immensity can pierce,*
> *See worlds on worlds compose one universe,*
> *Observe how system into system runs,*
> *What other planets circle other suns,*
> *What varied being peoples ev'ry star,*
> *May tell why Heav'n has made us as we are.*
> *But of this frame the bearings, and the ties,*
> *The strong connections, nice dependencies,*
> *Gradations just, has thy pervading soul*
> *Look'd through? or can a part contain the whole?*
> *Is the great chain, that draws all to agree,*
> *And drawn supports, upheld by God, or thee?*

The following is his 'hope' stanza:

> *Hope humbly then; with trembling pinions soar;*
> *Wait the great teacher Death; and God adore!*
> *What future bliss, he gives not thee to know,*
> *But gives that hope to be thy blessing now.*
> *Hope springs eternal in the human breast:*
> *Man never is, but always to be blest:*
> *The soul, uneasy and confin'd from home,*
> *Rests and expatiates in a life to come.*

It goes without saying 'hope that springs' eternal finds its roots in an eternal place. King Solomon wrote: *'Yet God has made everything beautiful for its own time. He has planted eternity in the human heart, but even so, people cannot see the whole scope of God's work from beginning to end'* (Ecclesiastes 3:11).

The hope that Peter had and the hope we too can have in Christ springs from the eternal. Our ephemeral life with all its trials and difficulties and eventual physical death can derive true hope that is grounded not in the machinations of man but in the eternal; the eternity of our Maker who imparts eternal life and hope that is only found in Him. Jesus, the Son of God and the Son of Man, who came from eternity into time to be born and live and die and rise again and go back to eternity, and is coming again at a date that has been set in God's diary, offers us this eternal life. That's exactly what He said to those who believe in Him. *'And I give them eternal life, and never shall they perish to the age, and never will anyone seize them out of My hand'* (John 10.39). Solomon tells us that we cannot see the whole scope of God's work from beginning to end, we cannot fathom it all, we can't work it all out in our finite minds. How can the finite possibly fathom the infinite? Who can grasp God's overall complete plan from beginning to end? Who can fully discover the depths of His wisdom and understanding?

God doesn't tell us everything about our here and now, never mind the future, nor do we understand the bliss we will experience in heaven; instead, our blessing for now is to have hope, including the hope of Heaven that springs eternal. If we put our trust in Him, we can say *'I have hope, because Hope has me.'*

Yes, God has indeed 'set eternity in the human heart.' In every human soul there is a God-given awareness that there is something more to this life on earth and this transient world.

And with that awareness of eternity comes a hope that we can find true hope and real life and ultimate fulfilment not afforded by vanity in this world.

God has given us His Word where we can trace the unfolding drama of redemption and hope for humanity from the beginning to the end. All made possible through the sending of His one and only Son. Herein are the treasures of wisdom that mankind longs for, found in our Lord Jesus Christ *'in whom are hidden all the treasures of wisdom and knowledge'* (Colossians 2.3).

The promise is given to us in Scripture for those who put their hope in God: *'I will give you hidden treasures, riches stored in secret places, so that you may know that I am the LORD, the God of Israel, who summons you by name'* (Isaiah 45.3).

There is a longing in the human soul. There is a knowing that there is something more than what we see and know around us every day. There is more. We have a deeply implanted awareness of the reality of God and the hope He gives but we have masked it, denied it, thwarted it, dismissed it, laughed at it, spurned it, rejected it, but it is still there; that insatiable longing for the more, for the I AM. We have replaced God; the Great I AM with ME FIRST and with our own gods to worship. It's really what one would call practical atheism, living as if God does not exist.

There have been many atheists that have turned away from their atheism and believed in the existence of God. One former atheist, scientist, and now a Christian Apologist, Marilyn Adamson, having been solid in her atheistic faith for many years, began to look again at what she called 'the possibility of God'. The concept of God was something that she could not get off her mind. As a confirmed atheist she was searching for God and as she continued on her journey she records: *I saw some evidence for God that was both factual and logical. The parts particularly convincing to me were the properties of water and the earth's position to the sun. It was all too perfectly designed, too perfectly put together. My faith in 'nothing behind it all' seemed weaker than the possibility of God.*

Lots of questions were written down over the years, lots of philosophers and brief systems were considered by her intelligent, insightful, and inquiring mind. Then, for logical, historical, and scientific reasons, she broached the possibility of the existence of God. Eventually she came to a point where, having weighed up all the evidence, she was able to say from an intellectual perspective that she could move from the 'possibility of God' to believing in the existence of God; to then exercising faith in God. Here are her own words: *Then came another decision I needed to make. I knew I had to act on that conclusion. Just intellectually concluding God existed was way too light. It would be like deciding ... aeroplanes exist. Faith in an aeroplane means nothing. However, if you need to get somewhere and an aeroplane is the way, you have to decide to act and actually get on the plane. I needed to make the decision to actually talk to God. I needed to ask him to come into my life.*

And she did just that. Now Marilyn testifies to a personal relationship with God and has found true hope. Check her out on Google.

You may have heard the phrase *'Ask Jesus into your heart.'* That's what Marilyn did. Just so that we understand what is meant by this, we need to be aware that when the Bible speaks of our heart, it does not mean our anatomical heart which pumps blood throughout the body. You would not say to the one you love, *'I love you with all my blood pump.'* We speak rather of the heart, as the Bible does, as it relates to the metaphysical core of who we are. The heart is the place from which our being, our awareness, our hopes, desires, and our love flows, all are birthed here. It is the place from which we believe and determines how we behave. It is from this place that we truly worship.

God has placed eternity in our hearts. Listen, believe, accept, enter into a personal relationship with God and the words from the famous passage in St. Augustine's Confessions will have even greater poignancy for you personally. *'You have made us for yourself, O Lord, and our heart is restless until it rests in you.'*

DAY THIRTY-THREE

JUST A PIE-IN-THE-SKY HOPE?

The prism of the Word: Psalm 19, Psalm 42, 2 Corinthians
5.1-10

Putting food on the table - the proof of the pudding

The phrase *'pie in the sky'* was coined by the Swedish-American
activist Joe Hill in 1911 when criticising the Salvation Army's
philosophy, which he perceived as their *'concentration on
saving the souls of the hungry rather than feeding them.'* He
used it in one of his songs while leading a radical labour
organisation.

Long-haired preachers come out every night,
Try to tell you what's wrong and what's right;
But when asked how 'bout something to eat
They will answer with voices so sweet:
You will eat, bye and bye,
In that glorious land above the sky;
Work and pray, live on hay,
You'll get pie in the sky when you die.

The man who was crucified on a cross upside down would
take issue with Joe. That man was Peter, who entered into the
fullness of his eternal hope via crucifixion. This hope, rather
than being pie in the sky, incentivised him to make an impact in
life on earth, by virtue of this very hope. For those like Joe who

say that the Christian faith is a crutch and this hope is an opt out whilst waiting for the next world, nothing could be further from the truth. Let's hear what Peter has to say about how to live in this world with our eye on the next.

Peter certainly had his feet on the ground. It's all about how we live down here. Here is the proof of the pudding. It is not all about Heaven and going there, it's about living here and now. Peter addresses leaders specifically but what he says also applies to everyone in how we should treat one another. There is the need to be caring towards others.

'Watch out for others and be eager to serve God. Leaders are not to lord it over the people. And look out for others, not for what you can get out of it, and be a good example, a good role model for others on how to live right in a world that has gone wrong' (1 Peter 5.1-43).

It's a future hope but it's also a very practical hope about living authentically and effectively in the here and now.

'The day is surely coming when the Great Shepherd will appear, and He is going to reward those who do His will on the earth. You will receive a never-ending crown of glory and honour. It would be amazing to have even just one crown to lay it at the feet of the King of Kings and Lord of Lords' (Revelation 4.10).

Peter addresses the young people (5.5). They are encouraged to accept the authority of their leaders. And then everyone is exhorted to put on kingdom clothes – the robes of humility. 'Dress yourselves in humility as you relate to one another.' There is no place for arrogance here. Be the opposite of the mocker in a world of muckers and mockers. 'Mockers are proud and haughty; they act with boundless arrogance' (Proverbs 21.24).

Then Peter tells us that the great and awesome God of glory and eternal hope is so interested in us and our world that He opposes the proud and gives His grace to the humble. So He calls upon us all to humble ourselves under the mighty hand of God so that at the right time He will lift us to a place of honour. And the God of all hope – this wonderful, amazing God – well, we can give our worries and cares to Him because He cares for us. He cares for you!

'*Humble yourselves, therefore, under God's mighty hand, that he may lift you up in due time. Give all your worries and cares to God, for he cares about you*' (1 Peter 5.6,7).

An indifferent world does not care for God and even when we are cold and are indifferent, He still cares for us and brings us back again and again and again. He is the God who, in spite of suffering in the world, restores us, supports us, strengthens us, and places us on a firm foundation, because all power belongs unto Him for ever. This is the sure place of true hope – in the Grace of God and in the Power of God and in the Care of God.

At the end of the short letter (5.12), Peter tells us that he has written it to encourage and assure his readers. Everything is in God's gracious plan, and He gives us His grace. We are then exhorted to stand firm in this grace. So, you can see from this one section of First Peter (chapter 5) that Peter has a lot to say about living a life that makes a positive and powerful impact in a world that is opposed to God. We are to live in the plan and purpose of God, and to be included in His plan is a massive incentive for living to please Him down here before we go up there.

What we do here will have eternal consequences in the world to come, not least our final destination, depending on who we have pinned our hopes on down here for time and eternity. Why not review the short letter of Peter again and note down all the things he has to say about living in this present world. His focus is very much on the here and now, not only the there and then;

although they are not mutually exclusive, rather they both go together and one impacts on the other, either for our good and glory or to our detriment and destruction.

Remember, however, it's not about working our way there to earn it because we can't, but rather it's about living fully and authentically and freely because we have been born again into this living hope.

Joe got it oh so wrong. It's not about *'pie in the sky when you die'*, it's about being *'sound on the ground when you're around.'* Then, when the day comes to go home, it's eternal glory. *When by His grace I shall look on His face, that will be glory, be glory for me.*

'Pure and genuine religion in the sight of God the Father means caring for orphans and widows in their distress and refusing to let the world corrupt you' (James 1.27).

Queen Elizabeth II
(21ˢᵗ April 1926 – 8ᵗʰ September 2022)

On this day, as one completes a review of the thirty-third day in our exploration of hope, the sad news has reverberated around the world that her majesty, Queen Elizabeth II, has passed away peacefully at Balmoral Castle in Scotland on the 8ᵗʰ September 2022. The outpouring of grief speaks volumes of the high esteem in which the Queen was held. President Macron of France in his moving tribute said: *'To you she was your Queen; to us she was The Queen.'*

Queen Elizabeth II was the Queen of the United Kingdom and the Commonwealth realms from 1952 until her death. Her reign of seventy years and 214 days was the longest of any British monarch in history and the second longest of any sovereign country in history. The nation and the world will mourn a monarch who was a remarkable public servant. As a humble servant of her people, the Queen carried out her duties consistently, impartially, and unswervingly for over seventy years.

'The memory of the righteous is a blessing' (Proverbs 10.7).

What was her secret for such humble, unstinting selfless devotion to her calling, and her deep love and affection for all people without distinction in terms of race, colour, religious belief, and political outlook? The truth is we cannot understand the Queen without reference to her Christian faith. In her coronation service the new Queen was presented with a Bible, described in the coronation as *'The rule for the whole of life ... and the most valuable thing that this world affords.'*

The Queen's life and testimony makes it clear that she took these words very seriously. As a follower of Christ, her whole life was one of service. Her life was rooted in the Bible. Her faith made a real difference during the highs and lows of life; she was enabled to be a stable and enduring presence and influence in her own nation and across the world.

The Queen was a Patron of the Bible Society from 1952 when she acceded to the throne. The following is a quotation from Queen Elizabeth II, on 3rd August 2022, summing up the source of her inspiration for living in such an unselfish and godly way, and of the eternal hope she possessed.

'Throughout my life, the message and teachings of Christ have been my guide and in them I find hope.'

May King Charles III and we do likewise.

DAY THIRTY-FOUR

HOPE AND THE BEGINNING OF THE UNIVERSE

The prism of the Word: Peter chapters 1-5.

Marilyn Adamson, Scientist: The consistency of Pure scientific findings

I remember a nickname we had for one of our teachers at high school; *'Neanderthal man'*. He talked a lot about this subspecies of Homosapien theory. His nickname was obviously unknown to him but in our boyhood skulduggery we thought he certainly looked like his 'distant relative'.

Then there was the science teacher who told me to stand outside the door of the class when I suggested that his grandad may well have been an ape but mine certainly wasn't. That did not go down too well. Even then it was frowned upon to question the great Darwin and his origin of the species. And today, to say you are a creationist, well we are the ones who are now called the Neanderthals, for our position is viewed as outdated and even preposterous. We hear the taunts: *'God indeed and He made it all? You cannot be serious!'*

We evolved? The evolving is going well, isn't it? A fragile and fearful world. Professor John Lennox states in his book, *God's undertaker: Has science buried God?* the following:

The world of strict naturalism in which clever mathematical laws all by themselves bring the universe and life into existence, is pure (and, one might add, poor) fiction. To call it science-fiction would besmirch the name of science. Theories and laws do not bring matter/energy into existence. The view that they nevertheless somehow have the capacity seems a rather desperate refuge ... from the alternative possibility ... Trying to avoid the clear evidence for the existence of a Divine intelligence behind nature, atheists scientists are forced to ascribe creative powers to less and less credible candidates like mass energy and the laws of nature.

Peter tells us that we do have an archenemy and he is described as going about like a roaring lion, seeking those he may devour. And it would seem he is making quite a success of it. Everything to do with God and God's Word is fair game and no place or person is too insignificant for the enemy to sow his weeds (yes, weeds) of doubt and confusion, particularly in relation to the origin of everything. It would suit us humans, as Fyodor Mikhailovich Dostoevsky wrote in The Brothers Karamazov: *'If God does not exist, then everything is permitted.'*

The enemy's mission is to destroy, and he is a liar from the beginning and 'any lie will do' as long as it gets the job done, which is the belief that God is either dead or irrelevant and the world and everything in it are here by chance. When some of the greatest intellectuals on the planet are the proselytes for such teaching and have the boundless enthusiasm of a tent meeting preacher, then the world takes note – they must know the answers given their IQ. But do they? Do they really? Perhaps IQ should stand for *incisive questioning* as well as intelligence quotient. And we shouldn't rule out *'phenomenal dud'* as it does not simultaneously denote a wisdom quotient. One has met some highly intellectual people who, let's say, seem to lack wisdom. The vernacular here would be *'They're not wise in the head.'*

We need to stop taking things at face value just because some well-known academic indicates a certain belief or the latest theory, we don't need to be alarmed and just accept it. We need to watch our influencers because not everyone has our wellbeing at heart, or our desire for true hope either. We need to look at the evidence and we don't need to be trained astrophysicists to find out if we are being cajoled into a black hole for thirty pieces of iron. Could Tyndale be right?

In the 1500s an Englishman named William Tyndale was talking with a friend about the need for everyone to be able to know God by being able to hear and read the Bible for themselves. At that time, it was illegal to own a copy of the Bible in the English language. Bibles were only allowed in Latin to make sure only the highly educated could read and explain it to the 'ignorant' masses. That's the IQ again! The phenomenal 'dudes' or 'duds' would tell us what to know and think. Tyndale's friend wasn't sure ordinary folks needed to know the Scriptures. He thought it might be good enough for the Pope to know the Bible in Latin and then tell all the English speakers what it says. To this Tyndale replied, *'I defy the Pope and all his laws, if God spare my life, I will make a boy that driveth the plough know more of the Scripture than thou dost.'*

On September 6th, 1536, William Tyndale was killed and then burned at the stake for his passion to see every person, even a plough boy, have access to all of God's truth. Interestingly now that most of us have access to the Bible, the enemy's tactics have changed. You don't need to read it now because it's just a book and, sure, some of the greatest minds have not accepted it. And then we have the usual 'full of contradictions' view of the 'expert', who, as I write, is suddenly an expert of Covid-19 and vaccinations and is now an expert on European politics since the horrible and unjustifiable war on Ukraine by the bunker aggressor Putin of Russia. You get my point.

Let's get to work then to consider just one aspect of how things really are, or in reality, the lie of the enemy who seeks to devour us. Science shows that all matter that exists, and time itself, and even space come from the same source. Today many in the scientific community believe that the universe started with a massive explosion of energy – it is now commonly referred to as the 'big bang'. This singular event started everything, the beginning of the beginning of space and time. So, something outside of space and time caused everything. The existence of everything comes from this cause. So far so good, we are still all on the same planet, I mean page. It does make sense. So what scientists are saying is that our universe started, and it was not always there. It was brought into existence. On the BBC recently the news reporter referred to the big bang 'fact'. It's taken as a fact now.

This belief came from studies in the late 1920s where galaxies were seen to be hurtling away from each other at phenomenal speeds. Something was causing this – some massive force. Edwin Hubble surmised that this was the direct result of a big bang that started the universe and so it is believed to be the evidence of that primaeval explosion from a single point of origin that filled the darkness with light, and the Universe is still expanding as a result. It all began at a moment, in one hundredth of a second and at temperatures much hotter than our hottest stars, the universe came to be, came into existence, and light filled the utter dark. There was darkness and then there was light.

Would the boy at the plough be out of place now reading 'In

the beginning, God created the heavens and the earth' (Genesis 1.1.)?

And then the boy at the plough reads on: *'And God said, "Let there be light," and there was light. And God saw that the light was good. And God separated the light from the darkness. God called the light Day, and the darkness he called Night. And there was evening and there was morning, the first day'* (Genesis 1.3-5).

The Bible in the hand of the plough boy is the only sacred text of all major religions that simply describes so vividly and accurately what scientists have only lately discovered – there was an explosion of light and a beginning to our universe from outside of the universe itself. And you can't bring in the laws of physics here because they did not exist then. Everything began without them. The universe actually produced the laws of physics.

So there was a singular start to the universe and everything in it with an 'almighty' burst of light', and even atheists and agnostics are on record that *'This cosmic explosion was literally the moment of creation.'* And then they go further and tell us, with all their enthusiasm about the beginning and how it began, *'The universe flashed into being and we cannot find out what caused it to happen.'* This conclusion does not sit comfortably with those in the atheistic scientific community because to observe a reaction and not be able to document a cause is terribly unsettling, to say the least.

One writer concludes, *'For the scientist who has lived by his faith in the power of reason, the story ends like a bad dream. He has scaled the mountains of ignorance; he is about to conquer the highest peak; as he pulls himself over the final rock, he is greeted by a band of theologians who have been sitting there for centuries',* and plough boys too, may I add.

Undaunted with the evidence, and to leave God out of the

picture, rather I should say, the universe, other's ideas and postulations were proposed to trump the notion of God the Creator. So the notion was to advance the theory of the 'steady state' universe. This means that the universe is infinite in age and therefore no creation was required. Good, that's God sorted out once and for all. It's all infinite and that's how everything came to be and continues to expand. Unfortunately, the idea had some serious flaws and was in fact disproved by science.

The theory of steady state hit the wall because it was discovered in the 1960s that radiation had not always existed but came from one singular source, the original moment of creation. In 1996 NASA's Cosmic background explorer confirmed this too. The levels of hydrogen, lithium, deuterium, and helium that exist in the universe today confirm this as well; a single source at a single moment. And so, the implications of the theory of the big bang are momentous. You either go for an unknown cause or you accept the conclusion that God is the cause. Even such a position has to allow at least the idea of the possibility of God; even for the most hardened anti-God-minded individual.

Remember our friend Stenger who in his quote about the 'multiverse' said, *'Surely, then, it is ludicrous to think that humanity ... is the special creation of a divinity that presides over this vast reality.'*

Well, he takes the view that the universe may be uncaused and may have emerged from nothing. You can't make this stuff up. Others have said, well the universe is here, that's all. However, as Marliyn Adamson, the former ardent atheist, said:

It is one thing to state that something is eternal, and therefore no 'cause' is necessary. But it is entirely different to scientifically observe the start of something, the instantaneous beginning of something, and then try to say that it had no cause.

Marilyn goes on to state:

Pure scientific findings consistently point to only one conclusion: the universe had a singular start, an explosion, where everything we know – the universe, time, space, scientific laws we observe – all had a beginning. If you have ever wanted to believe in God, but certainly did not want to do so in contradiction of known scientific facts, science provides you reason to believe that God exists and powerfully created all things.

The Bible says: *'Lift your eyes and look to the heavens: Who created all these? Do you not know? Have you not heard? The Lord is the everlasting God, the Creator of the ends of the earth ...* (Isaiah 40), *'for he commanded and they were created'* (Psalm 148.5).

Here is our hope – our Hope is God and in God, our Creator, our Maker. You can know the Author of the universe, He wants us to have a relationship with Him. He tells us in His Word. If we seek to know him, God says, *'I will be found by you'* (Jeremiah 29.14).

God says: *'Let not the wise man boast in his wisdom. Let not the mighty man boast in his might. Let not the rich man boast in his riches. But let him who boasts, boast in this: that he understands and knows me'* (Jeremiah 9.23,24).

Peter says: *'God opposes the proud but gives grace to the humble. So humble yourselves under the mighty power of God, and at the right time he will lift you up in honour'* (I Peter 5.5b,6).

Humble scientists, humble plough boys, humble earnest seekers, and honest doubters included, we all have an opportunity to know the God who brought about the beginning of the universe. Do we want to begin a relationship with God?

We can start today. Do we know God? Then we can deepen our relationship with Him and get into His Word and get to know Him more. Tyndale was right after all.

Solomon, that wisest of men, tells us:

He (God) *has made everything beautiful and appropriate in its time. He has also planted eternity [a sense of divine purpose] in the human heart [a mysterious longing which nothing under the sun can satisfy, except God] – yet man cannot find out what God has done (His overall plan) from the beginning to the end* (Ecclesiastes 3.11. AMP).

DAY THIRTY-FIVE

YOU AIN'T SEEN NOTHING YET!

The prism of the Word: Job 38, Isaiah 40. 10-31, and Psalm 14

Whatever you do, get to the Cross

One popular writer observes that many people live with two strong feelings – past regrets and future fears. This can lead to what one could call *'Entrapment in the prison house of regret and anxiety.'*

There are people who live with a life full of regret over things that happened in the past, or things that they intended to do in the past but never got around to doing. For some these feelings oscillate between past regret and future fears. Intense fear of the future also grips us and what is going to happen are things over which we have no control. The answer in many ways is to focus on the here and now, which is easier said than done. Many people are so caught up with either living in the past or the future that there is no room or interest or even strength to live and flourish in the now. In the therapeutic context, the therapist seeks to deploy a toolbox of skills to help the person to develop the ability to live in the here and the now.

Too much reminiscing and too much anticipation can lead to both stagnation and procrastination in the present. Such a way of living just compounds our sense of regret and anxiety. We live in a languishing state of being which is a mere existence, not a life which could be lived to fulfil its potential and flourish in the great every day of life and living.

Those who write on such important subjects and have a genuine desire to help people, often out of the depths of their own painful experiences, share important and meaningful observations and learning, having experienced the brutal anvil of suffering and pain. One key answer that they have come up with is *'choice'*. Sounds very simplistic and is again easier said than done. The argument is that we can choose to become conscious of the present and decide to live there. Thus, the first step to a peaceful life and an improved life is to choose to live in the present.

Peter would go so far with such thinking, certainly in terms of living for today. But he also has shown us that reconnection with God is the key to peace which was made possible by the blood of His Son Jesus shed on the cross for us. The work of atonement and its appropriation as we choose to follow Jesus brings us peace with God and is the foundation upon which all peace can flourish.

This is where the cross features and is pivotal to our lives on a daily basis and indeed our eternal destiny. If we are going to get anywhere in life, we need to get to the cross. Just to clarify, when we say, *'get to the cross'*, this is not a physical cross but rather it is the cross work of our Lord Jesus Christ. We need to get to the place of humility and surrender and bow before the Lord who died on that cross for us to take away our sins. We need to accept Him as our Lord and Master. Only then can we embrace, appreciate, and understand the mystery of the cross work on our behalf. Here is the beginning of hope, hope in the perfect life, the sacrificial death, and the glorious resurrection of our Lord Jesus Christ, and in His return in majesty and glory. The cross is the central event in world history. It is the most important event in the history of the universe when the incarnate God shed His blood for us. It was ratified by God the Father in the resurrection of His Son from the dead and is made known in this the day of grace by the Holy Spirit. One God in Trinity and Unity and diversity in three persons.

The cross answers and settles the regrets of the past and the fears for the future and how to live in the here and now. Here is the hope of the Gospel. *'He made peace through the blood of His cross'* (Colossians 1.20). The significance of Christ's work on the cross is that He will overthrow the damage effected by the fall for all of creation. He gives us peace with God and His peace in our hearts. The past is settled, the future is in His loving hands.

Peace I leave with you; My [perfect] peace I give to you; not as the world gives, so I give to you. Do not let your heart be troubled, nor let it be afraid. [Let My perfect peace calm you in every circumstance and give you courage and strength for every challenge (John 14.27).

The cross enables our reconciliation to God. This reconnection with God by virtue of the new birth into His family gives us the power to live for Him today in the here and now. The past has been dealt with and the future is secure, leaving us to get on with the divine art of living today in the way He intended us to live and grow daily in our relationship with Him and develop and realise our God-given potential. We can live according to His plan and purpose.

Our daily walk with God keeps us living in the present. The art of worship and prayer are essential ingredients to living in the present. Even secular writers have said to use prayer if it helps to get in tune with our inner self. We do so, but we must align with God first. This leads to an awareness of who we really are, a self-acceptance, as well as an alertness and an active state today and every day.

Such a way of being has been described as a state of *'active waiting'* and is another key component that secular writers have come up with today to help people live in the present. So we anticipate a future event but we don't down tools and spend all our time in the future, rather we are incentivised to live today in the light of that expected event. For the believer this is our confident hope. Rather than rendering us useless today, active waiting renders us powerfully present in the now because we anticipate the future; we are not overwhelmed by it or too enthralled by it to waste a precious day. We live for today, not for an empty and unfulfilling hedonism, but for a holiness and a wholeness designed and intended for us as set out in the Divine Hope manual, the Bible.

We are all aware of the term 'absenteeism.' Employers have absentee policies in place for their employees. One of the main reasons for absenteeism from work is mental health related problems. In the mental health arena, another term came into vogue some time ago to describe people who were at work but who in reality are not fit to be there. People who perhaps are suffering such psychological unwellness with unhealthy stress and anxiety so that they are unable to fulfil their role. The word is 'presentism.'

The word is used in other contexts too but in mental health it basically means reduced productivity when employees come to the workplace and are not able to fully engage or perform their tasks, or do so at lower levels as a result of ill health. The inference we can draw here is how many of us are suffering from presentism in life itself? The Bible and God's way of living give us the blueprint to our being fully present in life. Everything takes on significance every day.

'*Whatever you do, work at it with all your heart, as working for the Lord, not for human masters, since you know that you will receive an inheritance from the Lord as a reward. It is the Lord Christ you are serving*' (Colossians 3.23).

The amplified version puts it this way:

Whatever you do [whatever your task may be], work from the soul [that is, put in your very best effort], as [something done] for the Lord and not for men, knowing [with all certainty] that it is from the Lord [not from men] that you will receive the inheritance which is your [greatest] reward. It is the Lord Christ whom you [actually] serve.

This is what Jesus meant when He told His followers to be actively waiting for the return of their Master. The servant will wait actively because he or she does not know when the Master will return. The servant is not focused on the past, nor are they too busy overthinking the future. Yes, acutely aware. but living today in the awareness of the future and incentivised and empowered to live for today.

My boys are very competitive. One is into competing in Ironman events, the other into running in athletics which includes park runs and half marathons. Their chosen activities mean that they are active in the present. They engage in active waiting but that does not mean 'standing still'. Every day, without fail, they are engaged in some form of physical activity – running, swimming, cycling. There is an eye on the past in terms of times to beat and PBs, and there is an eye on the future in relation to the next big event coming up; but they are fully engaged in the here and now, and living each day with a structure and daily goals. How much more, then, is there the need for us to be actively present in the present and be fully engaged in the activities of the day, with an eye on the future goals?

One could argue that our achievements can only happen if we make the choice to be actively present each day and not live in the future or the past. One cannot help notice that for some superstars and celebrities there is a plethora of photos and references to past glories, when the band made albums decades ago, or when they made it big on the screen or the music charts. Obviously, there is a marketing ploy and introducing new audiences to some great stuff of which they would not be aware otherwise. The country that won the world cup on the football field twenty years ago would prefer to win it in the next world event. Past glories are great and great expectations for the future are admirable. We all have our dreams, but we need to live for today and in today.

As for my sons, the next competition in the future, whether it be a race or an Ironman competition, the big achievement can happen on that day, by being present on that day, but it is as much as being present today. Yes, the big achievement can only happen on that day, but it can also be a huge success because they took cognizance of the past and of the future but refused to live in both of them. They learned to live in the present. Jesus, the greatest Teacher of all, said:

That is why I tell you not to worry about everyday life – whether you have enough food and drink, or enough clothes to wear. Isn't life more than food, and your body more than clothing? Look at the birds. They don't plant or harvest or store food in barns, for your heavenly Father feeds them. And aren't you far more valuable to him than they are? Can all your worries add a single moment to your life? And why worry about your clothing? Look at the lilies of the field and how they grow. They don't work or make their clothing, yet Solomon in all his glory was not dressed as beautifully as they are. And if God cares so wonderfully for wildflowers that are here today and thrown into the fire tomorrow, he will certainly care for you. Why do you have so little faith? So don't worry about these things, saying, 'What will we eat? What will we drink? What will we wear?' These things dominate the thoughts of unbelievers, but your heavenly Father already knows all your needs. Seek the Kingdom of God above all else, and live righteously, and he will give you everything you need. So don't worry about tomorrow, for tomorrow will bring its own worries. Today's trouble is enough for today.

Notice the need to live for today and to live righteously and to seek the Kingdom of God first. You ain't seen nothing yet! By living in the present, you can focus on the now and this is where phenomenal achievements happen and, as to the future, there are eternal consequences and future rewards are possible and an inheritance is reserved in heaven for us. Find the right path today and walk it daily and do what He has called you to do.

If you are struggling over failure and finding it hard to get going again, take heart from what Jesus said to the Disciples. They had all failed, each and every one of them, they had run away when the going got tough. For some reason, we only remember Peter's failure, but they all scarpered when Jesus was arrested. Then they were hiding away for fear of what was going to happen. Huddled together. We are told that *'The doors were shut where the disciples were assembled, for fear of the Jews'* but Jesus turned up and said, *'Peace be with you.'* And then we read: *'Again Jesus said, "Peace be with you! As the Father has sent me, I am sending you."'* (John 20,21).

He was actively present with them, and He gave them His peace and He gave them a new mission. It's a new day, it's a new mission and boy did they take on the mission. You only have to read the book of the Acts to see that they seized the day. Carpe diem! So can we.

You ain't seen nothing yet. You will find the following in the meditation for today.

What a God we have! And how fortunate we are to have him, this Father of our Master Jesus! Because Jesus was raised from the dead, we've been given a brand-new life and have everything to live for, including a future in heaven – and the future starts now! God is keeping careful watch over us and the future. The Day is coming when you'll have it all – life healed and whole (1 Peter 1.3-5).

You ain't seen nothing yet in terms of what God has prepared for us in Heaven. *'But as it is written: "Eye has not seen, nor ear heard, nor have entered into the heart of man, the things which God has prepared for those who love Him."'* (1 Corinthians 2.9).

DAY THIRTY-SIX

MORE STARS THAN GRAINS OF SAND

The prism of the Word: The Message Bible Paraphrase, 1 Peter 1.3-5, 6-7, 13-16, 18-21, 2.11-12, 4.3-5, 7-11, 5.4, and 8-11.

Hope and just one grain

It's a cliché which has become very popular. It was Carl Sagan who wrote in his book on the Cosmos: *'There are more stars in the universe than all the sand grains on Earth.'*

This became a great way of trying to describe the enormity of space and its numerous stars. It's a great image to demonstrate the vast number of stars and the utter magnitude of the universe. One researcher, who was sceptical of this comparison, decided to try and calculate the number of grains of sand in the world. Using a reversed telescope eyepiece, he counted the number of grains of sand in a cubic centimetre; that's a sugar cube's volume of beach. Then he multiplied this number by the total number of cubic centimetres of beaches on earth. How he did that, the mind boggles, but good on him. He eventually did it and he got a very big surprise.

Astronomers had found a way to estimate the number of stars in the universe and so to calculate the number of stars he considered the number of known galaxies in the observable universe, which is now estimated at around 2 trillion. That's approximately 2,000,000,000,000 galaxies in the universe. Astronomers have also calculated that the number of stars in the Milky way is 100 billion stars, that is 100,000,000,000.

And so, taking into account the sizes of the galaxies compared to our galaxy, which is bigger than most, he used the figure of 100 billion stars for each galaxy. So, all the galaxies that exist in the universe are taken into consideration and they come in all shapes and sizes. Our Milky Way galaxy is a spiral shape, while others are elliptical, or egg-shaped, and many are irregular with a whole variety of shapes.

Using the Milky Way as the model, the number of stars was multiplied by the number of stars in a typical galaxy (100 billion) by the number of galaxies in the universe (2 trillion). The answer is an absolutely astounding number and totally beyond our comprehension. There are approximately 200 billion trillion stars in the universe. Or, to put it another way, 200 sextillion. That's 200,000,000,000,000,000,000,000!

Beginning to get the picture? He got a big surprise indeed. The numbers pretty much matched. There are, with the knowledge we have presently, about the same number of stars in the observable universe as there are sand grains in all of Earth's beaches.

To take it a step further, notice that the number of stars is calculated on the basis of the observable universe and not the actual universe since it is not possible to begin to tackle that part of the universe which is farther than the distance light has had time to travel across space and because we cannot see it we have no idea what's there. So it's limited to the cosmos within view. Next time you walk along the beach in your bare feet, remember the awesomeness of what is above you.

Mark Twain, in *Huckleberry Finn*, wrote, 'We had the sky, up

there, all speckled with stars, and we used to lay on our backs
and look up at them, and discuss whether they was made, or
only just happened.'

You may be thinking well, what have all these mind-boggling
numbers got to do with hope? Is it a hope of being temporary
residents here and moving onwards and upwards in one of Elon
Musk's space rockets to a home on another planet? Well
actually it's even more exciting than that and Jesus, as Son of
Man on earth, did speak of the stars. God also spoke of the stars
in the Old Testament, as did the ancient writers and poets. You
can find out more in the meditation 'prism of the word' for
today. Here are some quotations from the hope manual to give
us something to think about.

'And when you look up to the sky and see the sun, the moon,
and the stars – all the heavenly array – do not be enticed into
bowing down to them and worshipping things the LORD your
God has apportioned to all the nations under heaven'
(Deuteronomy 4.19).

'Lift up your eyes and look to the heavens: Who created all
these? He who brings out the starry host one by one and calls
forth each of them by name. Because of his great power and
mighty strength, not one of them is missing' (Isaiah 40.26).

'When I consider your heavens, the work of your fingers, the
moon and the stars, which you have set in place' (Psalm 8.3).

'The heavens declare the glory of God; the skies proclaim the
work of his hands' (Psalm 19.1).

'He determines the number of the stars and calls them each
by name' (Psalm 147.4).

I wonder if Carl Sagan had come across the promise God
gave to Abraham. Notice what it says in the book of origins,
Genesis. 'I will surely bless you and make your descendants as

numerous as the stars in the sky and as the sand on the seashore. Your descendants will take possession of the cities of their enemies' (Genesis 22.17).

The imagery was to emphasise how the nation would flourish and multiply and never be annihilated, even though despots over the centuries have tried to do so. Hitler tried too and looked at what happened to him. Jesus spoke of another grain. Not a grain of sand or a grain in comparison to a star, but of a grain of mustard seed. Just one grain. In fact, the grain of mustard seed is in effect a picture of hope. A grain of mustard seed is only 2mm but it can grow into a bush of upward 30 feet. In just one grain of mustard seed there is the potential for a miracle to happen, the miracle of growth and development and expansion and a flourishing life.

The grain of mustard seed is a symbol of faith. Our faith does not have to be some big thing, but rather just one little grain and from there great things can happen and great hope can spring forth. Hope can be born and grown and it's so great it can even move mountains. Everyone who encounters the vast universe, whether it is to look up on a clear night and see thousands of stars or go to an observatory and see the wonders of it all, we all must come to the place of decision. In any critical observation and analysis and understanding of it all, we must at the very least consider the possibility of God. Just to have one speck of faith is all that is needed.

This is what Jesus said, *'Truly I tell you, if you have faith as small as a mustard seed, you can say to this mountain, "Move from here to there", and it will move. Nothing will be impossible for you'* (Matthew 17.20).

One grain of mustard seed, a speck of faith can remove all

those mountains of defiance and doubt and resistance to the knowledge of God as the Creator, Sustainer, Saviour, and Lord over all. Yes, from one speck of faith can grow a personal relationship with the God who made it all and who came to earth as Emmanuel to live and die here and to rise from the dead. He came to the one and only habitable planet in the universe to die on a tree he had made, and He is coming back again to fold it all up and to make a new heaven and a new earth because this one is wearing out.

Look at it all – it's awesome – then look to Him, He is even more awesome. And with a grain of mustard seed faith, you can begin your journey to knowing God today. If you are on the journey, or if you have lost your way, or even lost your faith, it's time to bow the knee to Him now, as will all humanity on the last day.

Get into the Bible. Read through 1 Peter again. Notice how many times he talks about temporary residency here. God gives us eternal life above and beyond the stars, but it starts now, and we live in the power of His life today on earth with purpose, pleasing Him and knowing Him. Don't miss out. Allow that mustard seed of faith, that speck of faith to blossom and you will have a hope in your heart and an assurance and a peace in your soul that nothing can disturb. The universe is awesome, but God is infinitely awesome and yet He has all the time in the world for us because He loves us more than we can ever comprehend (John 3.16).

DAY THIRTY-SEVEN

MISSION IMPOSSIBLE?

The prism of the Word: Job 38.4-30

The Apollo 13 rescue mission and the 'lifeboat'

The Apollo space program was geared towards getting astronauts to the moon and Apollo 11 was the first manned mission to land on Earth's only natural satellite. The first steps by humans on another planetary body were taken by Neil Armstrong and Buzz Aldrin on July 20th, 1969. The moon landing was one of the biggest television events in history, reaching an estimated 650 million viewers. One remembers watching the grainy images on the TV. The broadcast from the moon was a massive technological achievement and was years in the planning; That's a story in itself. As a 12-year-old boy my mind wondered and also wandered into thinking, what if? What if they can't get off the moon? What if the spacecraft breaks down? What if something goes wrong? Can the astronauts be rescued and, if so, how? And by whom?

Then, in 1970, the Apollo 13 Spacecraft got into serious trouble after a smooth launch on its journey to land on the moon. Tom Hanks played the part of the Commander in the 1995 film *Apollo 13*. The real-life characters were, Commander Jim Lovell, 42, his lunar module pilot, Fred Haise, 36, and the commander module pilot, Jack Swigert, 38. They were settling down for the night after a televised broadcast when there was a sharp bang. The warning light came on, and those famous words that no one ever wanted to hear were uttered, *'Houston, we have a problem.'*

The problem turned out to be a major and potentially devastating one; they were losing oxygen into space. One of the tanks of oxygen had exploded. This was serious and if something was not done, it would be fatal. To make matters worse, the oxygen was not only needed for breathing but also to power the fuel cells that generated water and power for the spacecraft. The command module, where the crew lived, was quickly losing power. The situation looked hopeless.

The mission to the moon was aborted and the rescue had begun to get them home safe. NASA's top people were called in. Quick thinking was needed, and the only option was to move the crew to the lunar module which was designed to land on the moon. This became their 'lifeboat' in space to get them home safely. The lifeboat gave them hope; indeed, it was their only hope, otherwise they would be destined to be lost in space forever. The perilous journey involved many major obstacles, including the build-up of carbon dioxide and the fact that there was only enough oxygen for two people, not three. Also, it was designed for 48 hours on the moon's surface, not 90 hours to get them home. Given that the craft was on course to the moon, they had to get the lunar module on a free return on an earth trajectory to re-enter the earth's atmosphere, and then land in the Pacific Ocean.

The trip was a gruesome one with most electrical systems cut, including heating, to conserve power. Makeshift materials were used to get rid of the carbon dioxide whilst warning lights were going off. The crew could not sleep and there was very little water and little food. The temperature was low, and one side of the spacecraft was missing. But they clung on to hope.

All the while Mission Control was there to guide, advise, support, and care. The entry into earth's atmosphere was successful and, as they were about to splash down in the South Pacific Ocean, the crew moved back into the command module. The lunar module was then shed from the command module, the parachutes opened, and they splashed down safely after 142 hours of voyage time. It was nothing short of miraculous that they made it home safe.

The 'lifeboat' had been successful. It looked like mission impossible, but they made it and one of the astronauts was pictured a couple of days later holding a newspaper with the headline, 'Astronauts Safe.'

The Space Shuttle took over from Apollo and the primary role was to complete the assembly of the International Space Station (ISS). Plans were drawn up in the event that a rescue mission might be needed to bring back stranded astronauts and this embedded hope and confidence into all missions. These missions were designated STS-3xx, officially called Launch On Need (LON) missions. They were the pre-planned rescue missions which would be mounted to rescue the crew of a Space Shuttle if their vehicle was damaged and deemed unable to make a successful re-entry to Earth.

Coming back down to earth, so to speak, we all are acutely aware that something has gone badly wrong with the world we live in. Given the state it is in today, and the pervasive hopelessness that envelops the globe, oh how humanity needs a rescue remedy – a lifeboat big enough for us all. Man's ingenuity is such that all sorts of ideas are being floated to rescue mankind from impending disasters. The belief in the perils of climate change, as well as the imminent danger of nuclear war, are at the top of the pile of worries; throw into the mix food shortages, the cost-of-living crisis, the fear of further epidemics, and rumours of more wars, the need for real hope has never been greater. Some have even proposed setting up a colony on Mars so that the human race could survive, if and when this planet either implodes or is destroyed by mankind itself with the big boy toys of mass destruction.

The fact is we need a sure and steadfast hope. And so, we are reminded again from Peter that God is our only hope and he gives us a living and eternal hope if we put our trust in Him. The only real way to live confidently and expectantly in this world is to have a hope that not only transcends our problems, but gives us strength and vitality for living and making a positive impact for good in a world of so much evil.

The biblical analysis of humanity explains that the root cause of the problems in the world is sin. Sin is a dominant theme from the first book of the Bible (Genesis chapter three) to the last book (Revelation). The word *sin* is found throughout the Bible, and both the Hebrew and Greek languages share the same basic meaning. The Hebrew word חָטָא *(chata)* means 'to miss the target', or 'to lose the way', and the Greek ἁμαρτάνω *(hamartano)* means 'to miss the mark', 'err', or 'do wrong'.

Sin is when we transgress God's law and depart from His intended path. The apostle John tells us that *'Everyone who practices sin also practices lawlessness; and sin is lawlessness'* (1 John 3.4). The underlying idea of sin is that of law and of a lawgiver. The lawgiver is God. Hence sin is everything in the disposition, purpose, and conduct of God's moral creatures that is contrary to the expressed will of God (Romans 3.20; 4.15; 7.7; James 4.12, 17).

This sin problem impacts every aspect of life. We see the

breakdown of family life. Civic society is deeply impacted, and societal structures are being eroded and broken down. The defiance of authority and disrespect and contempt for law and order is rampant in every corner of the globe. The world of economics is also impacted by greed and the insatiable desire for more money and wealth. Politics too has been corrupted. The science field and the sphere of education has not escaped the attention of sin either. One of the major areas sin impacts us is in the mind, which theologians refer to as the *'noetic effects'* of sin. This means sin impacts our ability to think rationally, especially about God, who has made Himself known through general revelation (Psalm 19.1-2; Romans 1.18-20) and special revelation (1 Corinthians 14.37; 1 Timothy 5.18; 1 Thessalonians 2.13; 2 Timothy 3.16-17)

The destruction of nature and our natural resources is clear for all to see, and climate change is a major talking point on every continent. All sin and evil exist in connection with the wilful humans who manufacture it, and its effects are, more often than not, long lasting. Sin, when it is finished, brings forth death. We will all eventually run out of oxygen, so to speak, and die. If that was all we would have to say this book would be totally pointless. But there is hope and God has already provided a lifeboat.

No, He has not given instructions from space or even beyond the unobservable universe. No! He became a man. He was born into this fallen, sinful world and he came to die for us, to be our ransom from sin and death and hell. He made His home here. Then, at the age of thirty-three, He died and bore our sins in His own body on the tree. He was buried in a borrowed tomb, with a guard no less, to ensure, in the perverse thinking of the religious leaders of the day, that the disciples would not steal his body and say He has risen. On the third day, true to His word, Jesus rose again from the dead. After a number of irrefutable resurrection appearances, He then went back to Heaven. He is coming again to wrap it all up. Today, He is the lifeboat.

What if Jim or Fred or Jack had said, 'I'm not getting into the 'lifeboat', or Jim decided to try and get to the moon anyway? What if Fred decided to ask questions about the observable universe and how it got here, and Jack, well he decided to have a nap and maybe it was all a bad dream? Not on your life – they were only too glad of the lifeboat. It was their salvation. It was their redemption; it was their rescue. Perhaps this is your time to take the step of faith into God's lifeboat, His very own Son, and start living life to the full with a hope in your heart that nothing can destroy. Jesus said; *'The thief comes only in order to steal and kill and destroy. I came that they may have and enjoy life, and have it in abundance [to the full, till it overflows]'* (John 10.10).

Paul said, *'He (God) has delivered us from the domain of darkness and transferred us to the kingdom of His beloved Son'* (Colossians 1.13).

It was not some afterthought of God. The rescue was planned in eternity past. In the Bible we see God and His salvation on display. You need to step into the lifeboat today. The unfolding drama of redemption also begins in Genesis chapter three and ends by telling us that the time is coming when God will do away with sin and its effects, creating *'a new heaven and a new earth, in which righteousness dwells"* (Revelation 21.1; cp 2 Peter 3.13).

God wants us to be part of His plan and He has made a way for this to be possible and attainable in the here and now.

'We are redeemed with the precious blood of Christ, like that of a lamb without blemish or spot. He was foreknown before the

foundation of the world but was made manifest in the last times for the sake of you' (1 Peter 1.129,20).

Jerry Woodfill served as NASA spacecraft warning system engineer for Apollo 13. He is on record as saying that the spacecraft's successful return shaped more than his professional career. The event has resonated within him and shaped his view of God's role in fashioning events. His testimony is that, without divine intervention, the crew and Johnson Space Centre's mission control team could not have overcome the insurmountable obstacles they faced, and brought the astronauts home safely. Woodfill describes how the events relating to Apollo 13, and other experiences he went through not long after the space flight rescue, transformed him into a believer and he got into God's lifeboat.

In looking back on the space flight, he is on record as saying he saw the hand of God playing a role even when the explosion occurred. If the explosion had happened after the lunar lander had left the space module for the moon, the astronauts would have died because they ended up relying on the lunar lander and its power to return to earth. In his own words; *'An unrehearsed script seemed to be guiding the drama.'*

In the mysteries of life and its unpredictability, don't be unaware of the unrehearsed script guiding you to that place of faith and to this living hope which is eternal life. The phrase *'in Christ'* occurs about 180 times in the New Testament and 164 times in Paul's 13 letters. At the very end of his letter, Peter refers to the lifeboat when he says, *'Peace be with all of you who are in Christ'* (1 Peter 5.13b).

DAY THIRTY-EIGHT

TO INFINITY AND BEYOND

The prism of the Word: Ephesians Chapter 2

A real hope with endless possibilities

There is a courier van I see from time to time on my travels. The caption on the side of the van has caught my eye, and for those of us who live in Northern Ireland, it's very funny. The caption reads: *'To Finaghy and Beyond'*. Finaghy is a pleasant catchment area in South Belfast, and Captain Courier must have decided to use this catchy strapline to promote his premier business service. The captain is busy delivering all over the place, even to Finaghy and beyond. We are reminded of Buzz Lightyear's classic line, *'To infinity and beyond.'* The phase refers to infinity which, being infinite, cannot be reached. Thus, the expression has come to represent the idea of limitless possibilities.

The Bible tells us that God is infinite and yet he came to earth so He can be accessible and known, and therein lies infinite possibilities. Solomon addressed God in his prayer with the words: *'But will God really live on earth? Why, even the highest heavens cannot contain you. How much less this Temple I have built!'* (1 Kings 8.27)

David said: *'Great is our Lord, and mighty in power; His understanding is infinite'* (Psalm 147.5). Paul preached about this: *"Though I am the least deserving of all God's people, he graciously gave me the privilege of telling the Gentiles about the endless treasures available to them in Christ'* (Ephesians 3.8). Peter, the dealer in Hope, has a lot to say about the limitless blessings in the future for those who believe. Peter, in the context of hope, not only speaks of the present, i.e., we are born again to a living hope that starts here and now in the present, but also it's about the future; a future of endless possibilities with a certain hope which will blow our minds – *'eternity and beyond'*.

Peter's letter is very much in keeping with Biblical prophecy. For the uninformed, the Bible is a book about the future; it's an eschatological book. Most people don't realise that eschatology dominates and permeates the entire message of the Bible. This is one of the many facets of *'the prism of the Word'* that makes it unique. It is a book of predictive prophecy. The Old Testament provides hope for the future in the promise of the coming of the Redeemer, beginning in Genesis 3.15, and permeating the entirety of the Old Testament. You only have to read the Gospels to see how all the predictions about Jesus' first advent came true. That great eschatological event happened in the coming of Jesus in His first advent.

The blessings experienced by the Believer, exercising faith in Christ, in the present age are the pledge and guarantee of greater and infinite blessings to come when Christ returns in great power and glory, the next great eschatological event – the second advent, the return of Jesus Christ.

World events point to this and 'happenings ahead' were predicted throughout both the Old and New Testament too. When Jesus refers to Himself as 'the Son of Man,' this means much more than His identity with humanity. Tucked away in the prophecy of Daniel we find what this title really means:

In my vision at night I looked, and there before me was one like a Son of Man, coming with the clouds of heaven. He approached the Ancient of Days and was led into His presence. He was given authority, glory, and sovereign power; all nations and peoples of every language worshipped Him. His dominion is an everlasting dominion that will not pass away, and His kingdom is one that will never be destroyed (Daniel 7.13-14).

The second coming of Jesus Christ is the most important aspect of the New Testament. The emphasis is on the event, not on the time. One writer refers to the Bible as *'The sacred masterpiece.'* It was written over 1,400 years, covering 4,000 years of human history. There are some 1,239 prophecies in the Old Testament and 578 in the New Testament. 1,817 references in 18,352 verses. This predictive emphasis which permeates the entire Bible makes it unique amongst all other religious books. Almost every New Testament Book contains prophecies yet to be fulfilled.

So what does Peter have to say about the future? Well, there's quite a lot packed into his first letter. Here's what he has to say.

His readers are people of Divine destiny (1.2) with an inheritance that is imperishable, undefiled, and unfading which is reserved in Heaven (1.3-4) whilst living on earth being protected by the power of God through faith for a salvation ready to be revealed at the last time (1.5). There is going to be a big celebration of glory and honour when Jesus Christ is revealed to the whole world (1.7). Peter tells his readers to get ready and to put our hope in the gracious salvation that will come to us, and he repeats the words *'when Jesus Christ is revealed to the world'* (1.13). We are trusting in the Word of God which Peter tells us is eternal (1.23,25).

The people to whom he is writing are described as *'temporary residents and foreigners in this world'* and are to live as God would have us live. People will see our honourable behaviour, even if we are lambasted now, the day is coming when they will give God the glory when he comes to judge the world (2.11,12).

Christ is gone into heaven and is seated in the place of honour next to God, and all the angels and authorities and powers accept His authority (3.22). He will return and everyone will have to face God, who stands ready to judge the living and the dead (4.5). Then Peter says the end of the world is coming soon, the end of all things is near (4.7), so be ready. He has already said (1.20) that Christ appeared at the end of the ages – in the last days. His return is near, and it is soon. Be ready. For an explanation of the time factor, and what seems to be a delay in relation to the return of Jesus Christ, a reading of 2 Peter chapter three will explain this fully. Here is a brief quotation from the chapter: *'But do not forget this one thing, dear friends: With the Lord a day is like a thousand years, and a thousand years are like a day'* (2 Peter 3.8).

There is going to be a day of wonderful joy for the believer when He is revealed to all the world (1 Peter. 4.13). But there is a warning. What terrible fate awaits those who have never obeyed the good news? What will happen to godless sinners (4.18)? But if we trust ourselves to the God who created us, He will never fail us (4.19). Peter and those who believe in Jesus will share in His glory when He is revealed (5.1). The day is coming when the Chief will appear, the Great Shepherd. The question is, will He come back as our Saviour and Shepherd or as our Judge (5.4)? There is a crown of never-ending glory and honour to be awarded to those who honour Jesus. Then we have this awesome statement that in His kindness God has called you to share in His eternal glory by means of Jesus Christ (5.10). All power to Him for ever, Amen (5.11).

That's true hope! That's eternal hope! That's the hope that only the God of hope can give. Embrace Christ and embrace hope. Reject Christ and reject hope.

To infinity and beyond indeed! God is infinite.

'God is a spirit, infinite, eternal, and unchangeable, in his being, wisdom, power, holiness, justice, goodness, and truth. Scripture: "God is spirit, and those who worship him must worship in spirit and truth"' (John 4.24).

It has been said that our lives are but a moment in the light of eternity; but God wants the time we spend on earth to be purposeful and meaningful and lived in accordance with His divine plan. Make an impact for good and for God and then the endless possibilities of eternal life. *'For our light and momentary troubles are achieving for us an eternal glory that far outweighs them all'* (2 Corinthians 4.17).

DAY THIRTY-NINE

WHAT HAPPENED TO THE UNIVERSE?

The prism of the Word: 2 Peter chapter 3

How are you fallen from heaven?

The popular physicist Professor Brian Cox is on record stating that, as far as he is concerned, the future of the universe is only one of cessation and demise. It is indeed a bleak picture of the future from his perspective. This is one of his statements on the subject: *'The last star will slowly cool and fade away. With its passing, the universe will become once more a void, without light or life or meaning.'*

Although it's billions of years away, apparently, we need not worry too much about it. The last fading star is said to be the beginning of an infinitely long, dark epoch and all matter will eventually be consumed by monstrous black holes. Each of these in their turn will evaporate away into the dimmest glimmers of light. Space will continue its expansion ever outwards until even that dim light becomes too spread out to interact. Activity will cease. The end! Or is it?

The biblical view, as we have already seen, is a very different one. It's a positive eternal future of glory and the worship and celebration of God who made it all. But what of the universe itself? This cosmos of complexity and wonderment in which the earth is but a speck and which gives rise to all kinds of theories and speculations which are constantly changing in the light of new knowledge and information. No sooner has one theory appeared than it disappears like a shooting star and another takes its place.

Given that Peter has described the Bible as an eternal book and that God's word will endure forever, does it say anything about how it will all end? We would expect an eternal God to have an eternal infallible Word. Whilst the Bible is not a book on astrophysics or quantum mechanics, it has a lot to say throughout its pages about our world and our universe, how it all began, and what is going to happen to it. It is amazing the way we are told simply and effectively in such a succinct manner in Genesis about the beginning.

'This is the history (account) of the heavens and the earth when they were created' (Genesis 24).

A comparison with the book of Leviticus, which contains many chapters about sacrifices and offerings and the need to deal with ceremonial uncleanness to approach a holy God, goes into much greater detail about such matters, particularly about the creation of the universe. Is this not significant in itself? God was not out to prove anything to astrophysicists, or indeed any of us about creation; the evidence is more than sufficient. Yet God's primary purpose is about how we can know our Creator as our Lord, our Saviour, and Redeemer, and find our hope, our meaning, and purpose in Him. Having said that, let's think about the universe for a moment in the context of biblical revelation.

Tucked away in the great prophecy of Isaiah is a most interesting passage which sheds light on the mysteries of the universe in that something catastrophic happened in the aeons of the past. The revelation is not about a galaxy, or even a celestial star, but rather about a person. The person identified is referred to as the King of Babylon and the passage is about

God's judgement on Babylon. However, the king is unnamed, and no such individual known in the history of our world fits his description. Some commentators have referred to him as the King of the Underworld. The words are quite astounding.

How you are fallen from heaven,
O shining star, son of the morning!
You have been thrown down to the earth,
you who destroyed the nations of the world.
For you said to yourself,
I will ascend to heaven and set my throne above God's stars.
I will preside on the mountain of the congregation
far away in the north.
I will climb to the highest heavens
and be like the Most High.'
Instead, you will be brought down to the place of the dead,
down to its lowest depths.
Everyone there will stare at you and ask,
'Can this be the one who shook the earth
and made the kingdoms of the world tremble?
Is this the one who destroyed the world
and made it into a wasteland?
Is this the king who demolished the world's greatest cities
and had no mercy on his prisoners?' (Isaiah 1411-17)

Who is this shining star, the son of the morning who, with such pride in his own being, desired to arise about the stars of God and be like the Most High? Here we have the sin of pride!

'I will ascend, I will preside, I will climb, I will be like ...'

Jesus in Luke 10.18 refers to the identity of the person in Isaiah 14 when He said, *'I saw Satan fall from heaven like lightning'.*

Let's then look at another Old Testament passage, this time in Ezekiel chapter 28. Here we have a reference to the 'prince of Tyre'. He is the leader or ruler who is judged for his sin of pride, which is a universal offence. The judgement upon the prince of Tyre represents the judgement of God against a being that is not human, rather a celestial being. In fact, he is described as the 'anointed cherub'.

Then this further message came to me from the Lord:
'Son of man, sing this funeral song for the king of Tyre.
Give him this message from the Sovereign Lord:
"You were the model of perfection,
full of wisdom and exquisite in beauty.
You were in Eden,
the garden of God.
Your clothing was adorned with every precious stone—
red carnelian, pale-green peridot, white moonstone,
blue-green beryl, onyx, green jasper,
blue lapis lazuli, turquoise, and emerald—
all beautifully crafted for you
and set in the finest gold.
They were given to you
on the day you were created.
I ordained and anointed you (anointed cherub)
as the mighty angelic guardian.
You had access to the holy mountain of God
and walked among the stones of fire.
You were blameless in all you did
from the day you were created
until the day evil was found in you.

Your rich commerce led you to violence,
and you sinned.
So I banished you in disgrace
from the mountain of God.
I expelled you, O mighty guardian,
from your place among the stones of fire.
Your heart was filled with pride
because of all your beauty.
Your wisdom was corrupted
by your love of splendour.
So I threw you to the ground
and exposed you to the curious gaze of kings.
You defiled your sanctuaries
with your many sins and your dishonest trade.
So I brought fire out from within you,
and it consumed you.
I reduced you to ashes on the ground
in the sight of all who were watching.
All who knew you are appalled at your fate.
You have come to a terrible end,
and you will exist no more"' (Ezekiel 28.11-19).

Here we have more information about this proud celestial being. In his original state he was a magnificent resplendent being, created by God, and who is positioned in the hierarchy of angels, and he had what seems to be a significant, if not a preeminent place, in God's heavenly household. And given that he was located in Eden, the garden of God, was this not earth?

What we do know is that his heart was filled with pride because of all his beauty and his wisdom became corrupted, and God expelled him from the holy mountain of God and threw him to the ground. We don't have all the answers but what we do know is that this was the moment that sin entered into the universe, into our cosmos. A perfect universe created by God became contaminated with sin and became defective in some way. Is this what sent the universe into chaos? What we do know is that something happened at that moment when sin entered the universe.

Did God leave this creature in this state of chaos for a very long time, perhaps millions or even billions of years? What we have read in Isaiah and Ezekiel does predate Genesis. When we open the first page of the Bible we read: *'In the beginning God created the heavens and the earth'* (Genesis 1.1).

Then we read: *'The earth was formless and void or a waste and emptiness, and darkness was upon the face of the deep [primaeval ocean that covered the unformed earth]. The Spirit of God was moving [hovering, brooding] over the face of the waters'* (Genesis 1.2).

It seems to the author that there is a world (pardon the pun) of difference between verse 1 and verse 2. The earth was a waste, it was emptiness and there was darkness. And out of the chaos we are told the Spirit of God was moving upon the waters and God made the world into a habitable place for mankind whom He created from one man and one woman, having set the earth strategically in a solar system that ensured both its safety in the vast universe, and those who live on planet earth.

It was a perfect world for mankind. And God created them with a free will to choose the right and reject the wrong. For mankind there was one will, God's will, and they lived in perfection and harmony in relationship with God. But there were two wills in the universe, God's and Satan's. Man, through the sin of pride, decided to ignore the rules set down by God;

the fall of mankind took place and now today there are billions of wills in the universe. And sin came into the world and the evidence for it is death. Perhaps Satan thought that man would worship him, but no, everyone has gone their own way. So, sin entered the perfect world that God had made, and sin led to death, spiritual and physical death.

But in Genesis 3.15 God gave humanity hope, the hope of a Redeemer who would redeem us, but also redeem the world and the universe from sin. God addresses Satan with these words, and herein is the fountain of all biblical prophecy, centred on the seed of the woman, our Lord Jesus Christ, our Redeemer and the Redeemer of the universe. *'And I will put enmity [open hostility] between you and the woman, and between your seed (offspring) and her seed; He shall [fatally] bruise your head, and you shall [only] bruise His heel'* (Genesis 3.15).

Hold on to your hat, there's more about hope tomorrow and there is hope for your tomorrow too.

DAY FORTY

WHAT WILL HAPPEN TO THE UNIVERSE?

The prism of the Word: Isaiah 14, Ezekiel 28, Genesis 1.1,2,
and Genesis 3.15.

Behold, I make all things new

Given that this deadly destructive force called sin has in some way affected the entire universe and everything in it, what is going to happen to it? We have already touched on the notion put forward by some experts that the force of the rapidly expanding universe will lead to its eventual ending and the cessation of everything. Some estimates are that the universe is expanding at 1.7 times the speed of light and that this will lead to its eventual collapse and cosmic death and then perhaps a rebirth of some kind.

The experts tell us that the best evidence points to what is termed 'the big freeze', brought about by 'heat' death, in about twenty-two billion years' time. The universe will drift apart, star formation will cease, the skies will be black with stars fizzling out and all lingering matter gobbled up by black holes. This has been described as the universe's distant Armageddon.

Yet about a century ago it was believed that the Milky Way was the entire universe and was static; that's until Albert Einstein came along and postulated the notion of a universe in motion. One does admire those who dedicate their lives to seeking to know more about our universe. But now we must change tack. Even if one disagrees with people, one must respect those of integrity and honest seekers who really want to understand. Unfortunately, the enemy seeks to permeate all honest endeavours and sincere seeking and searching with the dust of what one could describe as an *'anti-God matter.'*

If we believe the universe had a beginning and is the work of a designer, an architect, a creator, God the Creator, then we would expect Him to have a plan about its shelf life, bookended by eternity past and eternity future. The Biblical emphasis is about a covenant relationship with God, and we are to worship our Creator. For example, we are exhorted in Psalm 95 to do just that.

O come, let us worship and bow down,
Let us kneel before the Lord, our Maker!
For he is our God
and we are the people of his pasture,
and the sheep of his hand.
O that today you would listen to his voice! (Psalm 95,6,7).

Given that it is an everlasting covenant, then we would expect God to have a failsafe plan for the future of His people, the world where we live, the universe, and heaven itself where God rules, reigns, and draws the redeemed to His nearer presence when physical life has come to an end on planet earth.

So if God made it all, and sin entered it all, and He came to earth to deal with it all and to redeem mankind on a cross, then are there any implications for the actual planet we call earth and for the universe itself? Does the Bible have anything to say about the end of the world and/ or the entire universe? And if so, what will happen to it all?

These are big questions and, for the sceptic, given the dates of the Bible books, how could they tell us anything of note or substance, or indeed of any accuracy as to its ending? Yet to believe that God is the Creator and that He gave us His Word, written down by men, who in fact were inspired by God Himself, then given it's God's Word, it carries infinite weight and absolute authority. Let's check it out. Where do we begin?

The Bible contains what we know as apocalyptic literature both in the Old Testament and in the New Testament. We tend to think of the book of Revelation, which is called the Apocalypse. We are thinking here though of what the Bible says about the cosmic apocalypse. The outcome of the cosmic apocalypse is not cosmic collapse, it is not total destruction but rather rebirth and renewal. Yes, the Bible tells us that the world will come to an end, but it will come to an end at God's bidding. And herein is the cosmic apocalyptic hope. There is going to be a new heaven and new earth. Jesus told us there would be renewal and rebirth.

There are so many references we could turn to, but we are going to look at several specific references that tell us what is going to happen in the future.

It's all wearing out! The world and the universe are all wearing out, it's all getting older.

'We know that the whole creation has been groaning as in the pains of childbirth right up to the present time' (Romans 8.22).

This is explained to us in Romans 8.18-30. And yet this passage is not about gloom and doom, rather it's about future glory and is brimming with hope. Even though the universe is wearing out, the future is full of hope. In fact, we are told that *'All creation is waiting for the future day'* (8.18).

The whole creation is waiting in great expectation of being made new. The whole universe is going to be reborn. The One who made it will make it new. This is almost 'by-the-way' because the focus is people, God's people, who have been reborn and have a future hope and the whole creation waits for the Lord from heaven to be revealed. So, for the universe and for the people who live in the world, there is the need for new birth. Sin and death will not win. God will rebirth the universe. And He is rebirthing people today – born again into a living hope.

The resurrection of Jesus is the guarantee that this is going to actually happen. That's exactly what Peter tells us in 1 Peter 1,3. We have been born again to a living hope *'because God raised Jesus Christ from the dead.'*

Then we have one of the most telling and revealing statements in the Bible about the universe, what happened to it and what will happen to it. *'Against its will, all creation was subjected to God's curse. But with eager hope, the creation looks forward to the day when it will join God's children in glorious freedom from death and decay'* (Romans 8.2-21).

We have already noted on a previous day that sin entered the universe. So, this amazing universe, in all its wonderment, has actually lost its former glory. The passage goes on to say:

For we know that all creation has been groaning as in the pains of childbirth right up to the present time. And we believers also groan, even though we have the Holy Spirit within us as a foretaste of future glory, for we long for our bodies to be released from sin and suffering. We, too, wait with eager hope for the day when God will give us our full rights as his adopted children, including the new bodies he has promised us. We were given this hope when we were saved. (If we already have something, we don't need to hope for it. But if we look forward to something we don't yet have, we must wait patiently and confidently) (Romans 8.22-25).

Death is not the final word for the earth's faith residents, nor is it for the world and the universe. God is on a mission to remove sin, evil, decay, and death and that mission will succeed; we already see it in the resurrection of Jesus from the dead. This was the day that changed everything, and God's redemptive history of everything is seen in the life and the death and the resurrection of His son, Our Lord and Saviour Jesus Christ.

This brings us to our penultimate passage for our fortieth day of exploration, Hebrews chapter 1. This passage tells us that God has, in these final days, spoken to us through His Son. To hear what God is saying today, we need to look to the Son in these final days. This terminology does not pose a problem at all when we read on and take this in its context. The writer goes on to tell us that God has promised everything to the Son as an inheritance. And here the universe is introduced.

'And through the Son He created the universe' (Hebrews 1.3.)

We are given glimpses into the mysteries of the Godhead with the Son being described as radiating God's own glory and expressing the character of God in His equality and deity and *'He sustains everything by the mighty power of His command'* (1.3).

The writer goes on to give more glimpses into the interpersonal relationship between God the Father and God the Son before coming back to the earth and the universe. The emphasis is on the eternal immutability of the Son, and this is what we read;

He (God the Father) also says to the Son,
"In the beginning, Lord, you laid the foundation of the earth
and made the heavens with your hands.
They will perish, but you remain forever.

They will wear out like old clothing
You will fold them up like a cloak
and discard them like old clothing.
But you are always the same;
you will live forever."
The text is a quote from Psalm 45.6-7.

There is so much more to say. Why not look up more references and find out more from the Bible and ask God for a greater understanding of truth.

When we come to the book of revelation we read:

Then I saw a new heaven and a new earth, for the old heaven and the old earth had disappeared ... He will wipe every tear from their eyes, and there will be no more death or sorrow or crying or pain. All these things are gone forever. And the one sitting on the throne said, "Look, I am making everything new!" And then he said to me, "Write this down, for what I tell you is trustworthy and true" (Revelation 21.1,4,5).

So here we have the truth of God's revelation; there is going to be a new heaven and a new earth. God is redeeming a people in the world to be ready to enjoy the next; where there will again be only one will in the universe, the perfect will of God, and there will be perfect harmony and peace and unity.

We have travelled for 40 days on this journey of exploration on hope – we have considered biblical hope. The Bible is the must-have hope manual and is brimming with the hope factor. Here are some examples.

'This hope will not lead to disappointment' (Romans 5.5).

'"For I know the plans I have for you," declares the LORD, "plans to prosper you and not to harm you, plans to give you hope and a future"' (Jeremiah 29.11).

'May the God of hope fill you with all joy and peace in believing [through the experience of your faith] that by the power of the Holy Spirit you will abound in hope and overflow with confidence in His promises' (Romans 15.13).

'For whatever was written in earlier times was written for our instruction, so that through endurance and the encouragement of the Scriptures we might have hope and overflow with confidence in His promises' (Romans 15.4).

'And now, Lord, for what do I expectantly wait? My hope [my confident expectation] is in You' (Psalm 39.7).

Billy Graham said, 'Man is a moral failure; God is our only hope.'

The author Rick Warren said, 'Without the grace of Jesus: A hopeless end. With the grace of Jesus: An endless hope.'

Author Tracie Petterson said, 'Our hope doesn't come from within – not in the sense of self anyway. It comes from God alone. If not, then it will crumble and blow as dust to the wind. You only have to fix your sights on Jesus."

Hope is found in a person, Jesus Christ. His Name is synonymous with hope. For us there is no other source of hope. He came to seek and to save that which was lost. He came to suffer, bleed, and die for us and forgive us as we repent. He came to rescue and restore. He came to call, draw, and love those who without his grace would continue to live for themselves. He came, and because he did, there is hope that sinners can be redeemed, and the world can be renewed. It really is true: hope is a person, and his name is Jesus.

Before Jesus went to the cross to do what he came to do, he detailed for his followers why he is the only hope for sinners. He made his identity and mission clear with these words: 'I am the way, and the truth, and the life. No one comes to the Father *except through me'* (John 14.6).

In these brief words, Jesus clearly explains why He is humanity's one and only hope. Notice the three reasons given by Jesus as to why He is humanity's only hope; why He alone is our only hope.

Firstly, He is the only way to God. Only he could bridge the great gulf between us and God. Secondly, He is the truth from God. He didn't just communicate God's truth; he is God's truth. He has not only revealed God's redemptive plan for us, He Himself is the Redeemer, the Saviour of the world. And thirdly, Jesus is the life. He does not only provide life, He is life, and He gives us life. He came as life to defeat the power of death and ignite eternal life in the hearts of his redeemed children.

Paul David Tripp says, *'Hope in the here and now and hope in the great forever that is to come rests on one set of shoulders. It rests on the almighty shoulders of Jesus, who is for you today the Way, the Truth, and the Life. He offers you what you have no power to provide for yourself: restored relationship with God, a knowledge of what really is true, and life that will never end. How's that for hope?'*

PROLOGUE

A SONG OF HOPE

The prism of the Word: John 14.1-6 and Hebrews 1.1-14.

Love the haven, Light that illumines, and Hope that inspires

George Matheson FRSE (1842-1906) was born in Glasgow and was the eldest of eight children. At the age of 17 he began to go blind. His fiancée broke off their engagement when he informed her that he was losing his sight. By the age of 20 he was totally blind. Undeterred by this terrible disappointment, he became a prolific author, hymn writer, and a great scholar. Many of his works can still be purchased today or accessed online. George was a brilliant student at Glasgow University and his wonderful sister was a tremendous help to him and even learned Hebrew, Greek, and Latin to support him in his studies.

He became a Minister in the Church of Scotland and was known as the blind preacher. He preached regularly to 1,500 people. On one occasion he was asked to preach before Queen Victoria. He took as his subject 'the patience of Job,' The queen was so impressed she asked for his message to be published so that it could reach a wider audience.

He did not consider himself as a hymn writerm but he wrote many hymns and produced a volume of these, and many are still in use today. Perhaps his most well-known and best-loved hymn is the one entitled *'Oh Love that Wilt Not Let Me Go'.*

The hymn was written the night of his sister's wedding. Later he recounted how the hymn was written. These are his own words.

My hymn was composed in the manse of Innellan [Argyleshire, Scotland] on the evening of the 6th of June 1882, when I was 40 years of age. I was alone in the manse at that time. It was the night of my sister's marriage, and the rest of the family were staying overnight in Glasgow. Something happened to me, which was known only to myself, and which caused me the most severe mental suffering. The hymn was the fruit of that suffering. It was the quickest bit of work I ever did in my life. I had the impression of having it dictated to me by some inward voice rather than of working it out myself. I am quite sure that the whole work was completed in five minutes, and equally sure that it never received at my hands any retouching or correction. I have no natural gift of rhythm. All the other verses I have ever written are manufactured articles; this came like a dayspring from on high.

And these are the words:
O Love that wilt not let me go,
I rest my weary soul in Thee;
I give Thee back the life I owe,
That in Thine ocean depths its flow
May richer, fuller be.

O Light that followest all my way,
I yield my flickering torch to Thee;
My heart restores its borrowed ray,
That in Thy sunshine's blaze its day
May brighter, fairer be.

O Joy that seekest me through pain,
I cannot close my heart to Thee;
I trace the rainbow through the rain,
And feel the promise is not vain,
That morn shall tearless be.

O Cross that liftest up my head,
I dare not ask to fly from Thee;
I lay in dust life's glory dead,
And from the ground there blossoms red
Life that shall endless be.

Through the trials of physical blindness and rejection, George Matheson came to place all his trust and hope in the love of God in Jesus Christ as his Saviour. As he thought of his sister's marriage, perhaps it brought back memories of that painful day when his fiancée said *'I will not be the wife of a blind man'*. But He had found his solace and hope in the God of love. A love that he describes in four simple but profound stanzas.

Notice how each of the four stanzas begins with a key word – Love, Light, Joy and Cross. Dr Hawn, a professor of sacred music, analysed the stanzas and noted that they are not only attributes of George's relationship with Christ, but also names given to Christ.

He states;

Love is a haven for a 'weary soul' and is as deep as the 'ocean'. The second stanza focuses on Light that illumines the way of the singer. Our 'flickering torch' is augmented by the 'sunshine's blaze' of Christ, the Light of the world. Stanza three is one of Joy – a joy that seeks for us 'through pain'. The 'rainbow' is a promise of hope following the rain indicating that 'morn shall tearless be'. The Cross is the theme of the concluding stanza. Through Christ's suffering on the cross 'blossoms red' are formed that lead to the birth of new life.

It is not a mere coincidence that our collection of reflections on hope is concluded at this point, focused on our Lord Jesus Christ and His wondrous cross. It is at the cross that redemption was accomplished and through His death there 'blossoms red, life that shall endless be.' The problem of sin was dealt with, that vile contaminant that has infected every person and every star and galaxy in the universe.

Our new birth in the resurrected Christ means that we are being made ready to share in this new Heaven and Earth wherein dwells righteousness. The only hope for humanity is found in this Roman gibbet where the Lamb of God took away the sin of the world, and this has not only personal significance for everyone who trusts in Him, but also cosmic significance and the renewal and rebirth of all creation. The Lord of love and light and Hope is coming back again. In answer to the question, 'Are you the Messiah, the Son of the Blessed One?' Jesus said, 'I am, and you will see the Son of Man seated in the place of power at God's right hand and coming on the clouds of heaven' (Mark 14.62).

'... straighten up and raise your heads because your redemption is drawing near' (Luke 21.28).

Look up! Look and live! Live in Hope!

It isn't a Humpty Dumpty Hope.

In Jesus Christ we find real, genuine Hope, faithful Hope in a fragile world.

A CONCLUDING PRAYER OF DEDICATION

Infinite and Eternal God, the Author and Custodian of true Hope, you alone are Divine perfection, power, strength, and unconditional love. No one is beyond your reach and the hope you offer. Nothing and no one is too far from you or too hard for you. Bless all who read this book and may they find in you their living hope. Open our eyes to see and give us the courage to take the steps we need to take.

Lord, we dedicate this book to you, the God of hope, and to all those who take the time to read it. In the words of the Apostle Paul; *'I pray that God, the source of hope, will fill you completely with joy and peace because you trust in him. Then you will overflow with confident hope through the power of the Holy Spirit'* (Romans 15.13)

Oh God our help in ages past
our hope for years to come,
our shelter from the stormy blast
and our eternal home.

Amen
ends ... a new beginning...

ABOUT THE AUTHOR

Graham Albert Logan is from Banbridge, Co. Down in Northern Ireland. Graham has worked in the field of mental health for over 22 years. He is trained in psychotherapy and has worked in several settings including mental health advocacy and management positions, supporting people with mental health problems. He has been involved in psychological wellbeing training and mental health conditions. In the secular world of wellbeing, he sees hope as a vital component for everyone and particularly in the recovery journey for mental health service users.

Having spent over 15 years in pastoral work, he has taken a keen interest in the biblical perspective on spirituality and wellbeing and how this relates to society today. This is his third book but is one which will appeal to a much wider audience as the previous publications were very much about analysis of scriptural text.

Graham has written this book with all kinds of people in mind, from the ardent atheist to the honest doubter, as well as the devoted believer. He challenges the reader to engage with the 40 short essays on hope and to make up their own minds.

He continues to work in the mental health arena and spends his spare time reading and writing and walking his beloved Harrier Hound Barney, his constant companion.

Printed in Great Britain
by Amazon